KITCHEN GARDENING IN AMERICA

Kitchen Gardening

in **A**merica: A HISTORY
by DAVID M. TUCKER

IOWA STATE UNIVERSITY PRESS / AMES

David M. Tucker is Professor of History, Memphis State University.

Authorization to photocopy items for internal or personal use, or
the internal or personal use of specific clients, is granted by Iowa
State University Press, provided that the base fee of $.10 per copy is
paid directly to the Copyright Clearance Center, 27 Congress Street,
Salem, MA 01970. For those organizations that have been granted a
photocopy license by CCC, a separate system of payment has been
arranged. The fee code for users of the Transactional Reporting
Service is 0-8138-1888-5/93 $.10.

⊛ Printed on acid-free paper in the United States of America

First edition, 1993

Library of Congress Cataloging-in-Publication Data

Tucker, David M.
    Kitchen gardening in America: a history / by David M.
Tucker. — 1st ed.
       p.   cm.
    Includes index.
    ISBN 0-8138-1888-5
    1. Vegetable gardening—United States—History. I. Title.
SB320.6.T83   1993
635′.0973—dc20   91-36309

CONTENTS

KITCHEN GARDENERS have grown edible plants for some ten thousand years without a written history and may still believe they need none. As they have declined in the population to a minority, however, they have become more interesting and their passion for green thumbs more curious to outsiders. In fact, these gardeners may even find their own story exciting and useful. History offers perspective on the craft of gardening. The historical narrative can illuminate the evolution of garden cultivation from Indian hills, English beds, and straight rows, back to English raised beds. It can describe the development of plants, fertilizers, and insect control for those millions who struggle with the same old problems. Kitchen gardeners are a minority, but they still number far more than the older types of food gatherers — hunters and fishers. Some twenty-nine million Americans grow vegetables, while only twenty-six million fish and fourteen million hunt.

Vegetable gardening might be considered one of the great conservative rituals. The craft comes from our peasant ancestors and their age of scarcity. Along with frugality and thrift, food gardening has been a survival skill taught by our elders. Preaching in that thrift tradition, John Wesley warned his Methodists in the eighteenth-century against wasting their time and money on "elegant rather than useful gardens." This line of division between ornamental and food gardens has been no absolute wall of separation but marks an essential characteristic of kitchen gardeners: they have been a traditional, practical people, stressing the importance of utility rather than beauty. For more than three hundred years these Americans have enjoyed the hope of planting, the pleasure of growing, and the joy of eating useful plants. They have shared a great folk ritual.

Americans have always written extensively of their experience with food plants, and their accounts can be harvested to tell their story. Developing a green thumb, being observant of the needs of plants, has led gardeners far beyond seeds and cultivation. Vegetable gardening has evolved beyond a survival technique enabling people to sustain an increasing population into a craft that is therapeutic and recreational as well as sustaining. The story moves beyond plants, tools, and tillage to the thoughts and aspirations of gardeners who have recorded their ideas ever since literacy swept the Western world. We are, of course, somewhat dependent on anthropologists to explain nonliterate native Americans, but beginning with the English who expanded into North America, gardeners recorded their worldview of vegetables, herbs, and astrology. In the eighteenth-century Martha Logan prepared her *Gardener's Calendar,* giving us the manual by which a Charleston goodwife managed her kitchen garden. As the traditional world of superstitious ancients fell before the enlightened mind of the eighteenth century, Thomas Jefferson kept a careful garden book to scientifically record his experience, banish superstition, and provide us with the clearest window on an Enlightenment gardener.

Gardens have always been connected with health and nutrition, but never more than in the nineteenth century when country people moving to town found urban death rates twice as high as those in their rural communities. Half the city children died in infancy, and the great cholera epidemics spread terror and promoted a renewed concern for gardening and vegetarian health.

Concern for health of the body, as well as the mind, has driven Americans to suburban rather than central-city living. Although historians usually explain the urban population shift to the suburbs as a flight from immigrants and overcrowding, the pull of the kitchen garden has always been a major attraction. Americans have sought both the employment opportunities of the central city and the good health of the country residence. Garden history thus includes the story of the suburban country life movement and concern for personal and family health, as well as nostalgia for trees and gardens.

Nostalgia for country living contributed much to suburban gardening; yet, these city gardeners quickly accepted the modern science of the nineteenth century. They rejected the Enlightenment worldview with its happy confidence in the balance of nature, where birds and beneficial insects controlled the pests, for the new Darwinian view of life as a struggle for survival and into which gardeners must enter with new chemical sprayers to defend their vegetables. Chemical gardening thrived virtually unchallenged from the 1890s until the 1940s when a feisty J. I. Rodale from Emmaus, Pennsylvania, launched a crusade to return to the muck and magic of traditional gardening. For a generation the war between organic and chemical gardening philosophies continued until a new concern with ecology emerged in the 1960s, giving the edge to natural gardeners: compost is good while chemical sprays are dangerous. But perhaps the professionals are right that plant roots can't distinguish chemical elements from organic or inorganic sources. Just as current gardeners are great environmentalists, so did the previous generation make great use of chemical technology.

A study of backyard gardeners is something more than the narrative of a craft or a nostalgic essay of simple toil and joy: the story of kitchen gardening offers a fresh and exciting adventure through American civilization as observed from across the garden fence.

ACKNOWLEDGMENTS

NO KITCHEN GARDENER is entirely self-trained; I learned the craft from my parents in small-town Arkansas where green thumbs were acquired in the rural tradition, without benefit of gardening books. As an adult, I have grown green beans under the shade of ancient red oaks in Memphis and tomatoes across the fence in the sunny backyard of my neighbors, the Robert Poppers. The suggestion of a fellow historian, Aaron Boom — a Swede from small-town Nebraska — turned me toward garden history. Aaron recommended writing a history of vegetable gardening, a project he had once considered for himself. The topic seemed silly to a serious social historian, but no study of American kitchen gardeners had ever been written, while multiple studies of more trivial academic questions were common. Garden history promised to be both pleasurable and utilitarian; the readers and I might even find the book helpful as well as fun.

Discovering this new field, where no historian had ever been, was exciting but troubled by wrong turns and errors. Most of the gardening literature had been penned by men, and my early work reflected the chauvinism of these sources until Kathryn Gleason of the University of Pennsylvania insisted that I give women their due recognition in the garden. A New York culinary historian, Karen Hess, whose Danish-American gardening roots are in Nebraska, saved me from gaffes with cookery and horticulture literature. Flora Ann L. Bynum taught me about Moravian gardeners, generously sharing her work and photographs of North Carolina. Peter Dryer, biographer of Luther Burbank, shared his knowledge of ancient Near East scholarship: the origins and gender of early agriculture are too dim to unscramble, and men are not yet written out of the first garden.

KITCHEN GARDENING IN AMERICA

1 : NATIVE AMERICAN GARDENERS

ardening began some ten thousand years ago, in a time only imagined by anthropologists, when humans had multiplied and spread around the globe, and their overpopulation created a food crisis. Then the traditional hunting and gathering techniques, by which people had eaten for about two million years, could no longer feed the growing population. The balance of nature had been reached for people; wild foods could not sustain an increased population. Male hunters, who provided the meat, and female gatherers, who provided wild greens, fruits, and nuts, could no longer maintain their food supply by traditional means.[1]

The story of the great food crisis may be only a myth; some scholars object that they can prove neither a food shortage nor the need for plant cultivation. But the story of a food shortage has the appeal of a true folk tale. Repeated African famines have occurred even in modern times. To alleviate such recurring food crises the weak and disadvantaged may have broken with the nomadic tradition and begun cultivating wild plants. Men may have played a supporting role in sustaining this means of feeding the population of the earth, but women probably invented the craft. They knew that some of their gathered seeds sprouted and grew abundant fruit when dropped in garbage heaps around campsites. The brilliant next step required con-

3

sciously planting, cultivating, and selecting those seeds most responsive to nurture. The domestication of a few plants enabled
humans to move beyond the primitive animal struggle for survival to a civilized triumph over hunger and rootless wandering.
This revolutionary development seems to have occurred inde-
pendently around the globe; in the Americas our original gardeners were natives of Mexico and South America. We know
nothing of their failures and disappointments but only of those
plants that native Americans found susceptible to cultivation.
Of the two hundred food plants gathered, only a handful were
to thrive in gardens. Perhaps the gourd responded most quickly
to human hands, providing edible seeds and a container that,
when dried, surpassed clay pottery in lightness, strength, and
durability. And from the Texas wild gourd evolved American
squashes and pumpkins.[2]

Generations of sharp-eyed gardeners and thousands of
years were required before native Americans transformed wild
plants into the corn, beans, and squash that American gardeners
were to celebrate. Seven thousand years ago natives in the Te-
huacan Valley of Mexico began to plant seeds of the wild pod
corn. These teosinte grass seeds were more the size of wheat
than modern maize, but their small flinty kernels delighted their
gatherers by exploding into popcorn when exposed to the heat
of the blazing camp embers. Seeds dropped accidentally in garbage heaps must have grown more luxuriantly than those in the
wild, catching the eye of shrewd gatherers. More than two thousand years of cultivating and saving the larger seeded mutations
continued before new types of corn developed, with most modern types requiring five thousand years of nurture. The evolution of Indian corns into modern varieties of pop, dent, flint,
sweet, and flour continued almost until the time that Columbus
discovered America and its gardens.[3]

So marvelous were all the native American plants that they
were carried back by European explorers and quickly entered
the diet of western Europe. In fact, historians credit American
garden crops with doubling the population of western Europe in
the eighteenth century. Before the arrival of the American seeds,
malnutrition kept Europeans vulnerable to infectious diseases.
The introduction of corn so raised nutritional levels in southern

Europe that the population of Spain doubled from five to ten million. What corn did for southern Europe, the South American potato provided northern Europe, more than doubling the Irish population from three million in 1750 to eight million in 1845, the year the fungus hit the potato crop, causing a million Irish to die from malnutrition diseases.[4]

As the cultivation of Mexican plants spread across North America four thousand years ago, northern women generally were the gardeners and men remained the hunters. The exceptions were those tribes in the desert Southwest with little to hunt. There, men took gardening away from the women, and male Pueblo and Navaho assumed dominance in their intensive irrigated farming.[5] Elsewhere in North America gardening remained a task for women, while men continued to hunt and provide meat. Only in the nonfood crop of tobacco would North American males assume primary concern for growing a crop. Men alone nurtured the magical smoke plant that native Americans offered to the spirits.

Accumulated cultural wisdom gave native American males additional supporting roles in furthering horticulture. Indian leaders usually located villages on river or creek bluffs overlooking fertile bottomland. Experience taught that plants grew best in the river basins that produced the tallest cane or the largest trees. Forest soils with their layers of leaf mold, sediment, and soft humus were more easily worked than the tough upland soil or the heavy clay of grassland. Clearing the land was heavy work. A new garden required more than a year of preparation by the men, who assaulted the trees in the spring with their stone hatchets, girdling the bark around the tree trunks and leaving the killed timber standing. The ruined forest stood idle until the next spring when the underbrush and some of the trees were burned off. The layer of ashes neutralized the acid soil of the forest floor, and the sweet loam of the new field could then be planted. The remaining dead trees with their falling limbs posed some threat to crops and required an annual cleanup and burning. Spring cleanup by men usually included breaking up the planting hills with digging sticks. The prepared spring gardens were then turned over to the women.[6]

Every American school child has learned that Indians used

fish fertilizer and taught this practice to the Pilgrims. Squanto is said to have greeted the Plymouth Pilgrims with "Welcome Englishmen" and taught them to throw three fish into every hill of corn. Recent academic skeptics have labeled this story of Indian fish fertilizer a myth, pointing out that Squanto had earlier been a European captive and surely learned to fertilize in Europe where the advantages of such plant food had been known since the time of the Romans. Even though Squanto had lived in England, he never planted corn by any imported technique. European gardeners never planted grain in hills; they broadcast seed rather than planting individual grains. Some Indians unquestionably used fertilizer. Natives of Peru and Chile applied not only fish but nitrate of soda and bird guano; Hopi and Zuni tribes of New Mexico applied fertilizer from bat caves. Colonial writers insisted that an Indian technique had been taught in Plymouth, but the practice of fish fertilizing must have been restricted to the Northeast where an annual herring and alewife run made fish available for old field fertilizer. Without spring fish runs or manure piles, most Indians had no convenient fertilizer and therefore simply moved when garden fertility declined. A shift in camp location also made firewood gathering easier for women, who had stripped the wood from an old campsite. Every ten to fifteen years men cleared new fields and moved the village to a new garden site.[7]

The one fertilizer understood by all woodland Indians must have been wood ashes. Burning trees and underbrush was more than a land-clearing technique. A native American explained to English botanist explorer David Douglas that Indians deliberately sought an open place in the forest with a fallen tree for their tobacco garden. They burned the dead wood and then sowed their seed in the ashes because "wood ashes made it grow very large."[8] Indian gardeners thus understood the beneficial results of ashes even without the chemical knowledge that it added potassium and lime to the soil.

Centuries of observation provided Indians with a garden calendar for planting spring crops. In New England, when the alewives ascended the coastal streams, when the oak and dogwood leaves grew to the size of a squirrel's ear, plants were safe from a killing frost. The heavens also provided a sure sign of spring when the bright cluster of stars known as the Pleiades disappeared after May 5 and signaled frost-free nights to follow. Even the Indian children knew the stars by name, and once the seven stars disappeared from the spring sky, the Great Spirit was honored and the garden planted.[9]

The forces of nature were appeased as an insurance policy for a bountiful harvest. Women ritually followed ceremonies of song, dance, and offering. Among the Iroquois, the tribal chief first threw tobacco and wampum in the ceremonial fire and addressed the creator: "Great Spirit . . . we thank thee for this return of the planting season. Give us a good season, that our crops may be plentiful."[10] Then the Iroquois women, led by their elected female chief who carried the seeds of three vegetables—an armful of corn ears, beans in her right hand, and squash in her left—marched around a kettle of corn pudding, accompanied by song and box terrapin rattle. This ceremonial means of making contact with the vegetable spirits, the dance to imitate and praise corn and her sisters, employed sympathetic magic to encourage the vegetables to flourish and yield their fruit. Honors to the food spirits continued with first fruits and then harvest ceremonies. And if some calamity threatened the crop, if, for example, rain did not fall, a thunder ceremony honored the thunder spirits.

Like prescientific peoples everywhere, native Americans could be accomplished naturalists in mastering techniques of gardening—basic soil analysis, field preparation, planting, cultivation, and harvest. These green-thumb skills surely contributed to the successful harvest; Indians possessed a body of useful knowledge proved by experience. Yet all human effort occasionally failed; drought or other disaster could bring the gardener's best efforts to ruin. So rituals and spells, with their explanations in tribal myths, were essential gardening tools along with garden work and nurture. No native American could plant seeds without those magical words and dances that made the soil fertile, the rains adequate, and the harvest abundant.[11]

Magic and technique may appear identical to the gardener. Both were surely accidentally acquired solutions that seemed to work. Both seemed demonstrated by practice. When an Indian woman first accidentally soaked corn kernels in hellebore root water she must have been greatly surprised to see a thieving crow poisoned and its drunken fluttering spooking the other birds from the field, saving the seed corn. Such an accidental poisoning surely led to a practice of soaking seed corn in what must have appeared to be magical root water. And perhaps a similiar fortunate accident demonstrated to the Hurons of the far north a technique for making the most of their short growing season. Squash seeds were said to have been forced to an early start by germination over the lodge fire. The women first powdered rotten stump wood into a light planting mixture to be put in bark boxes, planted, watered, and then placed high over the fire to be warmed by bottom heat. The magical sprouts could then be planted in the garden days before a seed would ever have sprouted in cold ground.[12]

Heaping soil into little mounds in the garden was another useful discovery that permitted plants to grow above cold ground. Where the soil has been too wet or too cold, gardeners have discovered that raised beds grow vegetables best. The Irish of the Bronze Age learned to garden their wet peat bogs by digging ditches and piling the soil along the sides into elevated beds for planting. Native Americans, from the ancient Mayans of Mesoamerica to the Hurons of the far north, also discovered that planting in hills, a variety of raised beds, proved more productive in all garden soils, elevating the plants above the wet and cold of early spring.[13]

Among the Iroquois and Shawnee, women gardened together as a group, electing an older woman as their head to direct their work. The chief matron led the women to the fields, which had been divided into separate family gardening plots of one to two acres. Each took a row of hills in the first family garden, planting in each hill four grains of corn dropped into separate holes made by a finger or short pointed stick. To avoid any appearance of favoritism, the women planted only part of the first family's garden. After completing one row of hills, three feet apart, across the plot, each woman moved on to the next plot, leaving behind a partially planted garden. When every garden of the tribe had one planted strip, the gardeners returned to the first field to complete the planting.[14]

In every seventh hill the gardener later planted climbing

beans of two main species—lima and common. Included among common beans were the kidney of Andean origin and the navy, black, red, and pinto of Mesoamerica. Because corn and beans grew up together, mistaken observers often said they were planted at the same time, but the wisdom of experience had taught that the corn should be given a head start on the beans. In Iroquois mythology, the climbing pole bean represented the wife of the warrior corn plant, growing up embracing the corn stalk. The plants were inseparable in the fields and often in the cooking pot where they were cooked together as the Indian dish succotash.[15]

Modern science confirms the native American wisdom of intercropping and eating both beans and corn. The corn takes nitrogen from the soil while a nitrogen-fixing bacteria, which adheres to bean roots, restores this major chemical requirement for plant growth. And in human diet, corn provides abundant carbohydrates but lacks sufficient protein, as well as one of the building blocks of protein, the amino acid lysine, which is abundant in beans. Together, the two make an excellent diet, especially when squashes were added with their fat and vitamin A.[16]

Native Americans never regarded squashes and pumpkins as wives of the corn warrior because they wandered too much from home and ran over the ground so fast that the warrior could never keep them at his side. The cucurbits could only be sisters, doing their intercropping tasks of spreading a flowing green mantle between the corn rows and keeping down the grass and weeds that otherwise would have thrived between the hills. Indians never practiced clean cultivation; they pulled weeds only from the hills. The broad leaves of the cucurbits, intercropped with corn, shaded the weeds and ground between the hills, preserving moisture for the corn. Long experience taught, however, that the various cucurbits—pumpkin, crookneck, scalloped, and winter squash—should be kept separate to prevent cross-pollination from mixing and diminishing the good qualities of each. These squashes were also planted later, after the corn had reached above the greedy grasp of squash vines, which pushed out over the ground between the hills of corn, choking the weeds. Squash could be planted between corn rows or in hills where the pesky crows or squirrels had destroyed the seed corn.

Summer crooknecks were most convenient on the borders of the cornfield, while the winter squash and pumpkins were located deeper in the corn rows.

On the garden borders Indians planted sunflowers of two special varieties that they had domesticated. The giant cultivated sunflower with a single head up to eleven inches across provided tasty seeds for food or oil for hair dressing. The second cultivated variety, the Jerusalem artichoke with its several small flowers, grew tubers like the potato. Chemical analysis has proved Indians correct in regarding the tuber as a nutritional supplement for corn. In addition, the Jerusalem artichoke is an important source of vitamin C, having three times as much as an apple as well as ten times the potassium. Once planted, the Jerusalem artichoke grew without cultivation, and unlike the potato, its tubers could be left underground to be dug any time between the fall frost and spring thaw.[17]

Indian gardeners seem eccentric in cultivating no greens, but with so many wild greens to gather, garden planting seemed unnecessary. In the spring, women could freely gather poke, wild asparagus, yellowdock, burdock, and milkweed from the uncultivated land. The various boiled greens were among the more than 175 wild foods that eastern American Indians gathered, while they cultivated fewer than 9.[18]

Seed saving of the cultivated crops required considerable care. Numerous colors — black, red, blue, white — and more than one hundred varieties of maize existed, including dent, flint, sweet, flour, and pop. Each tribe surely kept at least four corn varieties. Beans also came in many colors and more than a hundred varieties, including two main species — lima and common. With all the squash varieties of color and shape no tribe could have resisted keeping three or four.[19]

To protect the newly planted seed, men and children assisted the women. The fish buried in New England hills attracted raccoons, wolves, and bear, requiring day and night watchers for two weeks to prevent the seed from being dug up by animals eager for the rotting fish. Those seeds without fertilizer attracted only the smaller daytime visits of birds, squirrels, or chipmunks for the children to repel with whoops and arrows. A young black crow, caught by a snare and strung up by the feet, shouted excellent warnings to other feathered thieves. As the corn began to grow, deer could not be permitted to eat the young shoots. The ripening corn again brought invasions of raccoons, squirrels, crows, and blackbirds. Snares, deadfalls, watch houses staffed during daylight by children, and night patrols by men protected the crop from raccoons, bear, and deer.[20]

Indian corn required two cultivations. Ankle-high corn needed competing weeds pulled or hoed away from the hills. Second hoeing began with knee-high corn. Then women hilled-up a dust mulch to support the base of the corn plant, conserve moisture, and keep down weeds. This annual hilling created regular raised mounds across the land still visible in some ancient garden sites. Manufacturing the hilling tool, the hoe, seems to have been the work of men, who lashed a blade to the fork of a stout stick. Commonly, the flat shoulder blade of a deer could make a hoe, but clam-shell blades were sharper. A turtle shell or stone blade could be used, or even a limb torn from a tree by a storm could be quickly fashioned into a hoe, with the limb serving as a handle for the chunk ripped from the trunk, hardened in the fire, and then used as a blade. Such tools would have been crude instruments in sticky clay but were entirely satisfactory in the soft loams of Indian gardens.

Whites paid so little attention to the details of Indian garden nurture that we know virtually nothing of insects in the Indian garden. While corn and beans rarely fell to insects, squash surely needed protection from squash bugs. We can only assume that Indian women applied the same remedy on which whites could depend for more than two hundred years—the finger and thumb. With a sharp eye and a quick hand, gardeners could destroy the slow-moving bugs by daily examining the undersides of the squash leaves and smashing all culprits. Running the hand along the bottom side of the vine to crush insect eggs could have been the only prevention for the stem borer. Perhaps it was in part to wash off the grime of smashing bugs that Indian women finished the morning garden chores with a bath in a nearby stream before returning to the village for a feast of corn soup, hominy, or boiled cornbread.

The object of all kitchen gardens is eating and the pleasure from first harvests. The first seasonal dish from Indian gardens was yellow crookneck squash and green beans. The young squash could be roasted in the fire by covering them with a blanket of ashes and then heaping on hot embers for a slow bake.[21]

Indian women took great pleasure in announcing the arrival of green corn. Corn-on-the-cob time marked the peak of the garden season and typically called for a Green Corn Festival to celebrate the favorite dish. Pulled fresh from the stalk and laid, still enclosed in its green husk, under cold ashes topped with hot embers, baked corn-on-the-cob delighted all. Every woman also had half a dozen other green corn recipes, including an excellent porridge in which the corn boiled with meat, pumpkin, beans, chestnuts, and maple syrup. Large amounts of green corn could even be harvested and preserved as insurance against possible crop disaster. When broiled and parched the green corn stored even better than mature shelled corn.[22]

As the autumn sun receded to the south and the nights grew cool, harvest began for gardeners. Baskets of dry beans and squash were picked and transported from the garden to the residence. While planting and cultivation had been done in common, harvesting stood out as a family role in which the man might help, especially with the corn. Ears of maize were stripped from the stalks, thrown into the great harvesting basket, and carried to the lodge. There, the work again became communal as people gathered for evening husking bees. Corn husks were stripped back for women to braid together into great ropes of corn that were strung up indoors on the ridgepoles to dry. Every cooking fire fumigated the ears with smoke, forming a tar film to prevent damage by weevils and grain moths. The overflowing corn surplus could be dried on outside scaffolds and then stored in underground pits made waterproof by bark and grass linings and a covering mound of clay. These underground corn pits were equally secure for storing surplus pumpkins and beans.[23]

With her lodge piled high with braided corn, stacked and sliced dried squash, barrels of beans, sunflower seeds, and Jerusalem artichokes, a woman turned to gathering the wild nut harvest brought down by the first frosts. Hickory nuts, chestnuts, butternuts, and walnuts were brought in by the basket for the cold season. Winter brought the leisure for gardeners to become cooks and combine their wild and cultivated foods into endless varieties of bread, soup, and pudding. Men contributed their game from the hunt, but women gathered two-thirds of all food for the eastern Indians, growing most of it in their gardens.

2 : ENGLISH BEDS

English migrations brought a European gardening tradition to America in the early 1600s. Different seeds, tools, and tillage so separated the English from the native American garden that a single glance easily distinguished one from the other. The minds of these immigrant gardeners were an equally distinct creation of a different European culture. The two garden cultures shared only such general characteristics as being predominantly under feminine control, delighting in food plants, and having faith in magic.

England yet remained a prescientific society in which people believed in witchcraft, ghosts, fairies, and astrology. Human grasp of the world had increased so little since the days of the ancient Greeks that western Europe remained closer to the ancient civilizations and their astrological beliefs than to the modern world. Astrology—the belief that the movement of the planets control the fate of all living beings—impressed primitive peoples everywhere. As the sun appeared to alter its path across the sky in the spring, daily shifting its way north, plants began to flourish. When in autumn it shifted its path back to the south, vegetation died from killing frosts. Each month as the moon came to full view, the tides of the sea rose higher and weak-minded individuals, some Europeans believed, had fits of madness, called lunacy. The ancient Babylonians completed a

systematic study of these movements of the heavenly bodies—
sun, moon, Saturn, Jupiter, Mars, Venus, and Mercury—against
the fixed background of the stars that comprise the signs of the
zodiac to predict the change of seasons and to read the omens of
the gods. The Greeks and Romans further developed this collection of seemingly empirical data. The accumulated wisdom of at
least four thousand years contained answers for every human
question, and so Queen Elizabeth daily consulted her astrologer.
One courted disaster by making plans to marry, taking a medical
remedy, or acting in other important ways without consulting
the state of the heavens. Gardeners were to plant their seed only
after consulting the phase of the moon and the astrological sign.
The full system may have been too complicated for most;
garden writer Thomas Hill apologized that his discussion of
astrology might have been too complex for the common people
but assured them that, if unable to comprehend the proper
rules, they could simply purchase an almanac. These tables of
the daily positions of heavenly planets sold faster than the Bible
after the first printing of an English almanac in 1545. To be
sure, planting by the moon and stars was less ridiculous than
planting by the Christian calendar on which Good Friday
shifted as much as a month from year to year. In addition to the
charts and a calendar for gardening, the almanac purchaser received astrological forecasts of coming disasters along with lists
of markets, fairs, guides on travel, and medical advice.[1]

Astrology might seem in conflict with organized religion if
decisions were to follow signs rather than Christian teaching.
The two were usually reconciled with quotes from scripture that
seemed to justify astrology: "Let there be lights in the firma-
ment of the heavens to divide the day from the night; and let
them be for signs, and for seasons, and for days, and years"
(Genesis 1:14); "To every thing there is a season, and a time to
every purpose under heaven . . . a time to plant, and a time to
pluck up that which is planted" (Ecclesiastes 3:1–2). With these
two verses believers could take confidence that God had provided the signs for the direction of human behavior.

Religion and magic worked together, just as the Christian
church had absorbed old pagan Anglo-Saxon superstitions in
converting England to Catholicism. Pagan festivals became

Christian; leading the plough around the fire on Plough Monday now secured a Christian rather than a pagan blessing on the crops to be planted. Although the Protestant Reformation in the sixteenth century sought to ban the magic of priests, rituals, and saints days, efforts to depreciate miracle working had to wait for a new intellectual environment before magic could be killed. Protestants might pray directly to God for health, prosperity, and good harvests but still resort to other magical supports.[2]

Although still a preindustrial society, England no longer represented a simple primitive world. The population had long before settled down to rural village life, moving beyond tribal and feudal society to a market economy. Perhaps 80 percent lived in small agricultural villages, such as Goodnestone, population 276, where three gentry families, with their large manor houses, owned most of the surrounding land and employed fifteen servants and an equal number of laborers. The yeoman class of small landowners counted twenty-six thatched cottages along the village lane, half of which employed servants. At the bottom of Goodnestone society were the landless families — nine tradesmen (carpenters, brickmakers, a shoemaker), twelve laborers, and twelve poor men without regular employment. But even the poorest family on the village lane usually owned a cow and always tilled a garden behind its cottage.[3]

English women of all social classes managed their kitchen gardens. Customs firmly insisted that the woman's duty to feed and nurse her family began with a thorough knowledge of her garden herbs. A wife ignorant of herbs, medicine, and cooking could keep no more than half her marriage vows. She might "love and obey" but could not "serve and keepe," Gervase Markham lectured in *The English Hus-wife* (1615). Fitzherbert's *Book of Husbandry* (1523) also clearly assigned the kitchen garden to wives, declaring: "And in the beginning of March or a lyttel afore, is tyme for a wife to make her garden, and to gette as many good sedes and herbes as be good for the potte and to eat."[4] And Thomas Tusser, who also wrote for the literate 10 percent, gentry and yeomen who could read, declared:

> In March and in April, from morning to night,
> in sowing and setting, good huswives delight;

To have in a garden or other like plot,
To trim up their house, and to furnish their pot.[5]

The permanent English garden compelled the development
of a more intensive gardening than that of native Americans,
who moved on when soil fertility declined. Fertilizers were an
absolute necessity for English gardens, and the benefits of animal manures were known to all. In Thomas Tusser's sixteenth-
century picture of rural life, collecting manure and compost
were virtually daily recommendations. Tusser advised, in
rhymed couplets, that the cow and horse manure be cleaned
from the yard and stored in dung heaps for garden use.

Lay compas up, handsomely, round on a hill,
to walk in thy yard, at they pleasure and will.
More compas it maketh, and handsome the plot,
if horse-keeper, daily, forgetteth it not.

Lay dirt upon heaps,
some profit it reaps.
When weather is hard,
get muck out of yard.[6]

The practice of piling animal excrement, straw, and vegetable waste into compost piles for bacterial action to decompose
and turn into the gardener's elixir of dark humus extended back
to the classical Greeks and Romans, who knew the benefits to
the soil and plants if not the chemical and biological explanations why organic matter stimulated plant growth. If both the
Holy Bible and their former Roman conquerors enjoined English gardeners to "dig and dung" their plants, then no further
explanation seemed necessary. So the English not only put
manure in the soil, they put it in their watering cans to stimulate
their herbs with drinks of manure tea. But even the educated
English understood no more than the Romans, whom they still
read as gardening authorities, accepting such nonsense from
Pliny as "when you dung your garden, let the wind blow out of
the west, and the Moon decreasing of light." The Romans also
recommended the skin of a hyena or a crocodile at the garden
gate to protect the plants from hail stones, and eagle feathers to
save them from storm.[7]

The typical English gardener probably had neither knowledge nor access to Roman magical charms but merely followed the custom of digging and dunging. The garden soil was spaded to the depth of two shovel blades. To work a garden to the depth of eighteen inches or more the English practiced what they called trenching. Work began by spading a ditch across a garden bed, throwing the soil from the ditch aside, then digging in the bottom of the trench to work the soil to a second shovel or fork depth. Animal manure was then added to the bottom of the trench, with Tusser recommending even that of humans. This laborious digging resulted in a garden soil deeply mixed with manure and air to encourage root growth, good drainage, and heavy production. Trenching time occurred in November, after crops had been harvested. Tusser then recommended:

> If garden require it, now trench it ye may,
> one trench not a yard, from another go lay;
> Which being well filled with muck by and by,
> to cover with mould, for a season to lie.[8]

Gardeners knew winter frost beneficially froze and weathered garden soil. Then, before spring planting, the soil might again be dunged, dug, and arranged in beds. Raised squares and rectangles could be worked, planted, and harvested from the walkways around the beds. The gardener walked not on the garden soil where the roots grew but on permanent paths. Since the wheeled garden plow had yet to be invented, no reason existed for straight rows across the garden. Any bed design might appear in the garden. Elaborate geometric designs appeared on the covers of garden books for the gentry and noble families to copy. The common understanding required that garden soil be "digged, dunged and cast orderlye into Beddes."[9]

All English gardens required fencing. "Garth," the old English word for garden, meant a fenced enclosure. The creation of an English garden had always begun with the enclosure of the ground to keep beasts out of the herbs. The ancient wattle style, or woven fence, called for a ring of poles around the garden and then intertwined green branches and twigs to form the fence. A second style, the paling enclosure, probably began

English raised-bed gardening, recreated in New England. *Photo courtesy of Plimoth Plantation, Inc., Plymouth, Massachusetts.*

with sharpened stakes driven into the ground but evolved into the picket fence in which the pales were nailed or pegged to crossbeams and posts. The more permanent thorn hedge was a favorite of country people, but most prestigious were stone or brick walls, which cost the most in human labor but captured solar heat and warmed the walled plants in early spring and late fall.

The plants within the garden enclosure were all called herbs and grown for both food and medical benefits. Of the some fifty plants recommended in William Lawson's *The Country Housewife's Garden* (1617) and Thomas Hill's *A Most Brief and Pleasant Treatise Teaching how to Dress a Garden* (1563), only one-fifth would now be regarded as food plants. The others were for medicine, seasoning, and strewing. European gardening had traditional links with medicine. As Thomas Hill explained in *The Profitable Arte of Gardening* (1568), the wise men of Rome and Greece had established the principles of medical gardening, and the English must practice them to enjoy good health. The discussions of a plant sometimes devoted more space to its medical uses than to its cultivation and nurture. Hill's description of even spinach or onions reads like the label of an early medicine bottle, promising to cure countless complaints. Eating spinach with meat took away the pains and griefs of the throat, stomach, and back. The onion not only protected eaters from infectious diseases but healed wounds, killed warts, helped coughs, alleviated earaches and forgetfulness, and cured the bite of a mad dog if plastered on with a mixture of rue, St. John's wort, salt, and honey.[10]

The healing remedies of gardening books seem to have been copied directly from the herbals, botany bibles that had been copied and expanded for fifteen hundred years since the pioneer work of Dioscorides. John Gerard's *The Herbal or Generall Historie of Plants* (1597) required almost fourteen hundred pages to catalogue each herb with a woodcut, description, and list of virtues. Plants and planets were central to traditional medical practice of both professionals and the common folk. Folk medicine thrives when people are helpless against disease. The most educated of the age had no real protections against common illnesses or the great epidemics of bubonic plague, smallpox, and typhus, so the English took recourse in religion, magic, and their herb gardens.

Writers from the Romans to the moderns had recommended garden herbs rather than druggists or doctors. Heresbach's *Four Books of Husbandry* (1577) repeated that message, declaring:

> Nature hath appointed remedies in a readiness for all diseases but the craft and subtlety of man for gaine, hath devised apothecaries shoppes, in which a man's life is to be sold and bought, where . . . they fetch their medicines from Jerusalem, and out of Turkey, while in the meane time every poore man hath the right remedies growing in his garden; for if men would make their gardens their physicians, the physicians's craft would soone decay.[11]

The English country housewife daily practiced medicine with her soup pot. The pot supplied the evening meal; supper was then spelled "souper," identifying the last meal of the day as a liquid one to be supped. The day had begun for common people with a breakfast of barley bread, often consisting of a mixed flour including oats, peas, and beans. Cheese and bread provided lunch. During the afternoon the evening porridge pot had been simmering in the fireplace with a broth that might include a little meat and oatmeal, peas, or beans, along with greens, roots, and a few herbs from a list including alexander, borage, chives, fennel, leeks, mallows, marigolds, mints, pennyroyal, rosemary, sage, sorrel, succory, tarragon, thistle, and violets. These herbs were added not just for flavor but also for their presumed medicinal benefits, comforting the stomach, heart, liver, and head, while guarding against pestilence.[12] For an actual mutton pottage recipe *The English Hus-wife* suggested throwing into the boiling pot of water one cut-up mutton leg, violet leaves, endive, succory, strawberry leaves, spinach, marigold flowers, green onions, and oatmeal. When one-third of the liquid had boiled away, the stew was ready to be salted and served.

Virtually every flower in the garden grew not only for beauty but to supply specific medical remedies. The flowers, leaves, and seeds provided remedies for every problem known, from women's complaints to male baldness. For women, the fragrant lavender, violet, rose, and peony were especially desirable. The smell of fresh violets could cure a headache. Headaches as well as "women's private places grief" responded to rose juice in wine. Melancholy spirits lifted after a drink of rose leaf juice with honey. For labor pains and childbirth, violet syrup or basil juice or peony seeds in wine were helpful and assisted the delivery. The peony root purged the new mother and helped her rise from bed.[13] The herb garden actually included a few remedies that worked, such as the opium poppy to induce sleep and the lily of the valley as a heart stimulant. A spoonful of the lily of the valley remedy might bring a patient back from near death, but an overdose of this relative of digitalis, which is still a medical heart stimulant, brought on a heart attack.

A well-supplied medical herb garden required a list of additional pharmacy plants not normally placed in the cooking pot—angelica, betony, chamomile, clary, feverfew, lilies, dragon, dittany, elecampane, hyssop, lovage, licorice, rue, and valerian. These were specific remedies to be kept for the medical cabinet and not pot herbs for cooking and preventive medicine.[14]

Garden herbs provided another use as air fresheners and insect repellents. Strewing herbs were dropped in the halls and floors to be trampled underfoot. The danger of flea bites, which incidentally spread bubonic plague, and the annoyance of body lice, bugs, and flies may well have been reduced by strewing slightly poisonous wormwood and tansy. The natural insecticide pyrethrum comes from the painted daisy. Other insect repellents were chrysanthemum, feverfew, costmary, and oxeye. Wormwood received the specific recommendation of William Tusser:

> While wormwood hath seed, get a bundle or twain,
> to save against March, to make flea to refrain;
> Where the chamber is swept, and wormwood is strowne,
> no flea, for his life, dare abide to be known.

Other fragrant strewing herbs Tusser recommended were basil, balm, chamomile, cowslip, fennel, germander, roses, mints, sage, violets, and savory.[15]

Few gardeners had space for all the good plants listed nor did a majority have the ability to read an herbal, so the traditional gardener grew those herbs confirmed by family and village folklore as useful for strewing, healing, ointments, internal medicine, and nutrition. The same herb might be judged useful in each category, and in practice herbs were separated neither in the garden nor in the house. On the English kitchen table a green salad of alexander, artichoke, thistle, cucumber, cresses, endive, mustard, mint, purslane, radish, sage, sorrel, spinach, skirret, succory, tarragon, and violet would have been regarded as both food and medicine.

If pressed to name only those garden plants that prevented hunger, the English gardener would surely have named asparagus, cabbage and greens, peas and beans, and the root crops—skirrets, carrots, parsnips, turnips, and onions. For feeding the poor, boiled and buttered yellow carrots were Richard Gardiner's solution. His garden reform book omitted the "dainty salads" and offered utilitarian carrots, cabbage, beans, and roots as a solution for feeding the hungry of England.[16] But most British gardeners never suffered from that hunger; half of them at the end of the seventeenth century were eating meat regularly, and they continued to grow their herbs and flowers and to make their salads. Richard Gardiner's view did not represent English gardening, and the more "dainty" plants were certainly not to be banished from kitchen gardens by a mere book.

Not all English gardens were under feminine control. Royal estates and large country houses hired male professionals to grow their food. The elite style is best depicted by *The Compleat Gard'ner* (1693), the instruction book of Louis XIV's gardener, Jean de La Quintinye, who managed a twenty-five-acre kitchen garden built with transported soil on a lake bed next to the Versailles palace of the French king. Supplying the court tables with vegetables in every month of the year required organization and methods like those of the best market gardeners from whom Quintinye acquired his knowledge. *The Compleat Gard'ner* rejected astrological nonsense, offering instead proven advice on soil, seeds, plants, and the monthly list of tasks to perform. Quintinye directed his advice to wealthy gentlemen who were curious about gardening and wished instructions on selecting and directing their own kitchen gardeners.[17]

This French vegetable book was translated by an English gentleman, John Evelyn, who took a special interest in gardening.[18] Evelyn directed his own gardens at Sayes Court and wrote his own garden salad book, *Acetaria: A Discourse on Sallets* (1699), with instructions for vinegar and oil dressings as well as planting instructions for plants and roots eaten raw or blanched—from alexanders to wood sorrel. Evelyn reminded aristocrats that great men had traditionally retreated from public strife to spade in their own gardens. Evelyn even suggested that the garden might no longer be women's "province" in seventeenth-century gentry families. Writing of Roman women, he said "she who neglected her Kitchen-Garden (for that was still the Good-woman's Province) was never reputed a tolerable Huswife." But this redrawing of the feminine sphere was not absolute, for in an earlier passage Evelyn relied on traditional sexist stereotypes in distinguishing between the "Country-man's Field" and "Good-wife's Garden."[19]

In Evelyn's popular gardening almanac—*Kalendarium Hortense*—he advertised himself as a member of the Royal Society, a distinguished scientific group. Evelyn also associated with literary men and loved to quote his poet friend, Abraham Cowley, who had said: "I Never had any other Desire so strong, and so like to covetousness, as that . . . I might be Master at last of a small House and large Garden, with very moderate conveniences joined to them, and there dedicate the Remainder of my Life to the culture of them and study of Nature."[20] By combining science, poetry, and the wisdom of the ancients with aristocratic interest in gardening, Evelyn contributed to the respectability of male interest in food plants.

In the vast kitchen gardens of royalty and aristocrats, hired gardeners grew vegetables under the eye of estate owners. They planted only edible plants and roots in their food gardens, no ornamentals or medicinal herbs. Tradition was less prevalent in these aristocratic gardens, where science rejected astrology by the late seventeenth century. John Evelyn, for example, thought planting on Good Friday or by the phases of the moon was all delusion. Scientific skepticism and thirty years of experience had persuaded him of the falsity of old wisdom. He wrote: "Sow or Set any sort of Seeds or Plants, in all the several Quarters of the Moon, and I will promise you the same success in all."[21]

The gardening style that came to America in the seventeenth century, however, was not the aristocratic, scientific craft of John Evelyn but the smaller garden of traditional Europe. Many European women came to America with reluctance. Nostalgic and homesick for the old village, they dreamed of transforming and domesticating the strangeness of the land. To make America feel less wild and remote to them, they maintained homes and gardens in the familiar style. They exchanged cuttings, scions, seeds, and garden information to put their stamp on the landscape. Beds of asparagus and squares of herbs all tamed the new land. Mothers in America dreamed of creating "a pleasant home with a garden and flowers and creeping vines, and children and husband dear all at home, no more to roam." To refine the wilderness, to create a traditional image of home, women pursued their familiar English styles of gardening.[22]

English women carried their garden heritage to Plymouth Plantation and the other American colonies. For two hundred years they maintained the classical and medieval garden traditions.[23] They planted herbs while the moon increased, harvested during the decrease, and blamed the malice of heavenly bodies if their seeds or harvest failed. From the 1600s into the 1800s gardeners in America retained those distinctive characteristics of the English kitchen garden—astrology, herbs, raised beds, and garden fences.

3 : THE GARDEN OF THE GOODWIFE

I n our western tradition the goodwife has always been busy. In the Old Testament, Proverbs 31:10–31 describes the virtuous woman as doing more than washing, cooking, and cleaning: she also produced household goods and did the spinning, weaving, and gardening as well as buying and selling in the markets. The idealized woman's domain extended beyond the house, including the yards and the markets. Hebrew tradition continued among eighteenth-century American wives, who ruled in the garden, the hen and milk houses, and the kitchen and food cellars. Both town and country housewives were the managers of the kitchen garden.[1]

Women in the colonial kitchen garden have been largely invisible in the historical record because, denied formal education, they left few written records. No female diaries, for example, exist before 1750. It is not until after mid-century that a diary survived, recording the daily routine of Massachusetts gentlewoman Mary Holyoke, a physician's wife, who "Sowed sweet marjoram. . . . Sowed pease. . . . Sowed colliflower. . . . Sowed six weeks beans. . . . Pulled first radishes. . . . Set out turnips. . . . Cut 36 asparagus, first cutting here."[2]

The rare memoirs of an upstate New York girl recalled kitchen gardens as "the female province." Anne Grant claimed that, after the spring spading of the garden, "no foot of man intruded." Her Albany gardens were small, perhaps one-fourth of an acre, where goodwives excluded Indian corn, cabbages, potatoes, and roots for the more delicate kidney beans, asparagus, celery, salad greens, sweet herbs, and cucumbers, along with beds of flowers. In the words of Anne, these gardens enclosed in wooden palings were "extremely neat, but small, and not by any means calculated for walking in." These recollections were shaped by her later experience in England, where kitchen gardens for small families were said to require an acre and for large families not "less than three or four acres."[3]

American gardens also extended for acres when the women lived outside town. Pennsylvania farmers commonly reserved "an acre or two of ground" for their eighteenth-century kitchen gardens. German women especially grew "a variety of all vegetables" and were praised for horticultural skills by their English American neighbors. Germans were even said to have taught Philadelphians to plant more than turnips and cabbage. The prominent local physician, Dr. Benjamin Rush, observed: "Since the settlement of a number of German gardeners in the neighborhood of Philadelphia, the tables of all classes of citizens have been covered with a variety of all vegetables in every season of the year." And according to Rush, these gardeners on Pennsylvania German farms were usually female; "The work of the gardens is generally done by the women of the family."[4]

Bountiful vegetable harvests have been confirmed by probate court records, which tell social historians that vegetables became increasingly important in estate inventories. Where only 29 percent of the inventories listed vegetables in the seventeenth century, more than half in the next century listed roots—turnips, potatoes, onions, carrots—and cabbage also as being stored in the deceased's cellars. And if we may presume that half of the estates were probated during the warm seasons of the year, when the roots were still in the garden, we might conclude that virtually all families in the Northeast kept root cellars in the eighteenth century. While these inventories tell us nothing about the consumption of green vegetables—lettuce, asparagus, and herbs—they confirm that the Irish potato had become the most common food since Scotch-Irish migrations popularized this wonderful Peruvian vegetable in the early eighteenth century.

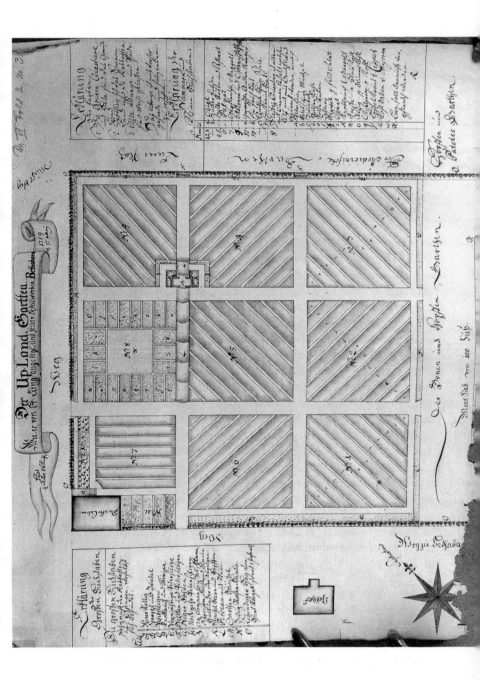

28

A German community garden with diagonal rows, drawn in Bethabara, North Carolina, on May 1, 1759. *Reprinted by permission of the Moravian Archives, Bethlehem, Pennsylvania. Translation and identifications of the plant lists reprinted by permission of Flora Ann L. Bynum.*

THE UPLAND GARDEN

As it was laid out by Bro. Lung and has been planted. Bethabara. Contains ½ acre, 26 rods.
1759 the 1st of May.

Road

EXPLANATION OF THE LARGE LETTERS

Letters on borders and walks:

A. Horseradish
B. Asparagus and onions
C. Parsley
D. Garlic and thyme
E. Last year's parsley
F. Cloves
G. Black beans
H. Still more parsley
I. At the summer house, flowers: daffodils, cloves, and lilacs
K. Gooseberries and hops
L. Gateway with grapes
M. Little garden house
N. Two grass (or sod) banks
O. Live hedge of dogwood only one year old
Road
Guest house
North
Road to Bethabara
The bean and hops garden
Scale of 100 feet

EXPLANATION OF THE COLORS:

1. Green sections and beds are vegetable plots.
2. Seed plots and border beds are reddish.
3. Walks and paths are white.

EXPLANATION OF NUMBERS AND SMALL LETTERS:

1, 2, 3 a. Lettuce
   b. Sweet peas
4, 5 Carrots and parsnips
6 Parsnips
7 Mangolds
9 Melons and Spanish pepper
10 a. Grafted quince stems
10 b. An early bed
   c. Quince tree nursery
   d. Cabbage bed
8 This section is planted only with seed brought from Germany:
   a. Parsley
   b. Turnip-rooted parsley
   c. Onions

d. Red cabbage
e. Beets
f. Celery
g. Corn salad
h. Chervil
i. Spinach
k. Garlic
l. Mangolds
m. Cress
n. Red cabbage
o. Radish
p. Caulifower
q. New-ploughed field
r. Cabbage
s. Spoonwort
t. Nasturtium
u. Kohlrabi
v. Majoram
w.
x. Empty – for transplanting
Mill road
Empty space
Medicinal garden
Hops and potato garden

The records also tell us that Indian beans had replaced the English pea in food storage and therefore probably in the supper dish.[5]

Travelers in the eighteenth century reported that every gardener had a cellar under the house for preserving vegetables through the winter. Gardeners also knew that one root was not to be kept in the cellar. The Swedish Peter Kalm reported that sweet potatoes, which gardeners were growing in Pennsylvania, did not keep in a damp cellar but must be stored buried in sand in a warm, dry upstairs room. The housewife who kept a good table not only gardened but also mastered the preservation of vegetables and their protection from ice, greedy microbes, and hungry rodents.[6]

A New York innovation in food storage protected the garden harvest with a Dutch cellar. In the eighteenth century St. John de Crevecoeur reported:

> We have another convenience to preserve our fruits and vegetables in the winter, which we commonly call a Dutch cellar. It is built at the foot of a rising ground which is dug through, about eighteen feet long and six feet wide. It is walled up about seven feet from the ground; then strongly roofed and covered with sods. The door always faces the south. There it never freezes, being under ground. In these places we keep our apples, our turnips, cabbages, potatoes, and pumpkins. The cellars which are under the houses are appropriated for cider, milk, butter, meat and various necessities.[7]

New Englanders insisted on root cellars as necessities, while southern gardeners usually managed without the cellar dug under the house or even one excavated in a nearby hillside. Where milder winters left the ground largely unfrozen, roots could be better preserved in the shallow Irish or Dutch "clamp" than in a warm and humid southern cellar. To build a clamp, or potato hill, the gardener waited for cold weather, until killing frost seemed imminent, then dug and dried potatoes to be laid on a straw bed in a dry sheltered spot. Straw and potatoes were layered until all the tubers were stacked up in the mound. The round tuber hill was topped off with a thatching of straw to protect the potatoes from rain. A trench was then dug around the heap, and the soil was thrown over the straw to provide further protection from wind, cold, and rain, while the ditch provided additional drainage to keep ground moisture and rot away from the harvest. Tubers protected in these hills were less inclined to sprout than those in a cellar.[8]

All Europeans had been accustomed to burying their roots for winter protection. Some growers packed and insulated with straw, but most preferred sand. Carrots, turnips, parsnips, beets, skirrets, salsify, and horseradish were pulled, their tops twisted off, and, after being exposed for a few hours of drying, were packed in layers of sand that were thought to resist rot even more than straw vegetable hills. Sand hill storage even worked for broccoli, cabbage, and cauliflower, although the gardener usually began by digging a trench for these in dry, sandy ground. The cabbages were pulled, roots and all, loose leaves were stripped away, and then the heads were placed upside down in the trench, covered with dry sand, and mounded over to keep out the rain water. The manuscript recipe book inherited by Martha Washington offered the following instructions for a turnip hill:

> TO KEEP TURNUPS ALL YE YEAR FROM SEEDING
> First cut of ye tops of yr turneps after michaelmass (September 29), & make a trench in ye ground yt is light & sandy . . . & lay in ye turneps, about 3 quarters of a yerd deepe your trench must be; & even as you have occasion to use them, digg them up, & cover up ye place again; this way will keepe them from seeding.[9]

With or without a cellar, an efficient southern gardener need not have been without fresh vegetables during winter.

The American colonial diet as well as the garden vegetables no longer copied precisely the English example. Sweet and Irish potatoes grew in colonial gardens and were roasted on the fireplace hearth. African okra grew in Philadelphia and southern gardens to thicken the supper soup. Indian corn provided the major grain for the family bread, which could be baked in a fireplace oven or on a hardwood slab placed in the ashes or boiled as Indian porridge. Indian beans grew in every garden for boiling or baking. Colonists had borrowed Indian squash seeds and planted their gardens "full of it." Pumpkins were commonly sliced and placed before family fireplaces to roast and then be mashed with butter, milk, eggs, molasses, allspice, and ginger to create an American pudding or, when baked in a crust, a pumpkin pie.[10]

Outside town, where more than 90 percent of colonial women lived, farm gardens were large, often one to two acres, with some plantation gardens covering six acres.[11] There, the Indian crops of corn, squash, and potatoes, along with cabbage, turnips, and sweet potatoes, were planted abundantly, requiring so much space and labor that the machines of the age—horse and plow—were used to prepare the soil. Individual squares of these extensive gardens sometimes covered a fourth of an acre and were laid out in rows like those of the farmer's cornfield.

The standard garden layout, from New England to the Carolinas, was the square or rectangle, divided down the center by a central graveled walk, wide enough for two passing wheelbarrows loaded with manure.[12] Surfacing of the path varied with the availability of materials; sand created an excellent walk and sea shells often paved coastal garden walks. A cross-walk usually split the divided garden into quarters. Another graveled walk followed the fence and fruit trees, six feet inside the palings, around the entire garden. These surfaced paths were designed for utility as well as pleasure. Dry footing permitted daily vegetable viewing without the bother of tracking mud back into the house. Wheelbarrows laden with water or manure cut no ruts in a graveled walk, especially if constructed according to the instructions of Philip Miller's *The Gardeners Dictionary* (1754), a widely owned plant manual in Britain and America. Miller recommended that new walks begin with eight to ten inches of gravel, packed and rolled down in muddy soil to bind the gravel into a hard surface.

Eighteenth-century garden layouts have been confirmed through garden literature and the material evidence. Landscape archaeology has located the walks, squares, and old fence post holes of historic gardens. An occasional eyewitness description recorded the plants within the pale enclosure. Outside Philadelphia the Robert Morris estate had been sold because of the founding father's bankruptcy and was acquired by Henry Pratt in 1799. The kitchen garden of the estate was described as an elegant square 330 feet by 297 feet, split by a central alley 13 feet wide and then subdivided by 10-foot-wide walks into twenty squares 58 feet across. Around the wooden fence a 3-foot border of snowballs, quince, and other flowering shrubs surrounded the entire garden. Each of the inside vegetable squares was bordered by decorative pinks and other flowers and herbs. The inside squares grew beans, peas, cabbage, onions, beets, carrots, parsnips, lettuce, radishes, strawberries, cucumbers, potatoes, and "much else."[13]

An even clearer picture of an eighteenth-century garden can be found by looking six years beyond 1800 into Bernard McMahon's garden book, which recommended that the 6-foot-tall board fence be lined with fruit trees, the inside squares lined with strawberries, gooseberries, currants, and raspberries, as well as aromatic shrubs of thyme, savory, and hyssop. Rows were recommended, rather than broadcast sowing, for peas, beans, cabbage, lettuce, endive, potatoes, artichokes, and Jerusalem artichokes. The rows were to run north and south so that plants could capture solar energy on both sides as the sun moved across the garden from east to west.[14]

The location of the kitchen garden, according to McMahon, ought to be "out of view of the front of the habitation." British landscape style had insisted on shifting vegetables away from front yards. While Miller's *The Gardeners Dictionary* offered a practical reason for the kitchen garden to be near the stables — so that "wheeling the dung" would require less time and expense — John Parkinson's *Paradise* (1629) had declared onions and cabbages to be offensive in smell and taste for English families. A flower garden instead, Parkinson insisted, should perfume the residence. This landscape style of hiding the kitchen garden may explain why none are visible in sketches and paintings of eighteenth-century homes. Kitchen gardens were necessities, put out of sight to the rear or far side of the better home, where their high walls would neither obstruct the resident's view from the front porch nor permit the gardening goodwife to be seen by an outsider from the street.[15]

If an acre of garden required the full time of one worker, could goodwives have been in charge of the more extensive farm and plantation gardens? Women did supervise these gardens. When Frances Ann Carter moved to a Virginia plantation in the forks of the Nomini River, after ten years in Williamsburg, she, and not her husband Robert, managed the garden. From the diary of her family tutor we know she "ordered the Gardener to sow lettuce and plant Peas" on February 8. She daily walked in the garden, checking vegetable growth and tree grafts and giving instructions to the two slave gardeners.[16]

While a few servants cultivated the plantation vegetables, all black families managed their own food gardens to supplement rations from the big house. Black families on the Carter estate planted their small plots of ground on Sundays, growing potatoes, peas, and other favorite vegetables. Most plantations assigned garden plots to slaves, who grew everything from tobacco and peanuts to watermelons and pumpkins.[17]

Farther south in the Carolinas, goodwives also managed extensive gardens. Eleanor Laurens, wife of a Charleston merchant, delighted in an exotic garden that included oranges, limes, sugarcane, and olives, as well as the more traditional vegetables, flowers, and fruit. When the Laurenses moved to a new house with a large garden built on land reclaimed from the river tide marsh, her husband wrote, "I live in the middle of a Garden of four acres pleasantly situated upon the River. . . . Mrs. Laurens takes great delight in Gardening & we content ourselves upon moderate Fare in a quiet rural life." Mrs. Laurens, according to her son-in-law, managed all the family gardens: "The whole was superintended with maternal care by Mrs. Laurens with the assistance of John Watson, a complete English gardener."[18]

The best example of a female gardener in Charleston, and probably in all of America, was Martha Daniel Logan (1702–1779). The daughter of a South Carolina governor, Mrs. Logan not only raised children but taught school in her home, sold garden seed and roots, exchanged ornamentals with John Bartram, and wrote out her seventy years of garden experience, which her family later published as a tribute to the late widow and as a means of assisting young female gardeners of Charleston.

Logan's *Gardener's Calendar* won great local applause for a generation, but because it appeared as part of a Carolina almanac and was never reprinted, it has been inaccessible to gardeners for a century and a half. The eighteenth-century origin and the female authorship make *Gardener's Calender* invaluable for kitchen garden historians. Mrs. Logan's work is a window into the gardening mind of the eighteenth century, the development of a planting calendar for specific local conditions, the belief in astrology, the craft of seed saving, the quaint but effective techniques for fertilizing, the long list of vegetables cultivated for the family, and a woman's ability to manage the fruit orchard as well as the garden.[19]

GARDENER'S CALENDAR
By Mrs. Logan

Known to succeed in Charleston and its vicinity for many years.

JANUARY
Plant out all kind of evergreens, either from roots or slips. Sow late pease and beans. Sow summer cabbage and parsley; the last at the change of the moon, the first at the full, that the parsley may grow luxuriantly, and the cabbage head well. Sow spinach for seed, in a small bed of rich land; but let it never be cut, and it will yield a quantity of seed. Plant out artichokes, which will bear in the fall after. Also plant rose and other trees, either for fruit, or ornament, except those of the orange tribe, as these are not to be moved till April. All kinds of flowering shrubs are now to be moved.

FEBRUARY
Sow all kinds of early melons, cucumbers, kidney-beans, squashes, asparagus, radishes, lettuce, and garden cresses, for seed. Sow late dwarf pease, and onion seed; and at the full of the moon, carrots, parsnips, and red beets, in beds prepared before wanted, made as follows; lay a quantity of dung on the beds, and turn them up repeatedly with a spade, very deep; then make them up about two feet broad, trench them in shallow gutters, in which drop your seed, cover them and let them lie. The middle of this month is proper for grafting in the cleft; if your trees have not

been pruned, they must not be neglected now. Set out fig trees —
plant out hops, and all kinds of aromatick herbs — set out cabbages, carrots, parsnips, turnips, &c. designed for next year's seed,
but they ought to be hanging up in some dry cellar since December.
Plant Irish potatoes. Sow oats, and reap in June.

MARCH

What was neglected last month, may be successfully done in
this: Sow French and sewee beans, all sorts of melons, &c. toma-
toes-seed, red pepper, for pickling — cellery seed for next winter,
which must be set out when of a proper size, and let grow all the
summer, in gutters where it is to be blanched. Plant another crop
of vines, rounceval pease, and transplant aromatic herbs. Now
trim orange and lemon trees.

APRIL

Sow cabbages, cauliflowers, and savoys, for next winter; (see
general directions after this calendar) but let them remain in the
nursery bed until August; when the rains set in, transplant them in
good rich land, laying their long stalks into the ground, up to the
tops, leaving out only the leaves; from these you will have early
cabbage and cauliflowers for winter. You may set out the savoy
plants, when they are of a proper size, and let them grow all
summer, as they will bear the heat without rotting, which neither
of the others will do. You may sow carrots and parsnips, but let it
be on the full of the moon, shade and water, to get up the seed.
Plant out orange trees, &c. but let it be done at the change of the
moon, watering them well, until they have taken root.

MAY

This month is chiefly for weeding and watering, as nothing
does well, either planted or sowed in it, unless you shade them.
You may sow endive or cabbage for the fall.

JUNE

Clip herbs for drying, and evergreens, if they are too much
grown, but not otherwise, as the heat will be apt to dry them too
much. If you have lost the last seasons for sowing carrots and
parsnips, you may now sow them; but the beds must be watered,
and then shaded to bring up the seeds; after the seed is in the
ground, you may lay over the bed some long litter or wet straw,
which must be taken off at night, and put on wet in the morning

until it comes up, then shade them with crotches and boughs laid over, until they are strong enough to bear the sun — remember to make your bed according to the directions given in February.

JULY

This month is only fit for weeding and watering; if you have showers, plant late French beans. Early turnips, onions, and carrots may be sowed the full of the moon, but will require the same pains to bring them up as the last month; early sallad will do with care. Be sure to water every thing designed for seed, as much depends on it; but this must be done only in the evening, while the hot weather lasts.

AUGUST

At the full moon, sow parsnips, carrots, radish, turnips, onions, cauliflowers, cabbages, endive, and savoy; all in shady places, except the two former, and these must be covered with boughs, to help their growth. Set out the plants sowed in April, as before directed, and be sure to water them constantly, if necessary, which will soon supply your garden.

SEPTEMBER

As we may suppose showers of rain are frequent, sow the following seeds: spinage, lettuce, water and garden cresses, chervil, endive, parsley, late cauliflowers; all those on the increase of the moon. Cabbage, radish, and turnips, on the full; set out monthly roses, at the change, give them plenty of water and dung; you may also inoculate with the bud. Large onions may be set out for seed about the end of the month.

OCTOBER

Dress your artichoke, taking away all their suckers, except three to each root, open their roots, lay about them a good quantity of untried earth and dung mixed, which method is proper in all cases where the roots are opened: if your plant suckers set them in places which have been dug out two feet square, and filled up with untried earth and dung. Trim and dress your asparagus beds, in the following manner; cut down the stalks, lay them over the bed and burn them; this done, dig up between the roots, and level it, then cover the bed, three fingers deep, with dung and earth mixed, and let it lie. You may plant cellery, set it in gutters; as it grows, hill it up. Sow raddish, and lettuce. Plant white and monthly roses, box, shalots, and evergreens.

NOVEMBER

Earth up cellery, which was planted out in the spring. Tie up endive for blanching. Continue to sow spinage, radish, and lettuce seeds. Plant Windsor beans. (A liquor to steep Windsor beans, to give the first shoot strength, is prepared as follows: take three quarts of sheep dung, two quarts of pigeons, four quarts of fowls, and six quarts of well rotted horse dung from an old dung hill; pour eight gallons of water on it, stirring it well and frequently; after standing twelve hours, pour off the clear liquor, and let your beans lie twenty-four hours in it, then plant them out immediately.) Sow early pease. Trim your monthly roses; and, at the full moon, open their roots and dung them. Sow cabbage for the spring; but screen them from severe cold, while very young. Prune your vines; and plant out red and striped rose trees.

DECEMBER

Prune and trim all kinds of vines, and fruit trees, except the orange tribe. Transplant all sorts of evergreen and other trees; all kinds of rose and sweet briars, honeysuckle, and jasmines. Sow late pease and Windsor beans, and set out onions for seed.

OTHER GENERAL DIRECTIONS

Sow all kinds of pease, squashes, melons, and the like in the increase, about or at the change of the moon. Cauliflowers and brocoli, at the increase; cabbages and all roots at the full of the moon.

THE MANAGEMENT OF CAULIFLOWERS AND BROCOLI

There are two seasons for sowing their seeds — August and April. The first season requires no trouble, but sowing the seed at the increase of the moon; and when the plants are of a proper size, set them out; when a little grown, weed and hill them up. If the weather is cold cover the bed all over with dung, about three or four inches thick, which will defend them against hard frosts, and in February they will flower. During their growth take care to pick off all the yellow or dead leaves at all times. In April you may likewise sow your seeds, if you did not do it in the fall; but it will do at any time from August to November, better than in April. When the plants are full grown, set them out in a nursery bed as thick as lettuce; where let them grow for a month or two; now pull them up again, and set them in a cold situation, pretty shady, and water them, if there is occasion, and let them remain until August or September, then pull them up a second time, and set them out in a rich soil, at the distance used for cabbages; where they will flower in January, and be much larger than those sowed in August. The beds are to be covered with dung, as is already directed. Flowering brocoli is to be managed in the same way. By transplanting these vegetables so often their growth is retarded; otherwise they would arrive at their full size by mid-summer, and afterward would, without flowering at all, rot and die.

A CERTAIN METHOD TO OBTAIN FINE CARROTS, PARNSIPS AND BEETS

Make your beds about two and a half feet broad, and dig them very deep. Lay on them a large quantity of well rotted dung. Dig them up again, and mix in the dung with the earth. Then trench across the beds, and sow the seeds three days before the full moon in February. When they are about one inch high, thin them, and leave at least three inches distance between each root, and you will have them very large and fine. They will not go to seed til May twelve months after, so that you may have them for use at least nine or ten months, if you sow a sufficient quantity.

A METHOD TO HAVE GOOD STRAWBERRIES
OCTOBER

Plant them in regular rows, on beds three feet wide, the soil should be rich, on each bed plant three rows of plants, fifteen inches distance, be careful to keep them clean, by frequent weeding, particularly when the fruit are set; take off the runners and leave the same space between each bed as it is broad; when these have borne fruit two years, dig up the intervals, and set your plants thereon, as before directed, and leave the old beds for alleys. Here the roots are to remain two years more, and when they have produced for two years, then change their soil entirely, for they should never remain longer on the same spot.

IF ANYONE IS DESIROUS OF OBTAINING GOOD SEED, LET HIM FOLLOW THE SUBJOINED DIRECTIONS

In December, before the weather is severely cold, choose some of your best cabbages, with the hardest heads — your largest and finest orange carrots, and your best parsnips, beets, turnips, and radishes; set these roots into dry sand in a warm cellar, where they will not freeze, and hang up the cabbages, with their heads downwards, covering them with some sort of cloths, to defend them from the cold. In this situation let them remain till February, when they will begin to bud out; then plant them out in your garden, into good soil, setting the roots and cabbages in the ground up to their tops, where let them stand and seed. Cut the cabbages across their heads both ways to help forward the seeding shoots; but do not cut deep. Give them constant watering, when occasion requires; and when the seeds are ripe, save them separately, that on the middle spire from the others on the side branches, and be most careful of the first, as these will produce much finer cabbages or roots, than the others. Choose out of your best heads of lettuce and mark them for seed; but do not transplant them, as they are not the better for it.

N.B. All water used for watering anything, is the better for standing in the sun, and in cold weather it is proper to put a little dung into the tub of water, as it helps the growth of your plants.

GENERAL DIRECTIONS IN REGARD TO FRUIT TREES

After trimming off all the dead parts and superfluous branches, it is a good way to shorten the last year's shoots down to four or five eyes, as these are the bearing branches, the fruit will be much finer. In December open the roots, and leave them quite bare, till the latter end of February, and in this time, scrape and pick out all the worms and insects which have been in them. And if you have trees which have been barren, cut away three or four of the leading roots of each tree, which by stopping its spreading into luxuriant branches, will make it produce fruit. This method is good for all trees, but must not be omitted to the apricots, especially in Carolina, without which they yield nothing.

TO KEEP WORMS FROM DESTROYING THE FRUIT TREES OF THE ENSUING YEAR

In the beginning of August, take common tar, and with a brush paint the bottom of the trees to about a foot high, and about three inches round the roots of the trees upon the ground, taking care to leave no shoot uncovered. This is the season in which these insects go up the trees to lay their eggs, which destroys the next year's fruit. This method has been proved by a gentleman in Carolina, with great success, particularly on the peach-tree.

AN INFALLIBLE METHOD OF KILLING WORMS IN THE ROOTS OF PEACH TREES

Scrape a little of the earth from the root, or body of the tree, so as to make a trench of two inches wide and one inch deep — let

this trench be filled with urine every morning, for some weeks —
then every other day; and after that once a week will be sufficient.
The volatile alkali effectually destroys the worms, and greatly promotes the vegetation of the tree.

When the elderly widow wrote out her acquired wisdom of
more than a half century of gardening in Charleston, she gave
us a sample of the mental calendar that every eighteenth-century
woman needed to feed and keep her family. In those days garden seed was not sold in paper packets with printed planting
instructions. The goodwife kept in her memory the survival wisdom necessary for saving her own seed from more than twenty
vegetables growing in her garden along with countless aromatic
and medicinal herbs. If the woman's thumb were to be green
then she had to closely observe the needs of plants and commit
those needs to memory or write notes to herself on the calendar
for next year. She mastered plant culture techniques for each
vegetable and the orchard sciences of grafting and pruning, insect control, and transplanting, as well as the preserving and
preparing for the table all her bounty of fruits and vegetables.

Although some people ridiculed astrology as grannyism and
old wives' tales, it is only fair to point out that when Mrs. Logan
married at fifteen years of age, Harvard College still taught
astrology as a science. Educated people picked their apples, cut
their timber, and planted their seed by the signs. Even after Mrs.
Logan died in 1779 American almanacs were still reproducing
the zodiac man and following the old tradition of assuming that
planets controlled weather, vegetables, and the human body. In
the shadow of the Enlightenment, astrology had continued to
thrive, and Mrs. Logan reflected the mainstream of eighteenth-
century popular thought when she recommended planting only
in the traditionally approved phase of the moon.[20]

While respecting the influence of the heavens, gardeners
maneuvered with all their wisdom against the seasons, nurturing
their plants to extend the natural growing months, screening
their seedlings from midsummer heat and covering them from
midwinter frost. In drought of summer they watered even
though they had no pumps, hoses, or drip irrigation equipment.
Shallow dug wells in Charleston provided garden water for the

labor-intensive chore of hand-watering thirsty garden plants.

The hum of industry in the kitchen garden produced much of the food and spice of life for the goodwife's family. Her tireless horticulture must have been satisfying, for in the language of the eighteenth century, "her garden was her delight." And as women began to write and keep diaries, they wrote "with special fondness and verve about their gardens," which may have given them more pleasure than any other household industry.[21]

4 : THE ENLIGHTENMENT GARDEN
OF THOMAS JEFFERSON

he new science of the eighteenth century created a gardener whose understanding broke sharply from traditional horticultural wisdom. No gods, no moons, no spirits were flattered to produce the harvest in the Enlightenment gardens of America. Nature's laws of growth and fruiting created the harvest without supernatural intervention. If the gardener only observed, recorded, and cooperated with nature's rules, then garden bounty appeared with the regularity of changing seasons.

Faith had retreated among the educated of the Western world as careful observations and scientific conclusions replaced magic and theology for explaining the events of the garden and the heavens. The new requirements of observation and experimental testing undercut ancient belief in magic and witchcraft, pushing astrology and the supernatural from the gardener's mind. If Copernicus, Galileo, and Sir Isaac Newton could discover the natural laws by which the movements of the planets were governed and the American David Rittenhouse could actually build a hand-cranked working model, then surely the observations and records of the natural laws of the garden left no place for supernatural intervention.[1]

Scientific truth, to be sure, is never heard by all. Ancient

beliefs stubbornly resisted the Enlightenment in farmer's almanacs, traditional communities, and old wives' tales, but for student Thomas Jefferson in the William and Mary College of the
1760s, the intellectually liberating Enlightenment view of the
universe swept away the older beliefs. Nature and its laws were
the creation of a God who designed and then ceased to interfere
with humanity or the planets. From the bible, only the Genesis
story of creation might be accepted as literal truth. Modern
people must throw off other shackles of darkness, superstition,
and traditional Christianity, developing their own powers of observation and reason to understand and use the laws of God and
the natural world.[2]

The new scientific interest in plants strongly appealed to the
educated. When Benjamin Franklin and John Bartram organized their American Philosophical Society in 1743 they sought
mastery of the natural environment by encouraging all experiments that "let light into the Nature of Things . . . increase the
Power of Man over matter . . . and multiply the conveniences
or Pleasures of Life." These concerns of the society specifically
included gardening. New gardening improvements were proper
scientific concerns, Franklin said, as were "all new discovered
Plants, Herbs, Trees, Roots, their Virtues, Uses, Methods of
Propagating them." Thomas Jefferson shared these utilitarian
scientific goals, joining the society in 1780 and becoming its
president in 1796. Throughout his own life Jefferson sought to
provide Americans with new plants, believing that "the greatest
service which can be rendered any country is to add a useful
plant to its culture."[3]

The scientific rigor of observation and note-taking enabled
Jefferson to write a natural history of his native state, *Notes on
the State of Virginia,* and also made him an important source
for later garden historians. Jefferson's garden notes, published
as *Thomas Jefferson's Garden Book,* provide the planting date,
exact location in the garden, and the arrival at the table for
every vegetable planted in his Monticello garden. Jefferson
often lapsed in his note-taking, but his precise data, covering
more than half a century, along with his general correspondence
and papers provide the clearest window in American history on
both a garden and a gardener's mind.

With Jefferson, a reader can even watch the construction of a retirement garden. Forty years as a political leader, and only a part-time gardener, were coming to an end as President Jefferson planned a new garden in 1808 for one of his chief occupations after retirement from public life. During those public years he had gardened in France and elsewhere, but his real garden had always been on the sunny south slope below the mansion on a Virginia mountaintop, which he had aptly named Monticello, or "little mountain" in Italian. The mountainside garden, however, had never received Jefferson's full architectural and engineering skills. In his last years in the White House he eagerly planned a model terrace garden. Directing from Washington, he instructed his overseer and labor force to begin leveling a flat forty-foot-wide terrace running a thousand feet along the southern slope. The enormous task of manually digging into the hillside, blasting out the rocks, and shifting dirt and rocks to the lower side of the terrace led Jefferson to alter his design from one to three separate "steps" within the terrace. But directions from Washington are not always followed, and Jefferson returned home to an incomplete terrace. The former president then supervised completion of his garden. Along the lower south side a fieldstone retaining wall rose twelve feet at its highest point to hold the garden terrace and to capture solar warmth for early spring planting.[4]

Below the acre kitchen garden terrace were seven acres of fruits and berries. To protect this entire eight-acre garden, Jefferson designed an enormous paling fence ten feet high. While still president of the United States he drafted exact specifications for his paling enclosure. The upright posts set in the ground nine feet apart were to be of decay-resistant locust. The cross rails of split poplar or pine supported seventy-five hundred pointed pickets of split chestnut. The overlapping pairs of five-foot-three-inch chestnut palings were spaced so close that even a young rabbit could not penetrate the enclosure.[5]

Jefferson arranged his kitchen garden in terraces with a creative deviation from the formal English tradition. No central alley split the terraces into quarters. Instead, the broad grass walk followed his retaining wall on the lower side, resisting erosion and permitting daily garden inspections without red clay leeching onto garden boots in wet weather. Above the walk, garden soil lay separated into Old World squares or beds. Each bed had a number, surely a scientific innovation over the old method. With 154 separate vegetable plantings in 1809, well beyond the power of any memory, Jefferson carefully noted in his garden book the species variety, location number, and date of planting. Vegetable plantings spilled over into the orchard below where the Jerusalem artichoke roots were buried along the fieldstone wall—no gardener would trust those wandering roots to remain in any orderly terrace bed. The various Indian maize for corn-on-the-cob—Erie, Pawnee, Cherokee, and sweet—were also banished to the orchard ground, along with the Indian pumpkin, Irish potato, African field peas, and watermelons. Sweet potatoes were a field crop, not even permitted in the orchard. Of all the Indian plants, only the green beans, limas, and squash were planted on the high terrace squares.[6]

The tomato, a South American native, also gained a favorite spot on the high terrace. Too often, garden historians assume Jefferson planted the tomato as an ornamental; they mistakenly think the northern European fear of the tomato still held in America.[7] The tomato, however, had won enthusiastic acceptance in both the south of Europe and America. *The Gardeners Dictionary,* by Philip Miller, reported on the love apple in 1754: "Italians and Spaniards eat these Apples, as we do Cucumbers, with Pepper, Oil, and Salt; and some eat them stewed in Sauces . . . and in Soups they are now much used in England." A Virginia cookbook compiled by a Jefferson relative and contemporary included more than a dozen recipes calling for tomatoes. Mary Randolph's *The Virginia Housewife* (1824) specifically called for tomatoes in the stew that was a favorite summer diet of Southerners. She called the dish "Ochra Soup," but Southerners would generally label it gumbo, the African word for okra. Her instructions were:

> Get two double handsful of young ochra, wash and slice it thin, add two onions chopped fine, put it into a gallon of water at a very early hour in an earthen pipkin, or very nice iron pot; it must be kept steadily simmering, but not boiling; put in pepper and salt. At 12 o'clock, put in a handful of Lima beans, at half-

Sketch by Lucia C. Stanton, depicting Monticello grounds with one-thousand-foot vegetable garden, stone retaining wall, and orchard, vineyard, and berry squares. *Reprinted by permission of Monticello, Thomas Jefferson Memorial Foundation.*

past one o'clock, add three young cimlins (squash) cleaned and cut
in small pieces, a fowl, or knuckle of veal, a bit of bacon or pork
that has been boiled, and six tomatoes, with the skin taken off;
when nearly done, thicken with a spoonful of butter mixed with
one of flour. Have rice boiled to eat with it.

Jefferson may have regarded this dish as representative of his
diet for he claimed to be largely a vegetarian. "I have lived
temperately," he said, "eating little animal food, and that not as
an aliment, so much as a condiment for the vegetables, which
constitute my principal diet."[8]

An edited work calling itself *Thomas Jefferson's Cook Book*
does not reflect this vegetarian emphasis; meat and dessert
dishes greatly outnumber the vegetables. This fabrication of a
Monticello cookbook by Marie Kimball was compiled long after
Jefferson's death. Some fifty recipes were copied from *The
Virginia Housewife* and may well have been used at Monticello,
but these dishes probably reflected Jefferson's entertaining menu
rather than his own pattern of eating. He entertained in the
elaborate planter style, serving hard liquor, which he did not
drink, and heavy meat dishes, which he regarded as unhealthy,
having written in his *Notes on the State of Virginia* that the hot
climate required instead "a free use of vegetable food, for health
as well as comfort."[9]

The bulk of the vegetables growing on Jefferson's high terrace were European greens and roots. After first planting
English peas in late March, Jefferson filled his garden with cabbage, lettuce, parsley, kale, tarragon, broccoli, cauliflower,
spinach, corn salad, endive, savory, and turnip greens. Then
came the roots—carrots, beets, rutabagas, salsify, parsnips, radishes, and onions. Successive plantings of the greens continued
into summer, along with eggplant, melons, and beans. Late
summer brought a fresh array of greens and turnips planted for
the fall garden. Even after frost killed his snap beans and Hot-
spur peas, Jefferson could continue eating Swedish turnips, lettuce, broccoli, corn salad, spinach, endive, and cabbage from
the fall garden.

Even winter never suspended Jefferson's daily fresh salad.
Earlier as president he had instructed his local market gardener

Restored vegetable garden at Monticello. *Reprinted by permission of Monticello, Thomas Jefferson Memorial Foundation.*

in Washington on the culture of Belgian endive for an extended growing season. The endive secret consisted of leaving the plants to grow undisturbed through summer and fall until after the first white frosts. The huge carrotlike roots were then dug and carried in dirt containers to the basement, where they sprouted new heads for harvesting every three weeks. An ample supply of roots guaranteed Jefferson his desired "sallad of endive every day through the winter till the spring sallading should commence."[10] Fresh, crunchy salads with a slight peppery taste were surely available for the winter Monticello table a century before rapid transportation brought fresh produce from market gardeners in Florida or California.

For boiled winter greens the Monticello garden offered something better than the common turnip or collard greens. Sprout kale may have grown in no other American garden in 1810, but Jefferson both grew and gave away seed for his "tender and delicious" winter vegetable, which survived snow and ice to repeatedly produce sprouts for cooking throughout the winter months from December to March.[11]

Conspicuously absent from the terrace were the medicinal herbs that had been so much a part of the old English garden. Jefferson the scientist seems to have had little confidence in either herbs or medical doctors, preferring instead to trust nature to restore balance to a sick body. For fevers or dysenteries, medical doctors who prescribed from experience rather than theory could be trusted for relief, but in most other cases the doctors were regarded as dangerous to health. Jefferson rejected bleeding, purging with mercury, and most medical theory. Only demonstrated results were persuasive to him. The new science of observation and testing by experiment had reduced miracle claims for most herbs. Where John Gerard's *The Herbal* (1597) devoted most of its pages to listing the medical virtues of each plant, Philip Miller's eighteenth-century *The Gardeners Dictionary* (1754) dropped the medical virtues entirely. As a professional gardener for the British Society of Apothecaries and a member of the scientific Royal Society, Miller could not reprint the old, unverified miracle claims. Sharing this new intellectual climate of opinion, Jefferson apparently found little merit in most traditional herbs, banishing them to the flower gardens of the front lawn for his granddaughters to supervise. Only once, in 1794, did Jefferson list the traditional herbs, and then he included them with the ornamentals.[12] Jefferson certainly believed some plants had medical value. In *Notes on the State of Virginia* he included twenty-one native medicinal plants, but these never grew in his kitchen garden. Perhaps medicinal and pot herbs had to grow with the flowers to keep Jefferson's garden properly scientific.

Experimental planting had characterized Jefferson's vegetables ever since his neighbor Philip Mazzei gave him Italian fruits and vegetables to grow in 1773. Swapping plants and seeds both locally and internationally gave Jefferson a variety from around the world. Friends from France sent seeds for the Monticello garden. The director of the National Garden of France annually sent as many as two hundred species of ornamental and garden plants. Jefferson's sprout kale, for example, came from the French National Garden. The Lewis and Clark expedition to the American West brought back new snap beans and salsify for Jefferson to grow. The salsify, or oyster plant, roots were stored like carrots for winter use and then fried in butter to be scarcely distinguishable from fried oysters. But when the Columbian salsify proved no better than the European root, Jefferson abandoned the American variety. No garden scientist kept failures or inferiors. Even Bernard McMahon, Philadelphia seedsman and author of *The American Gardener's Calendar,* could rarely supply all of Jefferson's requests for new plants. McMahon had never seen large Chile strawberries growing in America, yet Jefferson had planted them. The berries had apparently not survived his long absences from Virginia. The Monticello garden needed not just the wild Virginia strawberry and the Chile but the Hudson and the Alpine as well. The scientific eye that had once counted the one hundred small Virginia berries required to fill half a pint could never be satisfied with a single strawberry variety. And when Jefferson learned that his Alpine strawberries required "acres" to produce a dish, he moved them out of the garden into the field.[13]

Botany and horticulture were Jefferson's favorite sciences. They offered not only subsistence but "delicious varieties for our table, freshments from our orchards, the adornments of our flower-borders, shade and perfume of our groves, materials for our buildings, or medicaments for our bodies."[14] Botany offered the country family its major amusement and social entertainment. The addition of a single new plant for the diet of Virginians would have been a contribution as great as authoring the Declaration of Independence, and Jefferson experimented with Italian grapes, olive trees, sugar maples, pecans, upland rice, and benne—the sesame seed African slaves had brought to Georgia for baking with their bread and boiling with their greens. High hopes, however, for all these and other experimental plants never produced a great American success for Jefferson. But the plant search provided part of the horticultural stimulation that led Jefferson to say that he might be a gardener if he could begin life anew. Two years after his retirement from Washington he wrote:

> I have often thought that if heaven had given me choice of my position and calling, it should have been on a rich spot of earth, well watered, and near a good market for the productions of the garden. Such a variety of subject, some one always coming to perfection, the failure of one thing repaired by the success of another, and instead of one harvest a continued one through the year. Under a total want of demand except for our family table, I am still devoted to the garden. But though an old man, I am but a young gardener.[15]

The youthful curiosity of Jefferson ran to plant experimentation and natural observation rather than to chemistry, parasitology, or genetics. He assumed God to have made a perfect world of plants and animals; none others would ever be needed. People must merely experiment with nature's countless variety. The chemistry of growth required no similar experimentation. God had created a balance of nature, with plants providing food for animals and animals food for plants. Animal manures stimulated growth and also protected plants from the ravages of insects. As Jefferson told his son-in-law: "We will try this winter to cover our garden with a heavy coating of manure. When earth is rich it bids defiance to droughts, yields in abundance, and of the best quality. I suspect that the insects which have harassed you have been produced by the lean state of the soil.

We will attack them another year with joint efforts."[16]

In trusting nature to keep insects under control, Jefferson seems to have counted on both manure and birds. As a naturalist, he noted the joint return of birds and insects. The house martin arrived at Monticello between March 18 and April 9. Jefferson's favorite, mocking birds, wintered at Monticello, where the grandchildren were given instructions to do them and their nests no harm. Trees and shrubs were planted around the Jefferson mansion in hopes of attracting more birds. And the orchard below the garden must have been a nesting haven for the insect eaters.[17]

The value of birds for controlling insects had been developed by a fellow scientist in the American Philosophical Society. Dr. Benjamin Smith Barton had written a little book pointing out the noxious insect peril: America, already one of the most insect-infested parts of the world, seemed to have an increasing insect population. Insects were shifting from native plants to new garden crops, and little progress had been made in discovering remedies for insect damage. Birds were at least part of the solution, Barton said. Insects were the first food of almost all birds, even those who feasted on the farmer's fruit and grain. Certain smaller species especially deserved protection. In Pennsylvania the crested flycatcher, bluebird, woodpecker, and the house wren were great insect destroyers. House wrens were observed making forty to fifty trips an hour to feed their young with insects caught from the garden. In a twelve-hour day, even if only a single insect were carried at a time, each bird destroyed six hundred garden insects. Ten to twelve pair of these small birds were thought capable of protecting an entire garden, and Pennsylvanians had long built nesting boxes around their gardens. Thus Barton proclaimed for the scientific community the principle that people could assist in improving the gardening environment by encouraging some of God's creatures, birds, to diminish another pesky creature and therefore promote a better balance of nature.[18]

Jefferson and his enlightened generation may have manipulated the balance of nature a little but did not seek to overturn the laws. Even when nature's law of aging affected him, Jefferson made no protest. His retirement lasted seventeen years but his gardening only nine. By 1818 poor health, the loss of strength for his traditional half hour of exercise and soil cultivation every evening, and even an inability to tour the terrace beds forced him to turn management of the garden, as well as the plantation, over to his grandson. He still recorded his annual garden calendar but let T. J. Randolph plan and supervise the garden. A new hobby, creation of the University of Virginia, became Jefferson's major interest. Jefferson was, to be sure, insistent that the new university include a school of botany with a six-acre garden.[19]

Even in his last year and illness Jefferson retained an interest in food plants. When an Ohio newspaper reported cucumbers growing four feet long in a Cleveland garden, Jefferson wrote an old friend there for seed. "Although giants do not always beget giants," he wrote, "I should count on their improving the breed, and the vegetable being a great favorite of mine, I wish to take the chance on an improvement."[20]Jefferson divided the seed, planted his, and sent the other nine seeds to a gardening friend to multiply the chances of a cucumber success.

When Jefferson died on July 4, 1826, at the age of eighty-three, he left precise instructions for inscribing his tombstone. He omitted "gardener" from his list of accomplishments, as well as "President of the United States," and insisted that the marker be engraved

Here was Buried
Thomas Jefferson

Author of the Declaration of American Independence
of the Statute of Virginia for Religious Freedom
& Father of the University of Virginia

In the enlightened progress of humanity, Jefferson's declarations contributed to freedom. In the scientific pursuit and distribution of useful knowledge, his educational institution prepared the next generation to advance the general welfare. And the study of botany and gardening was surely part of the legacy that Jefferson believed he had passed on to Americans through his university.

5 : GARDENING FOR HEALTH

E arly nineteenth-century America fashioned a country life philosophy as a particular reaction to the alarming rise of urban deaths. As the population of New York City multiplied from sixty thousand in 1800 to some three hundred thousand by 1840, the accompanying mortality rates were horrible, especially for children; more than half died before they reached the age of six. Fear of urban sickness multiplied as the terrifying plague of Asian cholera ran through New York and other population centers. As an alternative to unhealthy urban life, all the positive aspects of gardening — vegetable diet, physical exercise, mental health, and country living — were united in one version of the good life in America.

The importance of vegetables had, of course, been recognized before the cholera years. Educated Americans had commonly complained that their countrymen unwisely departed from a healthy diet. Material abundance offered in America the great plenty of meat formerly available only to the rich and powerful. Most peoples had eaten mainly vegetable food throughout their history, except for isolated tribes such as the Eskimo whose environment provided no vegetables. The British ate more meat than the rest of Europe, with half the population dining on butcher's meat for the greater part of the main meal. Roast beef had become a national symbol for the British during the sixteenth century, but Americans moved beyond the British meat eaters, enjoying a daily fare of three meals of meat. The British had eaten only 147.5 pounds of meat a year, but an American widow's consumption of salt pork and beef increased from 156.7 to 209.7 pounds during the eighteenth century. Each widow surely supplemented her daily half pound of salt meat with substantial quantities of fresh fish, fowl, and game. This heavy increase of animal food in the American diet led educated observers to complain that Americans were eating too much meat and paying too little attention to their vegetable gardens.[1]

Bernard McMahon opened *The American Gardener's Calendar* (1806) affirming the link between health and gardening. All agreed, McMahon said, that fruits and vegetables were "necessary to health in all countries, especially in warm climates." In the South, Thomas Jefferson had criticized the "inexcusable" meat diet of the common people. In the North, where people ate much the same animal food, President Timothy Dwight of Yale College complained: "The food of the inhabitants at large, even of the poor, is principally flesh and fish; one or other of which is eaten by a greater part of the inhabitants twice or three times a day. . . . The proportion of animal food, eaten in this country," Dwight declared, "is, I think, excessive."[2]

President Dwight spoke as a gardener who believed his own hobby contributed to good health not only through a vegetable diet but also through exercise. As an overzealous student he had permitted himself only twelve mouthfuls of supper and four hours of sleep to provide additional study and reading time. The malnutrition and excessive reading by candlelight ruined Dwight's eyesight and health, forcing him to return home for a long recuperation under a physician's treatment of outdoor exercise. Walking and horseback riding brought recovery of health for all but the eyes. Dwight never again read for more than fifteen minutes a day. Throughout his remaining forty years of life, he continued vigorous exercise. In summer he cultivated a large garden with his own hands, working at least an hour every morning before breakfast. After the fall gardening season ended, he switched to walking, riding, and cutting firewood for exercise.[3]

In New Haven, Dwight cultivated the largest and best garden in the city. He experimented with strawberries, planting the local wild field and meadow berries along with the Chile, Hautboy, and Hudson. The wild Virginia became his favorite, responding to twenty years of gardening care, and perhaps cross-fertilization, by doubling its fruit size to three to four inches in circumference. Dwight closely observed the habits of all his vegetables and insects. When an insect attacked the roots of his watermelons, he discovered the pest and concocted a brew of burdock leaves and elder twigs to save the plants. In his vegetable garden Dwight found a lifelong challenge, delight, and therapy.

Gardening surely appealed to the Calvinist minister in Dwight, who approved useful and rewarding work. In his long poem *Greenfield Hill* he had recommended:

> Industrious be your lives;
> Alike employ'd yourselves, and wives;
> Your children, join'd in labour gay.
> With something useful fill every day.

Hard work and toil were rewarding.

> No life has blessings so sincere.
> Its meals so luscious, sleep so sweet,
> Such vigorous limbs, such health complete.
> A mind so active, brisk, and gay,
> As his, who toils the livelong day.
> A life of sloth drags hardly on,
> Suns set too late, and rise too soon;
> Youth, manhood, age all linger slow,
> To him, who has nothing to do.[4]

President Dwight did not specifically urge women to labor in the garden—perhaps he did not want to share his gardening pleasures—but he considered women's health damaged by a sedentary life inside the house. Until women took up outside exercise, Dwight said, they would continue to lose their "health, and bloom, and beauty" even before their thirties.[5] New England women may well have begun a retreat from the garden in the nineteenth century. The *New England Farmer* reported that women were not doing their part in the northeast kitchen gardens, which were miserably overrun with weeds. To be sure, farm women had much physical work in the house and never lacked for exercise, but still the male editor of the *New England Farmer* patronized farm women with the advice that after farmers did the laborious spring digging in the garden, "keeping the plants free from weeds should be attended to by the females."[6]

The preventive medicine practiced and preached by President Dwight reflected accepted health wisdom. Exercise and vegetable eating summed up Dr. Shadrack Ricketson's *Means of Preserving Health and Preventing Disease* (1806). If Americans insisted on leaving the healthy country life for town dwelling then they must exercise in the open air, "walking, riding, sawing, cutting, gardening." The Philadelphia physicians' *Journal of Health* agreed that vegetables, exercise, and avoidance of drugs and cities best preserved health. Nearly one-fourth of infant deaths came from diarrhea, an illness for which the *Journal* recommended the fresh air and sunshine of the country. In support of a garden diet the *Journal* quoted seventy-six-year-old Thomas Jefferson's advocacy of the vegetarian lifestyle.[7]

Vegetables as preventive medicine gained dramatic support in the 1830s when physicians proved helpless against the Asiatic cholera that spread out of India to become a terrifying global disease. Once a victim swallowed the waterborne cholera bacillus, it multiplied swiftly in the human alimentary tract, producing violent symptoms—diarrhea, acute spasmodic vomiting, fever, and death. Seemingly healthy individuals could, within hours, shrivel from radical dehydration, darken from ruptured blood vessels, and die. Cholera flourished in the great cities where the bacterium was transmitted by drinking water contaminated by raw sewage. More than seventy thousand New Yorkers fled the city in the summer of 1832, paralyzing business and allowing grass to grow in the streets. Among those who remained thirty-five hundred died.[8]

Physicians knew nothing of the comma-shaped bacterium and were not even able to agree on whether cholera should be classified as a contagious disease. Doctors generally assumed cholera to be only an aggravated form of diarrhea, produced by overeating, and to be treated by traditional bleeding and purging. These treatments of drawing blood and administering immense quantities of poisonous calomel, a chalky mercury compound, probably hastened the death of cholera victims and undermined the status of medical doctors. Ordinary folk had no trouble believing cholera contagious and medical remedies dangerous.[9]

The desperate public turned with more than usual attention to those who called for a return to the diet of the forefathers. Sylvester Graham, a troubled Presbyterian minister without a congregation, became the most famous and controversial of the new vegetarians. Graham packaged the old diet and exercise wisdom with a new rationale borrowed from reading in European physiology. From the French physician François J. V. Broussais he took the theory that all disease resulted from overstimulation, especially of the gastrointestinal tract. The theory offered a seemingly scientific support for Graham's opposition to alcohol, tobacco, medicine, excessive sex, and meat. If urbanites overstimulated their stomachs, of course the whole body malfunctioned and they succumbed to cholera or some other result of an unnatural diet. Graham told his New York audiences that cholera should be viewed not as a disease but as the natural result of adopting immoral urban diets and lifestyles.[10]

Graham would return to a bland vegetable diet without spices or stimulants. The contentious clergyman especially became the prophet of whole-meal bread, advocating a return to the homebaked bread of early Americans. The new generation of city dwellers had unwisely shifted to buying bread from public bakers, who used sifted flour from which the husks of grain had been removed to produce a finer, whiter flour. Graham's preference for whole-grain brown bread happened to be nutritionally correct, even though scientists then knew nothing of the food value of the discarded grain husk. Perhaps Graham sensed the value of indigestible bulk in whole grain for the proper functioning of the intestines, but he advocated unbolted flour because it was the more natural product. His suspicion of additives — bakers even added chalk to make whiter bread — led Graham to object to them, including yeast, and he thus became a promoter of unleavened bread.[11]

Most physicians had little good to say about prophet Graham, but Dr. William A. Alcott of Boston began the first health
food store in America for the purpose of supplying Graham
bread, as well as fresh fruit and vegetables grown on virgin,
unfertilized soil. Like most other health reformers Alcott had
once suffered ill health that did not respond to chemical medicines and then had turned to curing himself. His Boston vegetar-
ianism had preceded Graham's lectures, and his own more pro-
lific writings surely reached more Americans. He and not Graham served as president of the American Vegetarian Society.[12]

Alcott wrote guides for the housewife, assuring her that
"prevention is better than cure" and that she could prevent more
pain with her vegetable menu that the ablest physician could
cure. Plain, simple vegetables were healthier and more nutritious than beef steak, he assured his readers. A diet of bread,
fruits, and vegetables—potatoes, beans, corn, peas, turnips,
parsnips, carrots, squashes, pumpkins, and cabbages—would
save Americans from cholera. And how much better were these
vegetables and fruits grown at home. Of strawberries, Alcott
wrote:

> How pleasant to pluck them soon after sunrise, in all their native
> richness and freshness. The labor of gathering them, added to the
> rest of the stomach during the night, is the best preparation for
> their reception. In these circumstances, what more elegant break-
> fast can possibly be prepared—what more likely to raise the heart
> in thanksgiving to the bounteous author of all good—than a
> basket or dish of strawberries, just from their native vines and
> stems, with all the richness of fragrance and deliciousness of taste,
> which in these circumstances clusters around them? And who is
> there, with his mixed, heating, heated, greasy breakfast, might not
> well envy . . . his fortunate neighbor.[13]

Alcott, to be sure, had his more cranky theories: cold, dry,
mature vegetables were best. The zealot banned hot soups and
porridge, as well as corn-on-the-cob. If theory told him that
mature vegetables were more nutritious, then green corn and
green beans were rejected. And he had a special prejudice
against garden greens, which he found unappetizing unless
dressed with the prohibited seasonings—oil, vinegar, sugar, and

pepper. So greens were out. "Why should the healthy stomach be filled with such trash?" he asked.[14]

While the medical profession rejected Alcott and Graham as extremists, many physicians agreed on the superiority of vegetables. In 1835 the *Boston Medical Journal* printed Dr. Luther V. Bell's long essay on diet, criticizing the "overstimulating" meat that comprised too great a proportion of the New England diet. Bell thought most New England diseases to be a consequence of exhausting the body by overstimulating food. The population had departed from the simple diet of the first settlers, who had lived long lives on plain bread and milk for supper. After New Englanders unwisely shifted to meat three times a day, their health problems had then begun "requiring the employment of the lancet and other depleting measures to an extent unknown and unparalleled in other countries."[15]

The medical message of vegetables and exercise traveled to American women through Catherine Beecher's book on home management, *A Treatise on Domestic Economy* (1842). Most medical men, she said, traced disease and death to intemperance of meat eating. "To take meat but once a day," she wrote, "and this in small quantities, compared with the common practice, is a rule, the observance of which would probably reduce the amount of fevers, eruptions, headaches, bilious attacks and the many other ailments which are produced or aggravated by too gross a diet." And to secure the preferable vegetable food, women were urged to garden. American women of the wealthy classes were in especially poor health because they avoided fresh air exercise so common among ladies of other nations. "Walking and riding and gardening, in the open air, are practiced by women of other lands," Beecher insisted, "to a far greater extent, than by American females."[16]

Gardening and farming journals all preached the gospel of vegetarian health. One can read in the *Southern Agriculturist* that many flesh-eating Southerners died young or suffered from gout, rheumatism, or bilious complaints, while vegetable eaters lived into old age. Southern vegetarians shuddered to see the dining tables of their rash acquaintances in summer, "fuming with roast beef, boiled mutton, raving hot, nay, mad turtle soup; and not a single vegetable." Such a meaty diet invited "plague, pestilence, fever, dyspepsia, apoplexy, and every other distempter."[17]

Northern observers, and historians too, have mistakenly assumed that Southerners lived almost entirely on hog meat and hoecake. While pork and corn were the diet of the frontier, the march of civilization moved in the South as it did in the North. The older the settlement, the more extensive the garden. The new settler might make do with turnip greens, but the established farmer required collards and cabbage. Robert Squibb's *The Gardener's Calendar for South-Carolina, Georgia and North-Carolina* (1787) included the same garden vegetables found in Bernard McMahon's *The American Gardener's Calendar* (1806). While the Southern diet included more okra, sweet potatoes, and field peas, the vegetarian message of Southern horticultural magazines did not differ from those of the North.[18]

From North to South the agriculture periodicals urged farmers to devote more attention to healthful vegetable gardens with the greatest possible variety of edible plants, including all the greens. This association of vegetables with good health even added new species to the American diet. Rhubarb and tomato, for example, gained acceptance on American tables in the 1830s for reasons of health rather than taste.

The tomato had yet to gain favor in the Northeast before the arrival of cholera. A garden book could even declare that Americans "almost detested" the fruit in 1829. Only southerners and Westerners loved the vegetable then, with the editor of *Southern Agriculturist* reporting their elaborate attention to its culture: planting the seeds in hot beds during the winter month of February, later transplanting to garden soil, staking the plant to hold the fruit off the ground, and then even creating a special fall crop by cutting the top from a mature plant and rooting the cutting in the damp shade. Yes, tomatoes were in "high repute" in Charleston, where they were a main ingredient for okra gumbo.[19]

Out west in the Ohio valley, English visitor Frances Trollope discovered the American tomato in the Cincinnati markets in the summer of 1828. "From June till December," she said, "tomatoes (the great luxury of the American table in the opinion of most Europeans) may be found in the highest perfection in the market at about six pence the peck." Trollope soon rented a cottage for her family in a nearby village where she "had the pleasure of gathering our tomatoes from our own gardens, and receiving our milk from our own cow."[20]

In the North, few liked the taste of tomato. As the New York *Genesee Farmer and Gardener's Journal* explained, "There are but few people who are fond of them the first time they taste them." The search for good health, however, quickly forced Northerners to learn to love the red fruit. Judge Jesse Buel assured *Genesee Farmer and Gardener's Journal* readers in 1831 that "the tomato, from its anti-bilous properties, is highly conducive to health, and becomes, by a little use, one of the most desirable dishes upon the table." The "bilous" complaint referred to a multitude of serious indigestion problems, incuding cholera. Later correspondents even implied that the tomato protected families from cholera. One wrote that the red fruit "has been constantly used in various forms, at almost every meal during the last three or four seasons by myself and several acquaintances, whose health continued excellent even when the prevalence of the cholera banished fruits and vegetables from the table." Medical professors made no anti-cholera claims for tomatoes, but some did predict that the fruit would replace calomel as an internal medicine for diarrhea, dyspepsia, and bilous attacks. At the Willoughby University of Lake Erie, medical professors promoted the tomato remedy. The University of Maryland's distinguished Dr. Robley Dunglison more modestly pronounced the tomato "one of the most wholesome and valuable esculents that belong to the vegetable kingdom."[21]

In response to medicinal touting of the tomato a growing demand for the fruit doubled the tomato market in New York City during the summer of 1835. One bold market gardener, who had planted his entire farm with tomatoes, boasted of an $1,800 fortune earned from growing thc new vegetable of "ascertained wholesomeness," which New Yorkers now ate fresh or added to soups and stews.[22] An approaching winter season without the miracle fruit seemed unthinkable, and gardening journals recommended a recipe for preserving a bushel of the "healthful vegetable" until next summer's crop ripened:

> Take your tomatoes and pour boiling water over them, skin them;
> then boil them well, after which add a cup of salt, a table spoonful
> of black pepper, one of cayenne, and ounce of cloves, an ounce of
> cinnamon, and an ounce of mace, mix well, and put the tomatoes
> into small jars, run mutton suet over them and tie them up, either
> in strong blue paper or buckskin.

Newspaper testimony continued to advocate the tomato as a
miracle cure:

> In all complaints attended by torpor and inactivity of the liver and
> bowels, it is a speedy and sovereign remedy; for the sick head-ache
> ditto; for dyspepsia it never fails. For all . . . diseases of the kid-
> ney and urinary passages, it is worth more, and will do more good,
> than all other medicines put together. . . . For scrofulous diseases
> generally of the glandular system, it is one of the best remedial
> agents that can be found, if not the very best. All diseases of an
> occult nature, requiring the aid of mercury in some form for their
> cure, will yield more readily to the free use of the tomato.[23]

To no one's surprise, a new patent medicine, "Miles' Compound Extract of Tomato," appeared on the market by 1837.
And a decade later Robert Buist's *The Family Kitchen Garden*
could report that the tomato was universally grown by gardeners, occupied as much garden space as cabbage, and was
served on every table from July to October, raw, stewed,
stuffed, or fried. A new variety, Large Red, could grow to
eighteen inches in circumference. Hundreds of acres of market
gardens grew tomatoes for those urbanites who bought from the
city fruit and vegetable markets.

The cholera years also pushed a second vegetable, rhubarb,
into a favored position in the kitchen garden. The Asian rhubarb root had been for centuries a strictly medicinal plant used
as a purge and as a corrective and tonic remedy for the digestive
system. Using the red stalk rather than the root seems to have
been introduced in England by the mid-seventeenth century.
New vegetables frequently take a century to gain acceptance, as
did the Irish potato, and rhubarb seems not to have been intro-

duced into America before the 1770s. McMahon wrote enthusiastically about the use of the rhubarb stalks in pies in his 1806 gardening book, and it was as the "pie plant" that rhubarb was to gain popularity. The first terrible summer of cholera in America turned the plant into a sovereign remedy for diarrhea. The editor of the *American Farmer and Gardener* reported that his daughter had approached death from cholera infantum (diarrhea) before he baked a rhubarb tart and cured her in a single day. The *New England Farmer and Horticultural Journal* also reported, "During the present summer our children have had frequent attacks of summer complaint, and we have applied the usual remedies with little effect. In each instance we have been obliged to resort to the rhubarb at last." The new panacea for diarrhea retained its reputation. Four summers later, the *American Farmer and Gardener* reported rhubarb unequaled in curing "those distressing afflictions of the bowels which so affect our children and carry them off by hundreds each summer. No head of a family who regards the health of his offspring would be without some dozen plants in his garden, as in them he will have a sure and certain curative."[24]

Rhubarb surely tasted better than mercurous chloride when prepared according to the printed recipe: Stew a dozen rhubarb stalks in a pan with lemon peel, cinamon, two cloves, and sugar. The resulting marmalade could be served on dry toast to the sick child or converted into a pie with the addition of grated nutmeg, one-fourth pound of butter, one egg white and four yolks, and a pastry crust.[25] The addition of fats for the baked rhubarb pie runs counter to twentieth-century medical advice for diarrhea, but either pie or jelly were reported to have delighted and cured children. Perhaps the enormous amounts of vitamin C in rhubarb did have a salutary effect on various digestive complaints.

Rhubarb succeeded better in the North. This perennial from Siberia thrived in cool climates. The hot Southern sun wilted the pie plant and encouraged crown rot. Only by shading rhubarb could Southerners get their roots through the first summer. Surely the difficulty in growing rhubarb in the South prevented the plant from ever gaining a permanent place in either Southern gardens or diet.

Gardeners usually claimed that their hobby provided an additional benefit—mental health. Plants were reported to have a calming, tranquilizing effect, neutralizing the corrosive acids of commercial and social life. Anger, hostility, jealousy, envy, distrust, and revenge melted away in the garden. Rural scenes were soothing: "Graceful trees seem to wave a welcome to the gardener's footsteps; flowering plants, holding up their little cups to catch the dew, seem to smile upon him as he passes, and heavy laden fruit trees drop their ripe products into his hands, as if to reward him for his care. Yes! in the poor man's garden grow far more than herbs and flowers; kind thoughts, contentment, peace of mind, and joy for weary hours. A garden is a place of healing to the soul."[26]

Even on the southwest frontier, gardens were antidotes for unhappiness. In the Mexican borderland of Texas an American emigrant and real-estate developer, Thomas McFarland, kept a journal in which he wrote in 1839: "When the heart is troubled or the mind morose or feverish, a walk in a garden handsomely arranged, is sufficient to give relief. . . . A garden has a tendency to draw the mind from troubled thoughts." While growing enough food in his paled kitchen garden to "half support" his family, McFarland expanded his plant list to seventy-seven species, including not only greens and vegetables such as lettuce, cabbage, onion, garlic, mustard, parsley, kale, celery, peas, beans, squash, cucumber, radishes, carrots, beets, parsnips, turnips, okra, corn, tomatoes, Irish potato, and eggplant; but herbs—pepper, tansy, mint, sorrel, sage, thyme, rue, saffron, hoarhound, pennyroyal, fennel, marigold, and wormwood; fruits—peach, fig, raspberry, quince, plum, sour orange, melons, pomegranates, and strawberries; and ornamentals—althea, roses, pinks, cockscomb, poppies, sunflower, celosia, and iris. McFarland learned the Latin names and country of origin of most of his plants. And he experienced the pleasures of a "well arranged garden" and the joy of "Cucumbers!! Cucumbers!!" on May 19, "1st time this year eaten or ate today! We could have had them three or four days sooner, but saved the *first* coming for seed!"[27]

Beauty and bounty rewarded gardeners while their minds received constant stimulation by the growth and change of garden plants. "The germination of the seed, the development of the leaf, the growth of the stock and branches, the expansion of the flower, the swelling, maturing and gathering of the fruit, and the diversity in foliage, flowers and fruits" provided a succession of pleasant sensations.[28] The science of botany, soil analysis, and plant diseases provided a lifetime of intellectual challenge for the curious.

To be sure, an occasional garden hater could be found. An angry New England intellectual, such as Ralph Waldo Emerson, frustrated by an inability to write and unable to decide whether to embark on a British lecture tour, could lament, "The genius of scholarship & gardening are incompatible." Emerson took his frustrations out on the garden, especially after he bought three more acres and added to the garden:

> In an evil hour I pulled down my fence & added Warren's piece to mine. No land is bad, but land is worse. If a man own land, the land owns him. Now let him leave home, if he dare. Every tree and graft, every hill of melons, every row of corn, every hedge-shrub, all he had done and all he means to do, stand in his way like creditors when he so much as turns his back on his house. Then the devotion to these vines & cornfields I find narrowing & poisonous. I delight in long free walks. These free my brain and serve my body. . . . But these stoopings & scrapings & fingerings in a few square yards of garden are dispiriting, drivelling, and I . . . have grown peevish & poor spirited.[29]

But Emerson did not always hate his garden. "When I go into my garden with the spade & dig a bed," he said on another occasion, "I feel such an exhilaration & health from the work that I discover that I have been defrauding myself all this time in letting others do for me what I should have done with my own hands."[30]

Other New England romantics were garden lovers. Emerson's own gardener, Henry David Thoreau, created his literary masterpiece *Walden* by withdrawing from society to live with nature and his own garden. One passage in *Walden* especially reflects the therapeutic benefits of chopping weeds in the garden:

That's Roman wormwood, — that's pigweed, — that's sorrel, — that's piper-grass, — have at him, chop him up, turn his roots upward to the sun, don't let him have a fiber in the shade, if you do he'll turn himself t'other side up and be as green as a leek in two days. A long war . . . with weeds, those Trojans who had sun and rain and dews on their side. Daily the beans saw me come to the rescue armed with a hoe, and thin the ranks of their enemies, filling up the trenches with weeds dead. Many a lusty crest-waving Hector, that towered a whole foot above his crowding comrades, fell before my weapon and rolled in the dust.[31]

Thoreau has a great reputation for nonviolence, yet this passage is distinctly militant. Taking hostility and frustration out on the weeds and insects has always been a beneficial outlet for gardeners. This war on unwanted plants may be bad for weeds but is good for gardeners and their fellows.

Another New England romantic, Nathaniel Hawthorne, reflects the parental pleasure the gardener takes from plants:

The natural taste of man for the original Adam's occupation is fast developing itself in me. I find that I am a good deal interested in our garden; although, as it was planted before we came here, I do not feel the same affection for the plants as if the seed had been sown by my own hands. It is something like nursing and educating another person's children. Still, it was a very pleasant moment when I gathered the first mess of string beans, which were the earliest esculents that the garden contributed to our table. And I love to watch the successive development of each new vegetable, and mark their daily growth, which always affects me with a new surprise. It is as if something were being created under my own inspection, and partly by my own aid. One day, perchance, I look at my bean-vines, and see only the green leaves clambering up the poles; again, tomorrow, I give a second glance, and there are the delicate blossoms; and a third day, one somewhat closer inspection, I discover the delicate young beans, hiding among the depths of the foliage. Then, each morning, I watch the swelling of the pods, and calculate how soon they will be ready to yield their treasures. All this gives a pleasure and an ideality, hitherto unthought of, to the business of providing sustenance for my family. I suppose Adam felt it in Paradise; and of merely and exclusively earthly enjoyments, there are few purer and more harmless to be experienced.[32]

Out west in Indiana another New Englander, Henry Ward Beecher, provides another illustration of the psychic benefits of gardening. When the Congregational minister suffered nervous excitement from his work as a preacher, he turned to garden reading, not only the seed and fruit catalogues but also British and American works on botany and horticulture, including Loudon's *Encyclopedia of Horticulture*. Garden reading and especially physical work with his hands "soothed excited nerves," leading Beecher to expand his vegetable, fruit, and flower garden across two nearby rented lots. On the day his stillborn son was buried, March 11, 1840, Beecher set out onions, cabbage, and cauliflower. Gardening helped him survive, and his enthusiasm for the hobby was instrumental in his organizing an Indianapolis horticulture society that same year. Five years later he even took on the editorship of the *Western Farmer and Gardener*.[33]

Horticultural societies, such as the one Beecher organized in Indiana, propagandized gardening and the new creed of country life in America. These societies were nineteenth-century creations. Beginning with the first in New York in 1818, permanent horticultural societies multiplied a decade later with the founding of the Pennsylvania Horticultural Society and the Massachusetts Horticultural Society. Growing rapidly, ten societies organized by 1837, and their number further multiplied to forty by 1852. These societies did more than exchange information on fruits, flowers, and landscape gardening; they also advocated country living.[34]

The health and beauty of country living were invariably contrasted unfavorably with crowded, diseased, and immoral city life. The bigger the city, the greater the country life propaganda. In New York City, a Horticultural Association speaker confessed:

> When I pass through the streets of this great city, where the senses are continually assailed by noisome vapors, I am filled with wonders that thousands, who are not necessarily and exclusively confined to the city do not habitually escape from the crowded streets and stifling air as soon as the business of the day is done, and place themselves and their families in some pleasant cottage or statelier mansion . . . where they might breathe the perfume of

flowers, the new mown hay, and look forth upon the beauty and majesty of nature. Happy will it be, not only for the health, but also for the morals and intellectual character of our fellow citizens, when this practice shall become more general than it is.[35]

With so many beneficial and healthful assets, country life inevitably became stylish in urban America. The single propagandist who more than any other gave country living the approval of cultural style was Andrew Jackson Downing, author of *Treatise on the Theory and Practice of Landscape Gardening* (1841). An Anglophile who borrowed the British gardenesque landscape style, Downing took pleasure in describing country life as part of our Anglo-Saxon inheritance. Our English forefathers had been settled country gardeners, and we must return from our pioneer conquest of the wilderness and the equally crude struggle for riches to a more highly cultivated country life. To be sure, we had also inherited the warrior Anglo-Saxon love of conquest, such as the expansionist urge to overrun Mexico and to dominate the earth, but Downing preferred to promote the gardening inheritance. "We rejoice much more in the love of country life, the enjoyment of nature, and the taste for rural beauty, which we also inherit from our Anglo-Saxon forefathers," Downing wrote, wishing for Americans to become a settled people, unlike those Tocqueville had seen building a retirement home only to sell it before the roof was on. Optimistic Downing counted the growth of horticultural societies as evidence that culture was winning over primitiveness. Even as far west as St. Louis a society organized by 1847.[36]

Downing praised country living through his editorials in the *Horticulturist*. His suburban dream advocated a refined architecture, garden, and intellectual life in which builders created graceful, curved roads around beautiful cottages having the finest in fruits, vegetables, and ornamentals. All sensible people wished to retire to such a suburb, he believed, either wholly or partially, and now such cultured homes in the country were possible for New York City merchants. Railroads had made the country cottages possible by 1848, destroying "old notions of time and space" and permitting city people to live the good life among plants in the country air.[37]

Americans could now have the best of both worlds. They could work in the cities with their opportunities but live in the country where outdoor exercise along with a vegetable diet and the other relaxing country pleasures promised the healthy life.

The suburbs surely represented a compromise between ambition and prudent concern for health and comfort. Here, a person could have the money and culture of urban life, but garden with the pleasure and health of a countryman.

6 : SEED CATALOGUES AND STRAIGHT ROWS

The nineteenth century changed both America and its kitchen gardens. In that century the United States spread across the continent, tied itself together with a railroad system, built urban centers, and erected national corporations. Advertising in this new commercial age altered food growing by persuading gardeners to abandon their ancient practices of seed saving and laying out English beds in the garden. Propaganda pushed Americans into believing that they must get in step with the modern world by purchasing the products of commercial firms—garden plows and packaged seed.

For as long as people had gardened, they saved seed to plant the next year's crop. The ritual of seed saving—collecting, drying, labeling, and storing—required as much attention as preparing the soil for spring planting. Most garden vegetables self-pollinate and remain genetically consistent, but some, such as the squashes, require cross-pollination by bees who may well mix plant characteristics if more than one variety is planted in the garden. Growers who knew the rules of cross-pollination, and who resisted eating their earliest and best plants but allowed them to mature seed pods, could actually improve their heirloom seed year after year. Even if an occasional harvest were a disaster, and no seed were saved, or if family seed "ran out"— degenerated into undesirable plants—one could usually trade for fresh seed from a neighbor. Only a desperate, lazy, or profligate gardener, as well as one experimenting with new plants, must purchase seed from town.

Seed stores in eighteenth-century America imported a small supply of European vegetable and herb seed, offering a variety of peas, cabbages, lettuce, carrots, onions, and spinach from their bulk bags and barrels.[1] Seedsmen were also an important source of gardening information, writing the early gardening books. In Charleston, South Carolina, the seed importer Robert Squibb published *The Gardener's Calendar for South-Carolina, Georgia and North-Carolina* (1787), devoting 183 pages to a month-by-month essay of the gardening work to be performed in the South Atlantic states. In Philadelphia the seed and nurseryman Bernard McMahon published an even larger book, *The American Gardener's Calendar* (1806), which dominated the garden book field for the first half of the century, running through eleven editions.

The Boston, Philadelphia, and New York firms expanded into the smaller towns in the nineteenth century by sending out boxes of seed packets to be placed on commission with local merchants. The wooden seed box, filled with rows of paper envelopes, served equally well as a shipping container and as a store counter display rack. The paper seed envelopes in the box were an invention of the Shakers, religious sectarians whose New York communities began growing vegetable seed for the market in the 1790s. Shakers were the first to put seeds in small paper envelopes, and in 1795 the New Lebanon community sold $406 worth of beet, carrot, cucumber, and squash seed grown on its farm commune. As their seed business grew beyond the local area, the Shaker seed wagon became an annual precursor of spring across America.[2]

The secular seed companies of David Landreth, Grant Thorburn, Joseph Breck, and Frank Comstock were not slow to send out their own wagons, commission boxes, and advertising literature. Seedsmen introduced catalogues to the country dealers with vegetable lists and then added descriptions and planting directions. After the first catalogues by Goldthwaite and Moore (1796), Landreth (1811), and Thorburn (1822), competitive seed lists quickly grew so large that Indiana gardener

COPYRIGHTED 1887.   BY W. ATLEE BURPEE & CO PHILADA

THE VANDERGAW CABBAGE.

This new Cabbage, which we now offer for the first time, was procured two years since, at ten dollars per pound, from a famous Long Island Market Gardener, whose name it bears. Mr. Vandergaw has been selecting this variety for many years, and has sold the Seed annually to neighboring growers of Cabbage for the New York Market as high as $20.00 per ℔ and never less than $10.00 per ℔. Last year we obtained a few pounds at the latter price, expressly to distribute, gratis, for trial among our customers before offering it for sale. From all parts of the country comes *unanimous praise*, and we could fill many pages of our Catalogue with equally as strong testimonials as those published below. THE VANDERGAW forms large solid heads, much larger than *Early Summer* and almost as early. The quality is very fine and, like our famous Surehead Cabbage, it is remarkable for its certainty to head. The crop of Seed is so limited that *we can only offer it in sealed packets,*—each packet bearing a *fac-simile* reduced illustration of the above engraving.

Per pkt. 20 cts. ; 3 pkts. for 50 cts.

Every Plant Makes a Good Salable Head.

ALBERT W. KIDDER, Turin, N. Y., Oct. 7th, 1887, writes :—I am very much pleased with the Vandergaw Cabbage you sent me for trial. I think it is the best cabbage I ever raised. I set out *50 plants*, and *every one had a good salable head*. I shall want some of the seed for next year.

Weighed 20 Pounds, and Very Early.

F. A. BENSON, Biddeford, Maine, Sept. 22d, 1887, writes :—The sample packet of Vandergaw Cabbage you sent me last spring did extra well. Without any extra cultivation, it proved *a sure header*, and the heads were LARGE and COMPACT ; some WEIGHING 20 POUNDS. They are VERY EARLY and HAVE EXCELLENT TABLE QUALITIES.

Large Heads, Solid as an Apple.

CHAS. KRIEG, Akron, Ind., writes :—The package of Vandergaw Cabbage you sent me did very well, and was the best cabbage we had in the garden. The heads were LARGE and AS SOLID AS AN APPLE. It did much better than the Large Late Flat Dutch, and I consider it *the best cabbage I ever raised.*

A Splendid Cabbage for Early Market.

MYRON KENYON, Thurman, N. Y., Oct. 14th, 1887, writes :—The Vandergaw Cabbage is by far the best early kind I raised this season. Out of the trial packet you sent me, I had 125 plants, and they were fit for market on the first day of August. The heads weighed from 6 to 18 pounds each and are very much in shape like the Flat Dutch Cabbage. It is VERY HARD and crisp and is A SPLENDID VARIETY for early use. It is a *sure header* and is *of fine flavor.*

The Best for Quality and Productiveness.

L. D. MERRIT, Ironwood, Wis., Oct. 7th, 1887, writes : —Please accept my thanks for the extra seeds sent me last Spring. The Vandergaw is, without exception, THE BEST CABBAGE I EVER GREW here, both as to quality and productiveness. I set out 26 plants, and have 24 good solid heads, although the cut and cabbage worm and beetle have been uncommonly bad and the season very dry. They are just the cabbage for this climate.

Very Hard, Fine Grained and Delicious.

E. D. ROBINSON, Howlett Hill, N. Y., Oct. 7th, 1887, writes :—The Vandergaw Cabbage seed sent me last spring with my seed order, *I sowed, and set out 50 plants, which gave us 50 heads of* VERY HARD, FINE-GRAINED, DELICIOUS CABBAGE *and of good size.* We commenced using it fully 4 weeks ago, and considering the great drought we had and the heat of June and July, which checked its growth, makes it an early variety and much superior to Early York and Winningstadt, in my opinion.

LEONARD JACOBS, Derby, Conn., Oct. 7th, 1887, writes : —The Vandergaw is a splendid cabbage. It heads up well and the quality is excellent.

The Best Cabbage of 50 Kinds.

THEO. FOGLE, Tiffin, Ohio, Oct. 12th, 1887, writes :— It was very dry here the past season and we *had no rain for three months*, but the Vandergaw Cabbage did REMARKABLY WELL ; EVERY PLANT HAD A LARGE HEAD, which was hard and solid. I have tested 50 kinds the last 4 years, and find the Vandergaw the best I ever raised, and can recommend it to anybody.

J. M. EDELEN, Greenwood, Mo., Oct. 10th, 1887, writes : —The Vandergaw Cabbage did better than any other kind I set out, and for earliness I do not think they can be beat.

Read Burpee's PRIZE ESSAYS on CABBAGE and CAULIFLOWER.

Vandergaw cabbage. *Reprinted by permission of W. Atlee Burpee Co.*

BURPEE'S PERFECTION WAX BEAN.

Introduced by us last year, when, the supply being very limited, the seed was sold only in sealed packets, Burpee's Perfection Wax Bean has given splendid satisfaction. It was perfected by eight years' careful selection, and named in our honor by our friend, A. H. Ansley, of Yates County, N. Y., well known as an experienced grower of beans for more than a quarter of a century. In visiting Mr. Ansley the past summer, we were much struck by the exceeding beauty and purity of a ten-acre field of these beans which he was growing for us. It was a grand sight—the plants all uniform and vigorous in growth, free from runners, and so crowded with the magnificent golden-yellow pods (with not a sign of rust), that the whole appeared as might a field of gold. We quite agreed with Mr. Ansley, that "it was the finest field of beans in all New York." The illustration herewith represents two mature pods, natural size, and also a plant showing habit of growth. For *vigor of growth* and *immense productiveness*, it is *unequaled* by any other dwarf Wax Bean, the plants being loaded with the long, rich pods. One of our customers in Massachusetts, (Mr. Saml. Seagrave, of Uxbridge) has sent us a single dwarf plant of BURPEE'S PERFECTION WAX BEAN, on which we counted *fifty-seven matured pods.* In comparison with the Golden Wax, they are as early, or *earlier;* they are of more vigorous habit of growth, and have larger pods on a stronger bush, by which they are held well up from the ground; they have never blighted. Several other new varieties of dwarf wax beans were introduced last year, all of which we *carefully tested,* but found none to equal Burpee's Perfection Wax in productiveness or size of pods. The magnificent, large, golden-yellow pods are of the most handsome appearance and finest quality, being stringless, tender and of very rich flavor.

Per packet 15 cts.; per pint 40 cts.; per quart 80 cts., postpaid, by mail. By express or freight, per quart 50 cts.; 4 qts. $1.75; per peck, $3.00; per bushel $10.00.

Perfection wax bean. *Reprinted by permission of W. Atlee Burpee Co.*

Reverend Henry Ward Beecher complained of the "prodigal multiplication of varieties," with the William R. Prince catalogue of 1842 offending worst with sixty-one different beans, fifty-six types of lettuce, forty-nine cabbages, forty-seven peas, and thirty turnips. Beecher urged that Prince eliminate two-thirds of the listings. "We regard a very fat catalogue as we do a very fat man—all the worse for its obesity."[3]

Rather than following Reverend Beecher's call for puritan simplicity in catalogues, the seed companies were destined to exaggerate in a new direction by adding colored plates in the 1850s to create illustrations more beautiful than real plants. The firms also moved toward direct mail, with B. K. Bliss taking advantage of the post office's new three-cent letter rates by asking customers to mail in their seed orders. As catalogues were sent directly to gardeners they increased in beauty, size—some were even cloth bound in the 1860s—and superlatives. Most touted all their seeds rather than assisting the gardener in making selections, as did the old reliable Thorburn and Landreth. Gardeners immune to the challenge of selecting their own varieties might simply select Thorburn's small number one assortment for five dollars and receive sufficient seed to plant two acres, double cropped.[4]

Mail-order catalogues promoted prejudice against the bulk seed sold traditionally from bags, barrels, and bins by village stores. As *Miss Tiller's Vegetable Garden and the Money She Made By It* (1873) warned, buying locally could result in "poor vegetables and few of 'em . . . unless its a deal better than most village stores. You get fresher seeds from the large dealers, and truer to name. And as most of them post-pay everything right to your hands, it's just as cheap." The fictional Miss Tiller hawked seed catalogues of Vick and Gregory, running on for more than twenty pages with thick descriptions of more than a hundred named varieties of twenty-four garden vegetables. She ordered multiple beans, beets, carrots, corn, cabbage, cucumbers, cress, lettuce, melons, watermelons, pumpkins, parsley, peas, potatoes, radishes, spinach, squash, tomatoes, and turnips, along with single varieties of celery, eggplant, kohlrabi, okra, onion, peppers, parsnips, and salsify. For sweet corn she simply had to plant Vick's "Early Minnesota," followed by Gregory's "Mexi-

BURPEE'S NEW MAMMOTH SILVER KING ONION.

The Mammoth Silver King Onion, *named and introduced by us in 1884*, grows to a most remarkable size—*larger than any other variety in cultivation*, excepting only the New Mammoth Pompeii. The bulbs are of attractive form, flattened, but thick through, as shown in the illustration above. The average diameter of the onions is from 5 to 7½ inches—thus making the circumference from 15 to 22 inches. Single bulbs often attain weights of from 2½ to 4 pounds each. The skin is a beautiful silvery white; the flesh is snowy white, and of a *particularly mild and pleasant flavor*. So sweet and tender is the flesh that it can be eaten raw, like an apple. The Silver King matures early and is *uniformly* of large size and perfect form. Every one desiring the largest and handsomest onions, of the finest flavor, will be more than satisfied with the Silver King. *It cannot be too highly recommended*, either for family use, for exhibition at fairs or in restaurants, or for sale on market, where its size and beauty will prove very striking.

For several years we have offered cash prizes for the largest Silver King Onions grown from our seed. In 1885, Alfred Rose, Penn Yan, N. Y., won the first prize with two onions of the enormous weights of 4¾ lbs. and 4 lbs. 2 ozs. In 1886 our prizes were won by A. Banister, Meadows, Washington Territory, with an onion weighing 4 lbs. 11 ozs., and by T. B. Taylor, of Ellensburgh, W. T., with one weighing 4¼ lbs. The past season (1887) our prizes were won by J. V. H. Young, Arroyo Grande, California, and by George F. Montgomery, Pownal, Vermont, each with a Mammoth Silver King, weighing 4 lbs. 2 ozs.—all grown from seed in one season. We have sold the seed of this magnificent new Italian Onion very extensively, and it has everywhere given unqualified satisfaction. To continue this friendly competition, we again offer, for 1888, **CASH PRIZES OF $25.00 and $10.00** for the two largest onions raised from seed purchased of us this year—the onions, or reliable affidavits of their weights, to be sent to us before Nov. 1st.

Per pkt. 15 cts.; 2 pkts. for 25 cts.; oz. 35 cts.; 2 ozs. 65 cts.; per ¼ ℔ $1.00; per ℔ $3.50.

Burpee's mammoth silver king onion. *Reprinted by permission of W. Atlee Burpee Co.*

can" for midseason corn and the "Crossly" or "Trimble." For beans she insisted on an early crop of bush "Early Valentine" and "Dwarf Wax" to be followed by "Case Knife," which she described as "first class, string or shelled, green or dry, long pods, thick and crisp and tender," then "Concord" and "Giant Wax." For cabbage she ordered Vick's "Wheeler's Imperials," Gregory's "Cannon Ball," "Marblehead Mammoth," "Early Schweinfurth," and "Filderkraut."[5]

Miss Tiller's Vegetable Garden reflected actual New York state gardening practice in the 1850s and 1860s. Although the novel sold as fiction, it seems to have been autobiography. Literary criticism has decided that Anna Warner's novel "can hardly be called fiction at all," for she did not "possess the imaginative ability to transform personal experience into fiction." Anna simply told her own family experience. Her father, a New York City attorney and land speculator, had been ruined by the 1837 financial panic, and the family was forced to retreat up the Hudson River to a farmhouse on Constitution Island, opposite West Point Military Academy, where Anna and her sister Susan learned the skills of cooking, woodcutting, and gardening. They actually began writing best-selling novels because they needed the income. The great pleasure for Anna was gardening, and especially flower culture. After some thirty years of practice, she published an instructional manual—*Gardening by Myself* (1872).[6]

"Catalogues! Catalogues!" Anna Warner exclaimed, were the essential winter preparation for the flower garden. She confessed in *Gardening by Myself* that her family had declared that when others read novels, she studied catalogues. "What shall I get? How shall I have most show and sweetness with the least cost? For *what I can afford,* must come before what I want. One novelty will buy from five to ten old favourites: yet the novelties are so enticing!" Every reader of Miss Warner's *Gardening by Myself* learned that flower gardeners required not only the January catalogue but also the September bulb catalogues for fall planting.[7]

Mail-order catalogues gradually persuaded Americans to abandon the old custom of seed saving. Farmers, and a majority of town gardeners, had still grown their own seed in 1862, but for the postwar generation of gardeners, waiting for the seed catalogue became a cherished tradition. Seedsmen took full advantage of the railroad and the post office to overpower the gardeners with tantalizing engravings of fruit, flower, and vegetable promises. As catalogues ballooned in size, beauty, and promise, seed costs also went down because seedsmen turned from European seed sources and subcontracted the actual growing to American farmers in California and elsewhere.[8]

Before 1870, seedsmen commonly grew native American seeds—corn, beans, squash—on their own farms and imported the other small seeds from European growers. With the transcontinental railroad completed in 1869, sunny California became the great seed-growing center for carrots, endive, leek, lettuce, onion, parsnip, parsley, radish, salsify, and pole beans. Sweet peas were grown on farms there or in Utah, Idaho, Montana, Wisconsin, Michigan, or upstate New York. Sweet corn and vine seeds came from Nebraska, Ohio, New Jersey, Michigan, or California. Watermelon and okra grew best in the South. Europe still provided beets, mangels, cauliflower, rutabaga, and turnips, but the main seed-growing business had become American.[9]

With all seed firms sharing the same products, market advantage shifted to the most resourceful utilizer of the new national advertising. As printed announcements in newspapers and periodicals offered new seed catalogues at the beginning of each year, gardeners chose among seed books with hundreds of illustrations and as many as 250 pages of flower and vegetable descriptions. They could pay one dollar for the cloth bound *Vick's Flower and Vegetable Garden,* which advertised itself as the "most beautiful work of the kind in the world," or thirty-five cents for the *B. K. Bliss Annual,* twenty-five cents for the *D. M. Ferry Seed Annual,* or obtain free seed catalogues from Gregory, Dreer, Hovey, or Henderson. By 1880 the free catalogue offer had clearly triumphed. Then W. Atlee Burpee offered not only a free catalogue but also cash for growing seed from his firm. In 1882, Burpee offered $50 prizes for the three largest melons grown from his seed for the Cuban Queen watermelon. The following year, gardeners were promised $775 in prize money for trying a wide variety of vegetable seed. Scattered

AN EXACT LIKENESS, NATURAL SIZE, OF THE TURNER HYBRID TOMATO.

——THE TURNER HYBRID TOMATO.——

This distinct new variety, named and first introduced by us, has created quite a sensation on account of the enormous size of the tomatoes, their fine quality and the immense crops produced. Eli Gregor, Esq., of Fredericksburg, Ohio, sent us by express six magnificent Turner Hybrid Tomatoes, weighing 7 lbs. 13 ozs. Although averaging nearly **21 ozs. each**, these tomatoes were as smooth and perfect as an apple. Our prize of $25.00 the past season was won by Mr. W. H. Pierce, West Springfield, Mass., who sent us six handsome tomatoes weighing 7 lbs. 2 ozs. and of which the largest specimen weighed 25 ozs. We again offer a prize of **$25.00 cash for the six largest and best Turner Hybrid Tomatoes** raised from seed purchased of us this year. The foliage of The Turner Hybrid differs from that of nearly all other tomatoes, the large leaves being entire and not cut. It is a rank, strong grower, with thick stalks, and is **enormously productive**, *out-yielding all other varieties.* It grows quickly and is ready to market *very early* for so large a tomato. The fruit is *extra large* in size and *remarkably solid.* The illustration above is exactly the natural size of an average specimen which measured 4 by 4⅜ inches in diameter and weighed one pound. The average weight of the tomatoes is from 12 to 18 ounces, but many specimens reach 20 to 24 ounces in weight. They ripen up evenly and are entirely free from core. They make *the handsomest sliced tomatoes* we have ever seen, and have been pronounced by all who have tried them **unequaled in fine flavor** and table qualities. The form of the fruit is round and thick through, very smooth in specimens of medium to large size, and, while the extra large fruits are not so even in outline, they are equal in quality, firm and solid; the color is a very deep brilliant red. *The above illustration, reduced in size, with directions for culture, printed on every package of our extra selected seed.*

Per pkt. 15 cts.; 2 pkts. for 25 cts.; oz. 50 cts.; per ¼ lb $1.50; per lb $5 00.

Turner hybrid tomato. *Reprinted by permission of W. Atlee Burpee Co.*

throughout the Burpee seed catalogue were special offers to the gardener planting Burpee seed and producing the most pods on a Creaseback Pole Bean, the largest Mammoth Pumpkin, or the heaviest Turner Hybrid Tomato. Prizes were also offered for the best "How to Grow" essays for market gardeners. To obtain an advertising slogan, Burpee conducted another contest, announcing the winner, "Burpee's seeds grow," with full-page advertising.[10]

Burpee advertised into industry dominance during the 1880s. Purchasing space regularly in popular national magazines, as well as newspapers and farm journals, he had aroused gardener interest with cash prizes and then offered a free catalogue with "honest descriptions, truthful illustrations and colored plates painted from nature." The Burpee catalogue exaggerated less than Maule's 1887 *Annual,* which depicted huge cauliflowers the size of dining room chairs. Neither did Burpee claim to raise his own seed on the company farm but boasted instead of testing the grower's product on his own scientific trial grounds, growing three thousand seed samples a year and then ordering only the proven best from the professional growers to retail for his customers. Burpee modestly claimed to have won the nation's largest seed order through the "kind words of our customers," but the real key to his market growth had been aggressive national advertising. He purchased more advertising space than did his nearest competitors, Peter Henderson of New York City and James Vick of Rochester.

The *Burpee Farm Annual,* as his seed catalog was called, came bound in a color illustrated cover in 1888, with two special color inserts. Vegetables dominated, taking well over half the 128-page book, beginning with a dozen pages of new novelties such as White Zulu Pole Beans and Tom Thumb Pop Corn, and continuing with a wide selection of forty-six beans, thirty-two cabbages, twenty-one cucumbers, twenty-four herbs, nineteen squashes, and twenty tomatoes, for a total of seventy-three pages of garden seed. Only seven pages were devoted to farm field seeds. The last third of the book advertised flowers for the house and garden. The illustrated Burpee catalogue became a coveted item for gardeners to read, dreaming by the January fireside of spectacular crops to be harvested in the coming sea-

Painted back cover of "Burpee's Seeds." *Reprinted by permission of W. Atlee Burpee Co.*

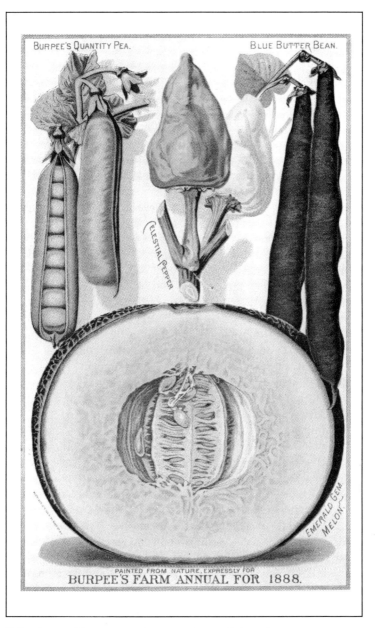

Painted vegetables. *Reprinted by permission of W. Atlee Burpee Co.*

son. And who would dare to place no order and perhaps be dropped from the mailing list for a free catalogue, which would grow in size to 220 pages by the twentieth century?[11]

Only a few of the some eight hundred seed firms in the business by the end of the century became national firms like Burpee. Most remained small regional houses within an industry remaining open enough for new entries into the business. Even in southwest Iowa a farm youngster could still aspire to become a seedsman. Five-year-old Henry Field is said to have been inspired by the 1876 *Vick's Floral Guide,* gathered seed from his mother's garden, packaged them in little homemade envelopes, and sold them to his Aunt Martha for fifty cents. In the 1890s Field began pricing his own garden seed lower than Burpee, selling and distributing from horseback around Shenandoah, Iowa. Then Field cranked out his own four-page catalogue with a hand press in 1899 and moved on to the mail-order business, constructing a seedhouse along the railroad track and sending out a folksy catalogue promoting "Seeds that Yield are Sold by Field." Henry hit the regional big time in the 1920s, especially after he built a radio station on top of his seedhouse and filled the midwest airwaves with country entertainment.[12] But even Henry Field had won his niche in the seed business by following the traditional seed catalogue art of presenting tempting illustrations of flowers and vegetables.

Catalogue advertising carried the illusion of new and wonderful plants for the garden. With eleven hundred known species and varieties of vegetables, old staples could easily be labeled "new and improved," illustrated in color, and described in such glowing terms that any gardener would want to try the seed. But only one new plant appeared in the Gilded Age. A black Virginian picked up a volunteer dwarf lima along the roadside in the 1870s, and after the bean passed through several hands, New York seedsman Peter Henderson brought out the new variety—Henderson's Bush Lima—to enable gardeners to grow limas after 1889 without the bother of staking with tall poles. But while truly new plants were rare, each catalogue gave the illusion of new wonders to plant along with the old reliables. With more old vegetable varieties than a gardener would ever plant in a single lifetime, perhaps the catalogues were not really false to the average gardener.[13]

"How fascinating have the catalogues of the nurserymen become! Can I raise all those beautiful varieties, each one of which is preferable to the other?" asked Charles Dudley Warner as he considered purchasing new strawberries although he already grew fifteen varieties on his three-acre suburban estate outside Hartford, Connecticut. "Oh for the good old days when a strawberry was a strawberry, and there was no perplexity about it," Warner lamented. "There are more berries now than churches; and no one knows what to believe. I have seen gardens which were all experiment, given over to every new thing, and which produced little or nothing to the owners, except the pleasure of expectation." The sensible Warner swore off planting the new catalogue novelties. "May Heaven keep me to the old roots and herbs of my forefathers!" he implored although he realized the futility of opposing progress. "Perhaps, in the world of modern reforms, this is not possible," he admitted, "but I intend now to cultivate only the standard things, and learn to talk knowingly of the rest."[14]

Even the cynical editor of the *Hartford Courant* capitulated to seed catalogues in 1871. By the 1880s gardeners who still saved seed of their own "raisin'," rejecting all "boughten" seed, faced ridicule in the garden magazines as ignorant rubes and bumpkins out of step with the enlightened age. Encouragement for seed saving could still be found in farm magazines, but half the farmers were said to buy garden seed.[15]

Only a gardener so reactionary as to ignore the seed catalogues would still be planting in English beds by the end of the nineteenth century. American garden reformers since the 1820s had urged the end of squares, crosswalks, and hand cultivation in the kitchen garden. The ancient division between field and garden culture should be abolished; garden crops should be cultivated just as the nineteenth-century farmer had learned to cultivate corn by horse-drawn implements. The horse-drawn cultivator could replace hand hoeing and weeding. Double plowing or subsoil plows could easily replace double digging and trenching. If farmers would only abandon the old English gar-

SPECIAL BULK PRICE LIST OF
Beans, Peas and Sweet Corn.

FOR MARKET GARDENERS AND OTHER LARGE BUYERS.—In the general list of vegetable seeds (pages 31 to 69, inclusive) all our prices include prepayment by mail to any post-office in the United States. Below we quote special low prices on Beans, Peas and Sweet Corn, by the quart, peck and bushel. At these prices we make NO CHARGE FOR BAGS, and deliver to express or freight office—the purchaser to pay transportation charges upon receipt of goods.

A comparison of our prices will show MARKET GARDENERS that BURPEE'S RELIABLE SEEDS can now be obtained at very moderate prices. We invite early orders, and request that when ordering, it may be distinctly stated whether the seeds are to be sent by express or freight. Otherwise, we will use our best judgment as to route. In every case WE GUARANTEE THE SAFE ARRIVAL OF ALL SEEDS IN GOOD ORDER.

☞ **MARKET GARDENERS WANTING OTHER VEGETABLE SEEDS IN LARGE QUANTITIES WILL PLEASE WRITE FOR SPECIAL PRICES.**☜ Please state plainly your business (whether Market Gardener, Florist, or Dealer in Seeds), and that you already have our Farm Annual for 1888. Address all applications to

W. ATLEE BURPEE & CO., Seedsmen,

Lock Box 1626 P. O.   PHILADELPHIA, PA.

BEANS—DWARF, BUSH, OR SNAP. *See pages 31 and 32.*

	Quart.	2 Quarts.	4 Quarts.	Peck.	Bushel.
Burpee's Perfection Wax. (*See page 7*)	$0 50	$0 90	$1 75	$3 00	$10 00
New Black-Eye Wax	40	75	1 25	2 00	7 50
Mont D'Or	30	60	1 10	2 00	7 00
Wax Date, Dwarf	40	75	1 25	2 00	7 50
Golden Wax	35	50	90	1 60	6 00
Dwarf German Black Wax	30	50	85	1 50	5 50
Crystal White Wax	40	75	1 25	2 00	7 50
Ivory Pod Wax	30	50	90	1 60	6 00
Dwarf Bonnemain	30	50	80	1 35	5 00
Early Etampes, or First of All	25	40	65	1 10	4 00
Best of All	35	55	90	1 50	5 50
Early Yellow Six Weeks	20	35	65	1 00	3 75
Early Mohawk	20	35	65	1 00	3 75
Extra Early Red Speckled Valentine (Best Round Pod Stock)	25	40	65	1 10	4 00
Refugee	20	35	65	1 00	3 75
China Red-Eye	25	35	65	1 00	3 75
The Goddard, or Boston Favorite	25	45	75	1 25	4 50
New Champion Bush	35	60	1 00	1 75	6 50
Green Gem, or Wonder of France	25	45	75	1 25	4 50
Canadian Wonder (Rose Bean, or Red Flageolet)	25	40	65	1 10	4 00
Royal Dwarf White Kidney	25	40	65	1 10	4 00
White Marrowfat	20	35	60	1 00	3 50
Prolific Tree Bean	25	45	75	1 25	4 50

BEANS—POLE OR CLIMBING. *See page 33.*

Golden Wax Flageolet. (*See page 25, crop short*)	50	90	1 75	3 00	......
White Creaseback. (*See page 24*)	45	75	1 25	2 25	8 00
Lazy Wife's. (*See page 34, crop short*)	50	1 00	......	.....	......
Tall Mont D'Or, or Butter Pole	40	65	1 10	2 10	8 00
Giant Wax (Red Seed)	50	90	1 75	3 25	12 00
Tall German Wax (Black Seed)	35	60	1 10	2 00	7 50
Early Maine, or Essex Prolific	40	65	1 10	2 10	8 00
Southern Prolific, or Kentucky Wonder	35	60	1 00	1 75	6 50
Marblehead Champion	45	75	1 25	2 50	9 00
Horticultural, Cranberry, or Wren's Egg	30	50	90	1 60	6 00
White Dutch Case Knife	30	50	90	1 60	6 00
Scarlet Runner	30	55	1 00	1 75	6 50
White Dutch Runner	30	55	1 00	1 75	6 50
New Extra Early Lima (Jersey)	45	80	1 50	2 75	10 00
Large White Lima	35	65	1 10	2 10	8 00
Small Lima, Carolina, Sieva or Sewee	35	65	1 10	2 10	8 00
New Challenger Lima	40	75	1 35	2 50	9 00
Dreer's Improved Lima	40	75	1 35	2 50	9 00
King of the Garden Lima	50	90	1 60	3 00	11 00

Special bulk price list. *Reprinted by permission of W. Atlee Burpee Co.*

1918 Field seed catalog. *Henry Field Collection, State Historical Society of Iowa. Reprinted by permission.*

den design and switch to the more efficient and economical straight rows, they would spare their wives senseless ancient drudgery. Yet, well past the Civil War, observers still found most gardens laid out on the European plan of small squares.[16]

Garden habits, like others, are resistant to change. And the old ways were not without their own points of superiority. Hand tools worked the soil into a better condition for planting. Raised beds warmed more quickly in the spring and produced earlier vegetables than the horse-cultivated rows. The old beds could be weeded from the walkways, even in wet weather, but no horse could be brought into the wet garden without damaging the soil structure, packing and puddling the clay particles.

When horses and plows entered the garden they endangered the flowers and herbs, especially those perennials that leafed out year after year without reseeding. Perennials had remained happily undisturbed in their old beds but could not live with the new plows and straight rows, so they were moved out of the garden, segregated from the annual vegetables in flower gardens. Or they might be abandoned entirely, and this was the intent of the drug trade, whose advertisements and sales of patent medicines were larger than those of the seed companies.

Until the middle of the nineteenth century, herbs remained a popular subject for American kitchen garden books. Commercial advertising then persuaded Americans to switch from garden herbs to patented medicines, which cost them millions without necessarily bringing better health. Within a single generation after the Civil War, sales of patent medicines rose from three million to seventy-five million dollars. Advertising surely helped sell the replacement for garden herbs; for instance, the manufacturer of a single patent medicine, Lydia E. Pinkham's Vegetable Compound, spent a million dollars a year promoting its commercial preparation. As bottled drugs rose in favor, old herbs disappeared from gardens here and in Britain. With the arrogance of a new generation, poet Rudyard Kipling ridiculed "Our Fathers of Old": "Anything green that grew out of the mold / Was an excellent herb to our fathers of old."[17]

If herbs were obsolete, then so were the English beds in which they were planted. With no beds to bar the way, a horse and plow could move straight across the garden. Even the garden fence no longer presented an obstacle. All fencing — whether stone, picket, or evergreen — had hampered horse-drawn cultivators, which required some ten to twelve feet of turning space at the end of each row. So the horse hoe remained out of the garden until the 1880s; then suddenly, the garden enclosure ceased to be necessary. The invention of barbed-wire fencing enabled the farmer to securely fence his animals inside the pasture and eliminate the need for the garden enclosure. So the garden fence came down, and the farmers freely tilled the vegetables with horse and cultivator. "We have tried the English garden long enough," gardeners concluded in 1890; "let us have an American garden for American farmers."[18]

In the towns, gardeners also dropped the English beds as American industry offered a substitute for the modern horse hoe. The wheel hoe had been invented by home craftsmen in the 1840s but had never caught on with more than a few market gardeners before English beds began to be replaced by straight rows. Then American industry mass-produced these hand-pushed garden plows, advertised them in the 1880s, and even succeeded in having them distributed as a bonus gift for subscribing to a newspaper. "Hoes, spades and rakes relics of the past," the *Arkansas Gazette* announced. "Every person having a garden should own one of these plows. A boy of ten can keep the garden in perfect order, doing better work than a grown man can do with a hoe." The wheel hoe sold for as little as two dollars, with the top-of-the-line "Planet Jr." going for ten dollars for a combined single-wheel hoe with attachments, including a cultivator, rake, plow, and seed drill. Now every home could have straight rows and mechanized gardening even without the horse.[19]

But could gardeners accept the new garden plow and abandon the ancient hoe that had given pleasure for generations? Garden literature had spoken fondly of the health benefits — soothing the spirit — induced by going among the vegetables. "There is probably nothing that has such a tranquillizing effect, and leads into such content, as gardening," Charles Dudley Warner said in *My Summer in a Garden* (1871). He specifically praised the use of the hoe. "In half an hour I can hoe myself right away from this world," he said.[20] Having learned from experience that the hot sun on his back and the hoe in his hand proved "better than much medicine," Warner and others of his generation were not likely to permit advertising to persuade them to let their hoes rust in the barn while they adopted the modern cultivation tool. There is evidence that the generation born before the Civil War resisted modernization into the 1890s, and one gardener surely spoke for them in *American Garden,* complaining that the wheel hoe was much too clumsy an instrument for an individual weed. Could the wheel hoe really be more efficient than the hand tool? "Scores of times during the season," the gardener asserted, "the ten or fifteen minutes one has to enjoy the flower, fruit and vegetable garden — and that would suffice for the needful weeding with the hoes we are celebrating — would be lost in harnessing horses or adjusting and oiling squeaky wheel-hoes."[21]

While obstinate traditionalists resisted the wheel hoe, iron industry advertisers as well as professional horticulturists emphasized that the new tool not only weeded rapidly but also saved moisture for vegetable plants by creating a dust mulch that checked evaporation and captured new rainfall. By the twentieth century all garden writers fell into line. "The wheel-hoe is the most important garden tool invented within a century," *Garden Magazine* said. And *Country Life in America* proclaimed it "the tool of all tools for the home gardener, the implement which is really indispensable, a perfect substitute for the horse-hoe, and the one piece of garden equipment which more than any other makes garden work effective and pleasant, even to the member of the family little used to outdoor work." According to this nineteenth-century writer, even a woman equipped with her "Iron Age," "Planet Jr.," or "Gem of the Garden" and attachments — rake, scraper, cultivator, and plow — could delight in working in the garden.[22]

Although the dominant culture announced a new American garden, the older European style actually survived for another generation in urban centers, where four million Italians immigrated in the generation after 1890. Italian Americans gardened in the traditional raised bed style that all European peoples, including the English, French, Germans, and Italians, had shared. The traditional medieval layout and practice may have appealed to new immigrants as a means of preserving cultural roots, a sense of stability, and a sense of well-being in a new country where much tradition was uprooted. Those who moved out to the end of the trolley lines where they might have space for growing herbs and vegetables gave America a pluralism in ethnicity as well as garden style.[23]

Outside immigrant neighborhoods, kitchen gardens became miniature versions of farm fields at the end of the nineteenth century, and for more than two generations efficient gardeners proudly pushed their garden plows between the vegetable rows before twentieth-century technology promoted the gasoline-powered rotary cultivator, raised beds replaced straight rows, and compost mulching replaced the dust mulch. For a time it seemed that only a few hand plows would be pushed into the twenty-first century, but in the age of ecology the wheel hoe has made a comeback. This nineteenth-century cultivation tool worked without noise, fumes, fuel costs, or expensive maintenance, although inflation raised the purchase price. The rediscovered wheel hoe of the 1980s sold in a low-wheeled Swiss model for ninety-five dollars or the American high-wheeled model for fifty-two dollars. Both the nineteenth-century innovations—the wheel hoe and the seed catalogue—remain permanent contributions to gardening.

7 : BALANCE OF NATURE IN THE GARDEN

ible readers in the Western tradition long assumed that all descendants of Adam and Eve had been sentenced to till a cursed ground plagued by thorns and thistles. Since Adam and Eve's expulsion from the garden of Eden, all gardeners labored by the sweat of their brows in the unfriendly soil, warring against countless hostile weeds and pests. In this antagonistic world all creatures crossing the garden fence were assumed to be hostiles, to be met with ruthless extermination by the beleaguered gardener.

Not until the eighteenth century did a more benign view of the gardener's world emerge. Then, with the physical mastery of the wilderness and the intellectual mastery of the laws of the universe, people were less fearful of nature and more willing to believe that God had created a benevolent design for His world. Rather than constructing a prison for punishment, God had created a generous world in perfect harmony where every force encountered an opposing force, resulting in a perfect balance. The wise Creator designed a planet in which the plants and animals were mutually necessary and beneficial.[1]

God had created noxious insects, but He had also created beautiful birds to eat the pests. Man, who early acquired a taste for eating songbirds, offended the new sensibilities of the eighteenth century that insisted he restrict his appetite for at least the most efficient insect eaters. Thomas Jefferson's botanist, Benjamin Smith Barton, advocated the official protection of the smaller house wren, bluebird, crested flycatcher, and woodpecker to preserve the balance against noxious insects.[2] While insects were the favorite food of almost all American birds, Barton said, these four special friends of the garden should certainly be saved from the cooking pot.

For most of the nineteenth century birds remained the main hope of naturalists and gardeners for keeping insects under control. Of course, gardeners would not leave the bugs entirely to the birds. Even Barton stepped in to save his cucumbers and squash by dusting the plants with tobacco and red pepper. Nineteenth-century gardeners had a variety of additional homemade dusts and sprays, including lime, soot, wood ashes, lye, tar, turpentine, salt, urine, soap suds, sulfur, wormwood, and elder or black walnut leaves. Yet despite these remedies, gardeners were more likely to intervene with mechanical rather than chemical means. For cucumber and squash bugs the forefinger and thumb were most recommended. Twice daily inspections of the leaves for crushing bugs and eggs were regarded as more effective insect control than even tobacco juice. A gardener might also put down an old shingle by each hill and destroy in the early morning all bugs hiding under it. Young chickens might be allowed to run in the garden and devour the bugs. For cutworms, destroying by soil cultivation or guarding against them by placing paper collars around plants served as the best remedies. For the cabbage looper, a cabbage leaf broken off every evening and placed on top of the cabbage could collect most of the worms during the night and find them waiting their physical destruction in the morning. Gardeners even had bug lights in the early nineteenth century—fires built on platforms to lure all the moths and night flying insects.[3]

The gardener's normal hatred of bugs was expressed by the novelist Nathaniel Hawthorne, who lamented that while his garden flourished like that of Eden, the plants suffered much more than Adam and Eve's. He noted in his journal:

I am forced to carry on a continuous warfare with squashbugs, who, were I to let them alone for a whole day together, would perhaps quite destroy the prospects of the whole summer. It is impossible not to feel bitterly angry with these unconscionable vermin, who scruple not to do such infinite mischief to me, with only the profit of a meal or two to themselves. For their own sakes, they ought at least to wait till the squashes are better grown. There is an absolute pleasure in taking vengeance on them. Why is it, I wonder, that Nature has provided such a host of enemies for every useful esculent, while the weeds are suffered to grow unmolested, and are provided with such tenacity of life, and such methods of propagation, that the gardener must maintain a continual struggle, or they will hopelessly overwhelm him?[4]

Why did nature permit a growing number of insect pests? Horticultural journals blamed not God but people's destruction of the songbirds. Because birds ate fruit and grain, farmers had permitted boys to roam their fields and shoot every bird they met. The custom of ritually shooting birds on election day in New England continued until mid-century, with all boys from age five to twenty going hunting for birds, killing ten to forty each, and then celebrating their gamebags. Americans then regarded a bag of songbirds as good eating. Not content with eating turkey and passenger pigeons, even robin redbreast served as a great table food. In the fall, when flocks of robins gathered, boys supplied the urban markets with birds, easily killing thirty dozen in a single excursion.[5]

Gardeners and naturalists in America and elsewhere sought to change the sensibilities of the public by explaining the role of songbirds in preserving God's balance of nature. Even robins occasionally ate a little fruit, but they more than earned their keep by devouring insect pests. Reverend Henry Ward Beecher asserted, "We charge every man with positive dishonesty who drives birds from his garden at fruit time. The fruit is theirs as well as yours. They took care of it as much as you did. If they had not eaten egg, worm and bug, your fruit would have been pierced and ruined. They only come for wages. No honest man will cheat a bird of his spring and summer's work."[6] The shotgun should never be pointed at songbirds. Those fruit growers who believed the birds took more than their fair share should instead drape nets over their trees or place stuffed cats in the branches to frighten the birds away. Unless boys stopped killing the songbirds, naturalists insisted, crops would all be overwhelmed by insects. As a correspondent to the *Horticulturist* declared:

> God provides a balance between insects and the feathered tribe; but man, in his cruelty and impiety, destroys the balance; and the insects creep upon his fruit to pay him for it. It is only after civilization has destroyed the birds of a country, that insects overrun it. The birds live upon insects. All agriculturists, gardeners, fruit growers, philanthropists, all good people should discountenance the destruction of birds. . . . So greatly has the stock of birds been reduced, that cultivators are beginning to be alarmed.[7]

Fruit growers, who suffered more than vegetable gardeners from bird raids, certainly spoke out in defense of the balance of nature. The New York Fruit Growers Club speaker for 1869 asserted: "We have destroyed our great forests that sheltered the birds; then we made war upon all of the feathered tribe, killing those that feed upon insects as well as those that feed upon grain and fruits, and in this way we have struck a balance against ourselves."[8]

To turn the balance back against insects, enterprising Americans imported a bird that did not need the forest but could build its nests in buildings. The first English sparrows were imported in the 1850s, and the birds continued to be purchased for twenty years. As colonies increased in Eastern cities, sparrows were sold farther west for a dollar a pair. But by the end of the 1870s, the sparrow's reputation rapidly declined. Although this European house sparrow needed no forest trees for nests, it was messy, noisy, and didn't eat insects. The sparrow preferred seeds and actually drove away insect eaters by taking the nesting boxes of wrens, martins, swallows, and bluebirds. The sparrow destroyed wheat, corn, and fruits, as well as vegetable buds. When the contents of sparrow stomachs were analyzed by the Department of Agriculture, only 14 percent contained any insect remains. The sparrow preferred to feast on partially digested grain from horse droppings. Farmers and the bird watchers in the American Ornithologists Union declared the bird a public enemy in 1885 and recommended shooting, trapping, and poisoning.[9]

Gardeners were less inclined to agree with the death sentence for the English sparrow. The most popular garden authority of the Gilded Age, Peter Henderson, defended the sparrow. "Since the European sparrows have favored us with their presence in such numbers," he wrote in *Gardening for Pleasure,* "insects of nearly all kinds have much decreased."[10] He believed the sparrow had destroyed the measuring worm and the rose slug. In his own examination of a sparrow's crop, the contents included rose slugs and aphids as well as seeds. Birds of all kinds should be encouraged, Henderson stressed, because gardeners could do little else to control insects.

The sparrow defense won support from a large majority of the gardeners who corresponded with *American Garden.* Readers judged sparrows a useful insect eater rather than a total nuisance that befouled buildings, destroyed wheat fields, and pugnaciously drove away other birds. Yes, sparrows expelled some native birds but not so many as were destroyed by boys, who could still sell robins for seventy-five cents a dozen in 1892. Perhaps individual sparrows had developed bad habits of fruit and bud eating, but, the *American Garden* insisted, "the whole race should not suffer for the bad habits of individuals." Birds were an asset gardeners thought well worth paying for. If sparrows created local problems, then community authorities could control the pests, but under no circumstances should boys ever be paid bounties to shoot any species of bird.[11]

The quarrel over sparrows reflected a new division appearing in the ranks of gardeners, with the farmers, Department of Agriculture, and scientific experts abandoning the old balance of nature theory for a newer, more ruthless approach to nature. Those scientists educated after the American Civil War grew up reading Charles Darwin's *Origin of Species* (1859), which undermined the assumption of a harmonious world governed by divine, mechanical, self-regulating laws of nature.[12] The Darwinians viewed nature as a harsh struggle for survival among all forms of life. Rather than maintaining a balance of existing plants, animals, and insects, nature's method of struggle forced evolutionary change. People, as a part of that Darwinian evolution, must take an active role in altering nature. They must enter the struggle on behalf of their plants and shoulder the chemical sprayer to destroy the enemies of their gardens.

The Darwinian idea of the struggle for survival required a generation before taking over garden literature; before the 1890s the concept of the traditional balance of nature still prevailed. Charles Dudley Warner, for example, laughed at the new theory in *My Summer in a Garden* (1871). "Talk about the Darwinian theory of development, and the principle of natural selection!" he said. "I would like to see a garden let to run in accordance with it. If I had left my vegetables and weeds to a free fight, in which the strongest specimens only should come to maturity, and the weaker go to the wall, I can clearly see that I should have made a pretty mess of it." Warner preferred to select his vegetables from the weeds with his own hoe. And when the striped bug attacked his cucumbers, melons, and squash, he sprinkled them with wood ashes and soot, making the plants repulsive, and then brought in a toad to balance the bugs. "The best thing to do is to set a toad to catch the bugs," Warner said, in affirming the balance of nature. When birds devoured his English peas, he turned to his tomcat, Calvin, and urged the bird killer to vigorously pursue instinct. The birds ate the worms and peas, and Calvin ate the birds in the round of nature. Of course, Warner never really expected to win the struggle against his garden enemies in nature. "This talk of subduing Nature is pretty much nonsense," he said. "We have got down the forests, and exterminated savage beasts; but Nature is no more subdued than before: she only changes her tactics — uses smaller guns, so to speak. She re-enforces herself with a variety of bugs, worms and vermin, and weeds, unknown to the savage state, in order to make war upon the things of our planting; and calls in the fowls of the air, just as we think the battle is won."[13] Warner's traditional view permitted people to intervene in the balance but never gave the illusion that such intervention could ever achieve dominance.

The confident new voice of Darwinian interventionism, and the leading spokesman of horticulture for more than half a century, who did promise dominance over nature was Liberty Hyde Bailey. Born on a Michigan farm in 1858, Bailey grew up read-

ing Darwin and Asa Gray's *Field, Forest and Garden Botany*
(1868). He studied botany at Michigan State and then worked
under Asa Gray at Harvard before becoming the college professor who elevated horticulture in the public understanding from a
craft to a science. Bailey became the great communicator between the public and the laboratory scientists who had discovered bacterial diseases of plants that, along with insects, might
be controlled by the new sprays. During a very long career,
Professor Bailey published sixty-six books, including the *Standard Cyclopedia of Horticulture* (1900). Bailey gained a popular
reputation as the horticultural genius of his time. "He is the
most inspiring teacher of our time," *Garden Magazine* wrote,
"and no books are meatier than his. His books are scientific and
they have in them the underlying principles of the old-time practical books."[14]

The young Cornell University professor even took on the
editorship of *American Garden* in 1890 to popularize the new
scientific horticulture. Bailey explained to readers that "disease
and insect injury of cultivated plants, like other diseases, are the
remorseless struggle for existence everywhere in nature." The
gardener must enter the struggle on the side of the plants. "In
your generation and mine, men must shoulder their squirt guns
as our ancestors shouldered their muskets." Perhaps people
could eventually learn to oppose disease with the natural forces
of parasites, birds, and crop rotations, but, for 1893, poison
spray offered the modern weapon. "The sprayer has come to
stay—for a generation at least—and we must all fall in with
it."[15]

Bailey led cheers for the new world of chemical controls,
insisting that gardeners could not rest on old methods and
habits. The modern world of challenge and change required
keeping up to date. Soils deteriorate, plant varieties grow old,
insects and plant diseases increase, so gardeners must respond to
the intellectual challenge with modern scientific methods. Gardeners might still take their new seed catalogue and dream of the
bountiful harvest of next summer but only if they included the
science of chemical control. Bailey preached: "Gardens should
be mapped and planned by the winter fireside. Formulas for
insecticides and fungicides should be familiarized, and materials

for making the compounds should be procured."[16]

The new chemical and spraying equipment manufacturing companies did, of course, advertise in *American Garden* and funded research in Bailey's college at Cornell. Yet Bailey never thought it improper to be associated with industry in the war against the inefficient methods of the past. Perhaps dusting tobacco snuff or sprinkling tobacco water with a broom had been all right for his parent's generation, but a modern would at least use the commercial tobacco preparation "Black Leaf 40" in a fine Hudson sprayer. The old botanical powders—pyrethrum from the flower petals and hellebore from the plant roots—were safe for people but lacked the persistence of the new arsenic compounds. The day of the new chemicals had begun after a farmer stumbled onto using green paint—copper arsenite—in 1867, and this Paris Green swept the spray market in the 1870s. In 1893 lead arsenic began to dominate the field. Certainly honey bees died along with a few careless human workers from the new poisons, but no one could deny that cheap white arsenic was a marvel of the new age.[17]

Bailey represented the arrogance of a new Darwinian generation willing to destroy all insects indiscriminately. The older generation, with faith in nature's balance, had feared poisons might harm beneficial insects who warred against humanity's insect foes. They had known that insects were eaten not only by birds but by other species of insects. In the old view, as insect pests increased so did insect predators, devouring the plant eaters and checking the damage. But once the belief in nature's balance had been replaced by a Darwinian faith in humanity's power to eliminate insects, garden authorities ceased to care about predatory insects and recommended that all gardeners purchase spraying systems. A generation of chemical use would follow before gardeners evaluated the new evidence and began to doubt that pests could be destroyed without destroying the planet. Then a new regard for the beneficial predatory insects would reappear.

Just as Bailey pushed chemical sprays so did he promote chemical fertilizers rather than barnyard manure for the garden. The artificial debate had started long before in 1840 with the leading German chemist, Justus von Liebig, ridiculing the old notion that manure and humus nourished plants. Only chemicals provided food for plants, Liebig insisted. Manure did include some chemicals but why not analyze the soil first and then apply only those chemicals needed. Liebig's ideas spread rapidly in the Western agricultural world but proved initially far too optimistic. His own commercial product proved to be insoluble and failed, much to the pleasure of gardeners in the 1840s who delighted in the proof that the all-wise Creator had provided the perfect fertilizer from animals. "No garden will be worth its culture," the *Family Kitchen Gardener* (1855) declared, "unless well supplied with manure every year. The present day is a period of considerable agitation on this all-important subject. We have tried several of the new manures, some of them to our loss and few to our advantage." So the conventional gardening wisdom remained that manure composted with vegetable waste and occasional dressings of wood ashes, bone meal, and bird guano grew the most abundant crops. Peter Henderson summed up the conventional wisdom best when he said, "It is a grave blunder to attempt to grow vegetable crops without the use of manures."[18]

Even the flower garden used horse manure as the major ingredient for its compost pile. "Handsome is," the ladies said, "as handsome does. Unsightly and unsavory—yet whoso looks therein may see a poetry and a meaning of which some fairer things are incapable." Ladies following the *Scribner's Monthly* recipe began their spring compost pile, collecting "once a month or so a barrow load of rich black earth from the street." All street vehicles were in 1871 pulled by horses, so everyone understood the meaning of "black earth from the street." Gardeners added to their compost pile all vegetable scrapings from the garden, a pail of warm soap suds every laundry Monday, and a shovel of lime "from time to time." Wonderfully did the compost pile change: "Mysterious alchemy, whose least law we fail to comprehend, is ever at work transmuting the refuse of the earth into its choice things." By next spring, the gardener had manufactured "the daintiest of dishes to set before garden kings . . . rich, black, crumbly loam, without malodor."[19]

The one variety of manure rejected by Americans was that of humans. Night soil had been collected by New York City and Boston firms that sold the product to farmers as late as the

1840s, but American prejudice against fertilizing with human waste, and the new technology of sanitary sewers and indoor plumbing, ended the use of this fertilizer, except by Chinese gardeners in the West. The Chinese had been attracted by the California gold rush, working placer mines along the mountain streams above Sacramento. Asians used their ancient wisdom to grow traditional Chinese vegetables—long green beans, cucumbers, cabbage, mustard greens, green onions, squash, bitter melons, and sweet potatoes—on their mining claims. Night soil, compost piles, and irrigation systems produced blooms even on hills and sand dunes.[20]

Chinese market gardens sprouted on the outskirts of California towns as the immigrants began to plant European and American vegetables. On the sand hills outside San Francisco, Chinese gardeners "transformed the sterile sand into the most fertile black earth." Journalists reported the city encircled by a "belt of greenness," small vegetable gardens "at the ends of unfinished streets, on the hills, valleys and slopes, on the roadsides, in fact, everywhere." In this fabled garden land without a winter, where state fair turnips grew to 30 pounds and beets to 125, the Chinese were said to do even better. "All the fruits and vegetables, raspberries and strawberries, under the care of the Chinese gardeners grow to a fabulous size," a visiting journalist said. "I have seen strawberries as large as small pears, heads of cabbage four times the size of European heads, and pumpkins the size of our wash tubs." Outside observers praised the superior Chinese culture of much hoeing and constant watering, but residents generally condemned the Chinese choice of fertilizer.[21]

Americans complained that Chinese gardens threatened their towns with disease and foul odors. "The evil consists mainly in the Chinese mode of cultivation, which is filthy and disgusting in the extreme," the *Auburn Stars & Stripes* complained. Not only was human ordure added to the compost pile, but "urine is kept in large earthen jars until it has acquired the proper degree of offensiveness, when it is poured over the growing cabbages and other vegetables." Newspaper readers were urged to boycott these gardeners: "Lovers of cleanliness should avoid patronizing heathens because of the filth used by them in their cultivation."[22]

Discrimination against the Chinese is one of America's sad stories. These immigrants were characterized as "the enemy" by the American working class because they performed better industrial labor while accepting cheaper wages. Union propaganda accused them of lowering the American standard of living, of being pagan aliens who would neither visit barber shops and cut their pig-tails nor adopt American values. While Chinese traditional fertilizer played no part in debates over excluding these Asians in 1882, the Chinese "honey pots" certainly won Asians few American friends.[23]

Not only Chinese fertilizer but also barnyard manure suffered a bad press in the 1880s. Fifty years after Liebig called for the end of manure, the *American Garden* and Professor Bailey agreed that he had been right. The great fertilizer debate finally turned against stable manure. Horticultural authorities now recommended that the city gardener abandon dirty, smelly manure and substitute clean Mapes' Garden Fertilizer, which gave the same lush growth. "Modernized horticulture, with modern implements, modern fertilizers and modern methods of culture" required giving up the old-fashioned ways. Experiments of Professor Bailey at Cornell had proved that twenty tons of barnyard manure did not produce so large a crop of tomatoes as 160 pounds of nitrate of soda.[24]

Professor Bailey's gardening books would tout the new artificials and omit manure except for a brief mention that if the soil structure were too heavy with clay then humus must be added to make it mellow and friable. A compost pile of leaves and other organic material mixed with some manure lightened the physical structure of the soil, making it easier to work. So manure might be considered as a soil conditioner but not a fertilizer. If the intention were to feed the plants, then the gardener should instead add specific chemicals—nitrogen, phosphorus, and potassium.[25]

Bailey might have told gardeners something about the exciting new discoveries of European microbiologists and organic chemists, who were finding that soil bacteria actually created plant food by digesting organic matter into simple chemicals. Organic matter and bacteria provided plant food as well as acting as soil conditioners, but Bailey still thought in the Liebig tradition. Garden soil remained a mystery to him. "You are wondering what is contained in this earth," he wrote in 1901. "Men have spent their lives to answer that inquiry and have died without making the answer complete. Compounds of potassium and phosphorus and silicon and nitrogen and many more; millions of microorganisms that you cannot see, and whose life no man knows; chemical activities too complex to be analyzed; moisture and heat and magnetism; physical forces so intricate and subtle that they cannot be measured—all these are in the laboratory that you are preparing."[26]

More than a little confused about the role of soil bacteria, Bailey simply ignored it in his garden manuals and proceeded, with boundless energy, to encourage gardeners to accept chemical science and do their duty in the evolutionary struggle to create a better plant world without insects and disease. While Bailey sometimes demonstrated a softness for "weeds" in the lawn—"if we cannot remove the dandelions from the lawn, then we should love the dandelions"[27]—no such toleration existed for pests that invaded the garden. There, people must do their duty for the plants and humanity.

The Darwinian faith in control of nature became the dominant belief among gardeners in the twentieth century. The faith in humanity's scientific control extended beyond the garden fence and the natural environment to economics and politics. All faith in natural laws decayed among the educated. The natural laws that Adam Smith had explained in his *Wealth of Nations* were now rejected as outmoded antique beliefs. By the 1930s a typical garden columnist could write, "Leaving matters to nature is as ruinous in gardening as it is in economics, world peace and metropolitan politics."[28]

8 : COUNTRY LIFE IN THE SUBURBS

uburban living has a long tradition because Americans have wanted both the opportunities of the city and the physical environment of the country. Since the early nineteenth century cities have represented money, culture, and progress. But these same urban areas also created the specter of crowds, crime, and disease, causing common people as well as intellectuals to shudder on approaching New York City. Yet cities were essential because the country products of rural and small-town New Englanders—their ideas and books—had to go to the city for distribution. So Americans sought to combine city opportunities with country living where home, children, and health were thought the natural life since the garden of Eden.

The alienation of Americans from their cities is usually dismissed as a rural nostalgia unworthy of serious examination. This longing for rural life is said to be a major human weakness, an irrational response to the city and industry, which altered the old agricultural life. The rush of nostalgia for trees, flowers, birds, pets, and even farm animals is associated with naive childhood memories. As the world turned increasingly to bricks, concrete, steel, and complexity, only an irrational pastoralism, it is said, could explain the growing popularity of gardens, camping, bird-watching, and rural writers.[1]

Popular fiction appeared in New York and Boston at the end of the Civil War. The humorous Robert Barry Coffin's *Out of Town: A Rural Episode* (1866) moved a writer one hour's ride from New York City into his "suburban retreat," with a half-acre garden and a milk cow, for the "health of wife and children." The more serious Charles Barnard's *Farming by Inches* (1869) moved a young, overworked Boston accountant with ruined health to a three-acre home just outside a New England manufacturing village. There, the city-born, Harvard-trained professional learned gardening from Bernard Mc-Mahon's *The American Gardener's Calendar* and Fearing Burr's *The Field and Garden Vegetables of America,* restored his health, and even earned a decent living for himself and his young wife. In reality the author had recovered his own health by moving out of the city, and so his novel is much like a how-to-do-it gardening manual. Readers learned intensive market gardening as the fictional Robert and Harriet Nelson read their books, buy two hundred wagon loads of manure at one dollar a load, construct the cold frames, plant the peas, harvest the lettuce, sell the cart loads of vegetables to merchants, and calculate costs, profits, and health benefits of country living.

Beneath the nostalgia for country living ran a rational concern for a healthy environment. Urban life threatened children because of its airborne and waterborne diseases. The frightening urban mortality tables of New York City in the 1880s were little better than those of the 1840s; one-third of all newborns died before reaching their first year. Virtually half died before reaching six years of age. The precise New York City census figures for 1883 count 28,972 children born, 8,668 dead in their first year, 2,660 in their second, 1,221 in their third, 787 in their fourth, and 525 in their fifth. Contagious diseases and impure milk were so hostile to bottle-fed babies during the summer months that going to the country offered the only real hope for survival. In rural districts infants were twice as likely to survive as in the city. Even in the healthiest American city of the time, Milwaukee, death rates ran double those of the Wisconsin countryside. The alarming urban mortality rates would not decline until the twentieth century. Nineteenth-century mothers did not have the scientific knowledge that polluted and unpasteurized urban water and milk brought on the deadly diarrheal illness, but their prejudices in favor of country air, milk, and water were surely sound.[2]

Country living promised a better environment for adults as well as their children. A new and distressing disease—nervousness—afflicted adult city dwellers. The new malady, identified and described by Dr. George M. Beard in *American Nervousness* (1881), afflicted those in the urban Northeast but not the rural South and West. While Beard and another famous neurologist, S. Weir Mitchell, advocated bed rest as their cure for the nervous exhaustion brought on by modern urban life, garden magazines recommended traditional outdoor exercise instead. "Gardening is the most beautiful, the most healthful and enjoyable employment for man or woman, for youth or old age," the *American Garden* proclaimed. Nine-tenths of sickly women would benefit from outdoor gardening, the magazine asserted. Prevailing "nervous disorders," "ill health," and "hysteria" would disappear once women took up gardening and nutritious food. The magazine insisted: "It is impossible for a woman to have 'nerves' or 'tantrums' if she turns her attention seriously to plants." For evidence, the magazine claimed support from "most advanced doctors" and from their own case history of a young woman who had returned from seminary study "in a decline," "melancholy," and "prostrated." When neither doctors nor rest in a health institute could cure her, she remained a hopeless case until she took an interest in cultivating and mothering flowers. Fifteen years later she was a happy mother, flower culturist, and kitchen gardener who testified: "If I had not been stimulated to take outdoor exercise, I would have died long ago!" So the *American Garden* assured its readers that growing flowers and helping in the vegetable garden would preserve the health of single women, childless matrons, and mothers.[3]

Belief in the therapy of horticulture extended beyond gardening magazines to journals of science, which also recommended "the quiet country home" and exercise in the open air as the best cure for nervous disorders. Work and play in the open air was said to make village children less nervous than their city cousins. "For male patients, gardening, in all its branches, is about as fashionable as the said diseases," Dr. Felix L. Oswald observed, "and no liberal man would shrink from the expense of a board fence, if it would induce his drug-poisoned wife to try her hand at turf-spading, or, as a last resort, at hoeing, or even a bit of wheelbarrow work." Physicians preferred gardening to sports and gymnastics because "labor with a practical purpose" enabled people "to beguile themselves into a far greater amount of hard work than the drill-master of a gymnasium could get them to undergo." Gymnastics offered only a poor substitute for the work ethic to those Victorians who had no garden to till. Men whose high stress and sedentary life in office buildings led to nervous dyspepsia (indigestion) were more commonly cured by the heavy tasks of preparing the garden soil. Every gardening advocate knew a story, such as seedsman Peter Henderson's, of a forty-year-old New York office worker whose dyspepsia had forced him to resign his position and retire to Bergen Heights. There Henderson persuaded the invalid to begin the cottage garden that restored him to rugged health through the pleasure and exercise of tilling the soil.[4]

Urban people understood the advantages of gardening and acted on those convictions by moving to the suburbs as soon as they were able to combine urban work with rural living. By the 1850s railroads and public transportation were enabling commuters to live in peripheral towns. In Chicago the population moved from the central city along the dozen railroads. By the 1870s Chicago boasted more than fifty suburbs, convincing its historians that "ninety-nine Chicago families in every hundred will go an hour's ride into the country, or toward the country, rather than live under or over another family, as the average New Yorker or Parisian." New Yorkers were actually just as attracted to the suburbs. Around Manhattan Island the population growth of the suburbs began to outpace the city in the 1840s when ferry boats allowed residents to escape to Jersey City or Hoboken, Williamsburg, or Brooklyn. Once across the Hudson, horsecar lines and then railroads carried commuters to the expanding suburbs in the 1850s. In Boston the same process occurred and has been traced by Sam Bass Warner, who explains the suburban ideal as a product of physical deterioration in the crowded city that drove the middle class back to the old rural ideal of the natural, moral country life.[5]

Suburban histories, from *Streetcar Suburbs* (1962) to John R. Stilgoe's *Borderland: Origins of the American Suburbs* (1988), have ignored the kitchen garden pull of suburbia. They see a landscape of streetcars, trees, homes, and front-yard ornamentals but overlook the vegetable gardens behind the houses. They recognize the negative push of the city, the pull of the rural picturesque, but never understand the drawing power of the kitchen garden in the country life movement. In fact, Kenneth T. Jackson, in *Crabgrass Frontier: The Suburbanization of the United States* (1985), even asserts that middle-class Americans "no longer needed herbs and vegetables from gardens." These historians overlook contemporaries who pointed to kitchen gardening as a major reason for suburban living among both workers and the bourgeoisie. Popular biographer James Parton, for example, then expressed the common belief in the importance of gardening when he declared that "separated from the soil, man never yet succeeded in thriving. At best, without it, he is a potted plant, and some of the pots are miserably small. I have visited many factories in New England, and I find that whenever the operatives have a good sized garden, with access to pasture for a cow, the people are healthy, contented and saving. . . . Whenever they are separated from the soil, as in some of our large and crowded cities, there is squalor, demoralization, and despair."[6]

A commuter from East Dedham wrote to the *American Garden* of his enthusiasm for the economic and psychological benefits of gardening:

> I live in a good neighborhood, close to a country station, ten miles from the city, where each house has its garden. . . . The families are not rich, but intelligent and of good taste. They like to make their salaries go as far as possible, to have something for concerts and journeys. . . . Each one raises potatoes enough for the year, summer berries and green corn for the season. Every house has its flower-border, gay with Gladiolus, Scarlet Geranium, Petunias, and Autumn Dahlias. Everybody says a garden is a great help.

The commuter actually criticized suburbanites for not planting even larger gardens, perhaps the entire seed catalogue, and also for not raising chickens, rabbits, ducks, and pigeons. Then they, like himself, could taste the greatest pleasure in life — anticipation of even greater success. "I see the house of my millionaire neighbor across the valley without envy. She can have no finer roses than I do from my little conservatory; no finer fruit than I grow myself; no better books than the great libraries give me; no prettier home than mine, with its flowers and shrubbery when grown; no pleasanter table; no better bed than mine, with its lavendered linen sheets. Yet I have these within the compass of $2000 a year, thanks to my garden."[7]

The longing for a kitchen garden affected the rich as well. A landscape architect who sought to profit from the new "half-country, half-town life" movement felt compelled to ridicule the horticultural fevers that led wealthy people to move from a city house to a country place where their kitchen garden, with Irish gardener, would prove an expensive luxury. Leave gardening to good professionals, Frank J. Scott urged in *The Art of Beautifying Home Grounds* (1870). The suburbanite should stick to grass, trees, and flowers. Rather than a garden, Scott promoted the smooth lawn, cut by one of the new hand-pushed mowers, as the most essential element of beauty in a suburban home. "Whoever spends the early hours of one summer, while the dew spangles the grass, in pushing these grass-cutters over a velvety lawn, breathing the fresh sweetness of the morning air and the perfume of new mown hay, will never rest contented in the city," Scott declared. But after praising the new lawn, and ridiculing the old garden, Scott gave in to the popular desire for kitchen gardens by including them in half of his landscape designs in the back of the book.[8]

Just as popular taste compelled architects to accept kitchen gardens, so were educators persuaded that the school, like the home, should have a garden. The idea of school gardens dates back to 1840 when Friedrich Froebel created *Kindergartens* for German preschoolers, but American acceptance emerged later as part of a popular wave of enthusiasm about nature. Children found nature trips more fun than the drudgery of letters and numbers. "The trees, the birds, the meadows, and the flowers — these are the things that delight the child," one teacher observed. "The country is the children's paradise." Nature study could even promise educational opportunity. The critical habit of direct observation, teachers declared, could best be taught by investigating nature to learn geology, botany, entomology, and ornithology. But for the urban teachers, plants and nature were usually inaccessible; public parks posted notices forbidding the plucking of a leaf or the breaking of a twig. The school garden offered the best hands-on teaching of biology and the interdependence of plants, animals, minerals, and people. Beginning with the Massachusetts Horticultural Society sending Henry L. Clapp to study European school gardens in 1890, American urban schools inaugurated gardens to bring nature to children along with all the progressive educational virtues of group cooperation, outdoor exercise, and modern science. The new educational fad even won applause from Harvard President Charles W. Eliot, who declared school gardens the best "living laboratory" and "as much a part of good school equipment as blackboards, books and charts."[9]

The popularity of school gardens surely owed as much to sentiment as to science. School gardens were also products of the wave of enthusiasm for nature study. The nature essay had begun with Henry David Thoreau's retreat to *Walden* and a kitchen garden. Then John Burroughs polished the form, giving simple country facts and placing humanity in harmony with nature. Beginning with an 1865 essay titled "With the Birds," Burroughs enchanted a generation with *Winter Sunshine* (1875). "Not a little of the sunshine of our northern winters is surely wrapped up in the apple. How could we winter over without it! How life is sweetened by its mild acids! A cellar well filled with apples is more valuable than a chamber filled with flax and wool." And in *Locusts and Wild Honey* (1879) he asks, "Lives there a country boy who does not like wild strawberries and milk? . . . Of all the small fruits known to man, none other is so deeply and fondly cherished, or hailed with such universal delight, as this lowly but youth-renewing berry." Burroughs preached that while the city abused ear, nose, and eye, nature soothed and healed, making people saner, healthier, and more contented. He fashioned a religion of nature, saying, "If we do not go to church so much as did our fathers, we go to the woods much more, and are much more inclined to make a temple of

them than they were."[10] By the turn of the century such sentimental nature books had begun to rival the novel in popularity.

While suburbanites might enjoy the sentimental side of nature, they sought to share their more practical craft of gardening
with the inner-city poor. The kitchen garden became a major
social welfare remedy for urban hunger in the worst economic
depression of the nineteenth century. When unemployment
reached 35 percent in American cities by 1894, the mayor of
Detroit began a charitable vacant lots program. Mayor Hazen
Pingree may have known of the British allotment gardens for
the poor, but, of course, the American sensibility never permitted acknowledging any British model, so Pingree offered vacant
lot gardens as his own original experiment. He acquired the use
of vacant land around the city, simply by asking the landowners,
and he acquired seed and tools by requesting that prosperous
citizens donate expense money for the charitable project. Almost a thousand needy families of Poles, Germans, and elderly
white and black Americans were then given plowed plots on
Detroit's 430 acres. And they grew more than forty thousand
bushels of potatoes that summer of 1894, along with enormous
yields of beans, squashes, pumpkins, pride, and goodwill.[11]

The successful Detroit experiment captured the attention of
charitable New Yorkers. Vacant lot gardens promised not only
to multiply every dollar contributed to five or six dollars worth
of food, but also to persuade the surplus city population to
return to rural America. The Detroit superintendent of the poor
emphasized that more than a hundred city families had already
moved back to the country. "The poor, hard-working people see
that upon a little patch of half an acre they can produce enough
to half support themselves, and it sets them to thinking. . . . If I
can almost live on half an acre, I could make a comfortable
living on a few acres, and they begin to figure on getting into the
country."[12]

Any movement back to the land reassured civic leaders,
who were worried over the prospect of urban violence and revolution if the unemployed were unable to find work. While they
feared that direct charity might destroy character, this vacant lot
program provided honest work, taught a useful rural occupation, and utilized wasted urban space. New York counted some

17,329 vacant lots below West 145th Street and uncounted acres of unused land beyond, but the New York Association for Improving the Condition of the Poor decided against the city lots, which might require police to watch the crops, and chose instead 138 acres on Long Island where eighty-four families received allotments, seed, tools, fertilizer, and a practical garden supervisor. By potato harvesting time these charity gardeners were reported to be as happy as children on a picnic, digging, storing, selling, and rejoicing. "The majority of them," the garden supervisor reported, "were anxious at the close of the experiment to go to the country and take hold of agriculture in a true and permanent way."[13]

Once New York endorsed vacant lot gardening, the Detroit plan quickly gained widespread national acceptance. Twenty cities and towns had tried vacant lot gardening in 1896, and the following year the remaining large holdouts—Chicago, Kansas City, Providence, and Philadelphia—became converts to Pingree's self-help program for the unemployed. While Philadelphia had been slow to join community gardening, its Vacant Lots Cultivation Association quickly became the major advocate of urban gardening, with published annual reports to advertise the charitable work.[14]

In the Philadelphia *Annual Reports* we learn that the first Philadelphian to apply for a garden plot had been a weak, emaciated widower who had been unemployed for six months and had become desperate about feeding his four children. On his large vacant lot of nine-tenths of an acre, he harvested and produced thirty bushels of potatoes, one hundred quarts of canned tomatoes, fifty quarts of corn, twenty quarts of canned beans, thirty gallons of tomato catsup, four bushels of turnips, one bushel of carrots, and one thousand celery stalks, as well as selling enough to purchase warm clothing for the family. Needless to say, a rosy hue had replaced the wan cheeks by harvest time.[15]

Philadelphia *Annual Reports* even recorded the ethnicity of its gardeners, creating a small window into cultural taste in gardening. The majority of plot holders were elderly ethnic Americans, white and black, but the Irish-born who came in second during the years of depression later dropped well behind Italians

and Germans. The Irish apparently were not vegetable lovers —
their dish of potatoes could easily be bought from the store. The
Italian diet, however, of eggplant, artichoke, broccoli, and zuc-
chini seasoned with garden-grown tomato, thyme, oregano, basil, and garlic led Italians to participate in the vacant lots program as well as to move to the outskirts of American cities to
grow their own vegetables. Love of gardening surely had ethnic
roots. The immigrant group that had abandoned horticulture
for urban life back in the eighth century — the Jews — never applied for Philadelphia garden plots. More than a thousand years
of city living had killed Jewish gardening tradition. When slum-
dwelling Jews in New York City were asked if they could use a
garden, they generally said "no" while Italians replied "yes" to
the same question. Italians, and most other immigrants, came
from rural backgrounds with a love of gardening that continued
even though they had moved to American cities.[16]

   While other cities dropped their vacant lot programs when
full employment returned, the Philadelphia civil leadership continued vacant lot farming to assist the old, the weak, and the
partially disabled who could find no place in the industrial system even in prosperous times. Philadelphia garden plots were
even increased in numbers to more than four hundred with the
intent of teaching gardening to more children and contributing
to the "back to the land" movement by "bringing country life,
with all its blessings of pure air, wholesome food, and health-
giving exercise, to the very doors of the slum dwellers."[17]

   Vacant lot gardening continued to be widely discussed as a
welfare solution, regularly reported in the charitable journals
such as the *Survey*, and passionately promoted by the New York
reformer Bolton Hall. When Chicago settlement workers from
Hull House revived vacant lot gardening in their city in 1909,
they credited the Philadelphia Vacant Lots Cultivation Association, as well as the request of their own poor, for creating the
new Chicago City Gardens Association, which borrowed eight
acres from the International Harvester Corporation and placed
a hundred poor families on one-sixth-acre plots. Each family
received seed and specific instructions for planting the 150-by-
36-foot plot. The Chicago philanthropists were sensitive to dif-
fering ethnic tastes and resolved to "allow our Italian farmers

plenty of room for garlic and peppers, our Irish friends potatoes, and our German contingent cabbages and kohlrabi," but
all received the same seed packages and a rather specific row-by-
row planting list:[18]

Onions, 8 rows.	Kohlrabi or Peppers, 1 row.
Parsley, 1 row.	Cabbage (early), 9 rows.
Parsnips, 5 rows.	Cabbage (late), 1 row.
Carrots, 3 rows.	Peas, 4 rows.
Swiss Chard, 1 row.	Beans, Spinach, 8 rows.
Lettuce, 1 row.	Potatoes, 10 rows.
Spinach, 1 row.	Potatoes or Squash, 8 rows.
Cucumbers, 1 row.	Sweet Corn or Beans, 4 rows.
Early peas, 2 rows.	Tomatoes, 12 rows.
Radishes or Cucumbers, 1 row.	Hubbard squash, 1 row.
Beets, Turnips, 4 rows.	Pumpkins, 1 row.

Urban philanthropists advocated not only vegetable gardens
on vacant lots but also resettlement of slum dwellers on homesteads in the countryside. Bolton Hall wrote his popular *Three
Acres and Liberty* (1907) and organized a cooperative Free
Acres Colony to relieve urban congestion and promote more
suburban self-sufficiency outside New York City. In Massachusetts, the state legislature created a Homestead Commission to
work with towns and cities in assisting laboring families from
the slums to establish suburban homes with room for children
and gardens for both play and profit. The Massachusetts program of state aid to resettle these urban working people who
earned only twelve to twenty dollars a week won overwhelming
support when put to a public referendum, thus demonstrating
that suburban gardens were applauded in the Northeast by the
vast majority of Americans.[19]

The day of the country life movement had arrived, with
reformers, educators, and the media agreeing that the drift of
history was moving from the cities to the new country life. The
market for outdoor life had been insatiable since the turn of the
century. When publishers churned out 142 books on country
living without a single commercial failure, Frank Doubleday
knew, in 1901, the time had come for launching his new magazine *Country Life in America,* with Professor Liberty H. Bailey

as editor, to sing the praises of the out-of-doors where "men are free," "where there is room, and where there are sweet, fresh winds," and to "portray the beauty of the land that lies beneath the open sky, to lure to health and relaxation, to stay the congestion of the city." With lush photographic articles depicting abandoned farms, wild and domestic animals, camping, canoeing, hunting, walking, winter sports, maple sugaring, harvesting, and kitchen gardening, *Country Life* packaged the joys and delights of rural living. Bailey's new magazine advocated suburban rather than farm living, saying, "The ideal life is that which combines something of the social and intellectual advantages and physical comforts of the city with the inspiration and peaceful joys of the country."[20]

The intoxicating spirits of country nostalgia could carry writers beyond the suburbs to advocate a clean break with the city into full-time farming in Vermont, Pennsylvania, or the Ozarks. "Cutting Loose from the City" portrayed the choice between New York City's crowded Henry Street market—with its struggling masses, its ugliness, its plague of tuberculosis—and the other alternative—the landscape along a rural road: "This is the Country—God's Country—with its pure air and green fields, and the lure of the open road. Which do you choose?" The "Cutting Loose" series carried testimonials of middle-aged professionals who had found restored health and happiness on farms scattered from New England to the Pacific Northwest.[21]

Professor Bailey of Cornell's Agricultural College strongly objected to what he considered a mindless romantic "back to the land" movement that sought to put city people on farms. As a country-born and academically trained horticulturist he insisted that none should enter farming without first graduating from an agricultural college. Success in the business of farming required money, knowledge, and experience that city people lacked. They should stick to gardening in the suburbs and move to the country only for a vacation.[22]

Naturally, a few "back to the landers" were offended by Professor Bailey's "wicked" efforts to discourage them. Men of forty were not looking for "success" or a "business"; they wanted instead "to live," and for three thousand dollars they could easily purchase a living in the Vermont hills, with a third of the money going for a one-hundred-acre farm, a third for tools and livestock, and a third to live on for the first three years until the kitchen garden could be supplemented by income from maple sugar, bees, or poultry. "The possibilities of a life on such a farm," Helen Dodd wrote, "are almost unlimited in the New England hills. Every farm has its woodlot, its big pasture that can be planted to forest if one does not keep cattle to use, its brook and steep little ravine that means a fairyland to children. Many have a maple grove and a sugaring outfit included; there is always lumber for cabinet work, stones and boulders for building, and the tillage land."[23]

Most city people, however, just as Bailey said, found all the country they needed in the suburbs. The nostalgia of farm life may have created as many literary essays as working farms. The success of *Country Life* produced a competitor, and the title of the new journal, *Suburban Country Life,* clearly labeled the real focus of the country life movement. *Suburban Country Life* explained that it wrote for "the man of moderate income who loves the country with its pure air and green fields, and who has selected a spot to his liking where he may enjoy his own vine and fig tree away from the noise and confusion of the city." The size of this suburban holding was precisely described as the "quarter or half an acre of ground about the house, the possibilities of fruit, flowers and vegetables, the getting into the soil with one's own hands."[24] The gardener who moved out from the city surely planted a more ambitious garden than city dwellers, and the Peter Henderson Seed Company capitalized on the new market, offering three kitchen garden seed packages — the city collection for $1, the suburban for $2.50, and the country for $5.

To ensure proper scientific advice for gardeners, *Suburban Country Life* hired an agriculture professor. Only one lyrical Liberty H. Bailey existed, but the new magazine's agricultural advice for suburbanites on "The Gentle Art of Killing Bugs" promoted the same chemical solutions. Every gardener must purchase a sprayer and a supply of kerosene emulsion for aphids, along with Paris Green or hellebore for the other little pests.[25] Suburbanites, it seems, were being instructed to trust chemicals and science rather than nature to produce the garden harvest.

To eliminate labor and backache from the suburban garden, the experts recommended the final abolition of the English bed with the latest tool of modern technology—the wheel hoe. With hand and finger work abolished, rakes and hoes could rust in old barns to the rejoicing of all except those dour Calvinists who complained, "But there was discipline for weeds and boys in the old checker-board garden." Purchasing the garden plow would not prevent a man from the pleasure of spading in the garden at the first break of spring. Professor Bailey could grow lyrical over the pleasure of digging in the dirt. "Do not delegate the work," he said. "Yourself thrust the blade deep into the tender earth. Bear your weight on the handle and feel the earth loosen and break. Turn over the load. You smell the soft moist odor, an odor that takes you back to your younger and freer days or sends you dreaming over the fields."[26]

Yes, *Country Life* argued, suburban life even led one man to give up golf for gardening. Tasting a neighbor's fresh strawberries or beet greens frequently led to the first experiment in gardening. The resulting testimonial in *Country Life* asserted:

> I shall never again be dependent upon such expensive establishments as golf-links or even tennis courts; give me a shovel, a hoe, and a packet of seeds, and I shall have fun wherever I am. . . . The mental interest and stimulus of gardening are far greater than those of any game, and the occupation brings a man into the pleasantest contact with his neighbors. If a man does not care for killing beasts and birds, if he finds games unsatisfying, if he enjoys an occupation which provides him with literature and keeps him in touch with many men, if he cares to have his children working with him, and likes to look forward to an employment for his old age— then I can imagine no better resort for him than "bending over dirt."[27]

The market for country life stories ran well beyond the suburban magazines and the periodical press to the major publishing houses, which sold several million copies of fiction and literary essays by Ray Stannard Baker and Dallas Lore Sharp. As the nation's leading urban reporter, Baker could not openly write bucolic literature recommending the desertion of the city. So under the pseudonym David Greyson he published *Adventures in Contentment* (1907), claiming to be a refugee from the pressues of urban life whose ruined health had been cured by country life on a farm. This successful novel and eight others, which sold more than two million copies, came in part from Baker's own lifestyle. *McClure's Magazine* had given him a six-month work year in 1902, which he used to write from East Lansing, Michigan, and later Amherst, Massachusetts. In the country, Baker had the freedom to spend mornings writing in his study amidst the works of Cobbett, Emerson, Thoreau, Tolstoy, and Muir, and then afternoons with the simple outdoor pleasures of the garden and the field.[28]

Baker argued that the home in the country restored his spirits and allowed him to withstand the urban frictions of muckraking journalism. Perhaps being married to a daughter of Liberty H. Bailey's botany professor, W. J. Beal, also helped him to enjoy the natural beauties of country walks, bird-watching, and gardening in which Baker took pleasure. "I like to see things grow," he admitted, "especially things I have myself planted, or bred, or tended. I like to go out of an evening after a day's work is over and I am tired, and walk about my garden and orchard, or down into my field. I like to see the young corn pushing up through the brown earth . . . young bees playing in front of the hives, blossoms coming thick on the apple trees."[29]

The best-read country essayist, after John Burroughs, was Dallas Lore Sharp, a Boston College English instructor who had been reared on Gilbert White's *Natural History of Selbourne* and the new nature study in the public schools. After publishing his first book, *Wild Life Near Home* (1901), Sharp wrote hundreds of magazine articles, many of which were later republished in his twenty books celebrating the life of the commuter. Sharp had no quarrel with city jobs: "The city is necessary; city work is necessary; but less and less is city living necessary." The day had passed when every person could live on a farm, but with the streetcar, railroad, and now the motor car, "the day has just arrived when every man's home can be his garden and chicken-pen and dooryard, with room and quiet and

a tree." People needed "something green and growing to cultivate, something alive and responsive to take care of." Children
needed open fields and woods. So Sharp worked in Boston for
the salary of a college professor but commuted to *The Hills of
Hingham* for an "adventure in contentment" on his fourteen
acres, "my fireside with my boys and Her, and the garden and
woodlot and hens and bees."[30]

Debate over suburban living never questioned the wisdom
of leaving the city but only whether such communities ought to
be planned to avoid the waste of transportation and the loss of
community participation. The planned garden community, popularized by Ebenezer Howard's *Garden Cities of Tomorrow*
(1901), advocated a self-contained community with industrial
employment but without the pollution and congestion of old
factory towns. Americans admired the English model towns of
Letchworth and Bournville, with their kitchen gardens and local
industry, but here as there the conventional unplanned suburban
bedroom community housed those who moved out from the
city. Architects for planned communities tended to overprice
their land values by designing expensive public buildings. Advocates for planners always had less influence than the opponents.
When planners sought federal sponsorship of European-style
farm villages for returning World War I veterans, commercial
farmers and their friends in the Department of Agriculture
killed the dream of city homes on country lanes.[31]

Garden cities remained the ideal of urban planners who
sought to humanize urban life by reuniting city and country. In
the 1920s the new name for decentralized cities became greenbelt
towns. The New York–based Regional Planning Association
promoted the idea of self-sufficient greenbelt towns surrounded
by farms and forest. The literary spokesman for these greenbelt
planners, Lewis Mumford, declared that cities could never remain the permanent habitat of people unless open space, parks,
and gardens were restored to the city. While the urban environment might be ruralized a little by utilizing the vacant lot program or the German *Schrebergarten* idea to give tenement dwellers a small cultivation patch on the outskirts of the city, only
decentralized towns promised to restore the livable city that had
existed before the industrial revolution. Unfortunately the plan-

ners' demonstration model of Radburn, New Jersey, did not open until 1929, the beginning of the Great Depression, which forced the town into receivership by 1931, converting this planned community seventeen miles from Manhattan into just another commuter suburb for white-collar workers. So suburban growth continued to be controlled by market forces, not by community planning.[32]

The crest of popularity for suburban living continued, but concern for health and interest in gardens lost their force as rising public health standards and medical control of infections made city living less hazardous. As the penicillin and sulfa drugs of city science killed bacterial infections in the 1940s, fewer Americans believed nature so essential for the healthful development of children. The new technology of refrigeration and frozen foods permitted mothers to obtain fresh vegetables from the supermarket, and home growing became more difficult. The reforestation of suburbia blocked out the sunlight for gardens and encouraged the multiplication of birds, chipmunks, squirrels, and raccoons, which revived in numbers unseen since the days of native American gardeners. Land developers of Levittown, Forrest Park, and the other postwar communities reduced the size of suburban lots, building only a ranchstyle house and no kitchen garden. The new suburbs were without rural flavor in the eyes of social scientists and novelists. These were no longer "country homes" but mere "dormitories" for middle managers in William H. Whyte, Jr.'s, *The Organization Man* (1956). Neither did the Connecticut commuter in Sloan Wilson's *The Man in the Gray Flannel Suit* (1955) express any interest in growing vegetables in the country but only in making money and preserving character in corporate America. Literary enchantment with suburbia ended with the 1950s generation of urban-bred intellectuals ridiculing the standardization of bourgeois people in rows of neat little toy houses. Suburbia continued to be the most popular place to live, but its lifestyle lacked literary defenders.[33]

9 : VICTORY GARDENING

T wice in the twentieth century Americans have grown food gardens as a patriotic response to wartime. The massive uprooting of ornamentals and the plowing under of golf links, front yards, and public parks has often been described as evidence of excessive government hysteria. But the truth is that the national government never led public opinion in either world war. Americans initiated victory gardening and then pressured the government to become a cheerleader for their patriotic efforts.

The war gardening of 1917 emerged from consumer fear of rising prices and actual food shortages. Threatened railroad labor strikes and the anticipated American entry into the European War created speculative food hoarding in the winter of 1916–17, leading to an inflationary price spiral that quickly doubled the cost of most food staples in New York City while onions soared 700 percent in cost and cabbages 2,000 percent. By February, 1917, the terrifying cost of food drove housewives to overturn and burn pushcarts loaded with exorbitantly priced food. On the morning that a federal grand jury began an inquiry into the price spiral, Russian Jewish housewives from the Lower East Side rebelled against rising prices. Overturning pushcarts and attacking food peddlers, a thousand women marched on City Hall to tell Mayor Mitchel: "We can't stand it any longer.

Our children are starving. . . . We must have food to give our children. . . . We come to you for justice and mercy, Mr. Mayor, and we ask you to appeal to the businessmen to make the prices of food such as we can afford to pay."[1]

A Food Committee ended the immediate crisis by importing carloads of rice, fish, and brown beans for bargain prices. Fear of famine and transportation shutdowns, however, continued among the six million residents of metropolitan New York, arousing a new interest in vegetable gardening. Wall Street bankers began plowing under suburban estates to plant potatoes; community garden advocates campaigned to turn all idle land into vegetable patches; and the Brooklyn Park Commission opened demonstration gardens and offered prizes to stimulate backyard vegetable growing. Across the New York boroughs— Manhattan, Brooklyn, and the Bronx—twenty volunteer community gardening organizations sprang up as America entered the war. To eliminate duplication and confusion, the city brought all organizations together under the Park Commission of each borough. Vacant lots and park lands were registered, soil fertility was checked, and gardening plots were handed out to eager, landless vegetable growers. Thus vacant lots, front lawns, and golf courses in the New York area were plowed not because of federal propaganda but because of actual consumer fear of famine.[2]

Not only in the urban Northeast but also across the heartland, volunteer community garden programs emerged in response to fear of food shortages. In Oklahoma City the *Daily Oklahoman,* which had been advocating city gardening for two decades, persuaded the local chamber of commerce on March 1, 1917, to support its plan to make their city the first to hire a trained horticulturist for overseeing an urban garden program. The city leaders in the chamber and the Rotary Club endorsed the *Daily Oklahoman* program, hired professor D. C. Mooring from the state agricultural college, and propagandized the citizens: "Every man, rich as well as poor, should have a garden. The rich man should do it to reduce demand. The poor man must have a garden in order to have the food he is accustomed to and needs. It is not difficult for the rich man to have a garden. If the poor man needs assistance he must be given it."[3]

Assistance for the poor was generous. First, the chamber of commerce borrowed fifty acres of city and private property, plowed the land, and divided it into individual garden plots. Free seed and gardening advice were also offered the poor. Twenty neighborhood inspectors assisted the garden superintendent, visiting and encouraging the gardeners. Free copies of a state university bulletin on home gardening were supplemented with daily "Your Garden" articles in the *Daily Oklahoman.*[4]

The wealthy were assisted by lavish flattery that asserted "the best people" were the most successful home gardeners. "Women of Better Class, Rather than the Needy, are the Best Gardeners," the society columnist asserted. "The best gardeners of the feminine sex . . . are the wives of men who are most successful in the professions or trades. We often hear that the poor remain poor because they are thriftless. That is very true, for if the poor were both industrious and thrifty, they would not remain poor very long." The columnist went on to interview several prominent ladies known for their good health, beautiful bodies, and sunny dispositions, which they achived from garden exercise and perhaps those European trips to bring back an exotic Italian bean or herb. The garden exercise of these ladies must have been limited because at least one had brought assistance from the family plantation in Louisiana. "Henry, the venerable negro servant, whose devotion to the family dates from those plantation days, plays an important part in all these home gardening enterprises," the reporter said. "He scorns all new and scientific methods. Consequently the garden potato crop must be planted in the dark of the moon, and all other vegetables on Good Friday."[5]

The school children were also enlisted in the Oklahoma City War Garden program, marched behind a fife and drum corps, encouraged by chamber of commerce orators, and promised two hundred dollars in prize money for a garden contest. One of the eleven-year-old first-place winners would later write:

> My name is William T. Adams. I live at 1008 East Sixth Street. In the fall I put a big load of manure in the lot. Early in the the spring papa had it plowed. I then smoothed it down and laid it out in rows. I planted my potatoes and my sweet peas in the mid-

dle of February, my beans, peas, lettuce, radishes, onions, spinach, mustard and beets, I planted about the middle of March. I sold about $10 of vegetables and we used that much. My mother canned 8 quarts of beets and 6 of beans. I now have a late garden of black-eyed peas, sweet potatoes, butter beans and turnips and a few beans. I sold $8 worth of sweet peas. I shall devote more of my time to sweet peas next spring.[6]

While Oklahoma City boosted its number of gardens by 450 percent, from 3,000 to 13,500, garden promoters emerged on the national as well as the local level. A wealthy New Jersey lumberman, Charles Lathrop Pack, moved quickly after the New York food riots to organize his own National Emergency Food Garden Commission to promote backyard and vacant lot gardening across America. Moving to Washington, his commission became a propaganda agency seeking to persuade Americans that taking up the garden hoe could be as patriotic a duty as bearing a rifle. Pack fed the newspapers daily stories intended to persuade Americans to put all idle land to work, learn the best gardening methods, and preserve their garden surplus. This private agency propagandized so energetically and resourcefully that the Department of Agriculture resented being elbowed aside as the gardening authority in the national capital.[7]

Once the national government declared war against Germany on April 6, 1917, President Woodrow Wilson asserted leadership, calling for every American to contribute in the war to establish democracy and human rights. Americans at home must sacrifice to supply the food so essential for victory. "Everyone who creates or cultivates a garden helps," Wilson declared, "and helps greatly, to solve the problem of the feeding of the nations; and every housewife who practices strict economy puts herself in the ranks of those who serve the Nation. This is a time for America to correct her unpardonable fault of wastefulness and extravagance."[8] To further propagandize the nation for the war effort, Wilson created a Committee on Public Information run by advertising executives whose artists, speakers, and salespeople assisted the Agriculture Department in a War Garden Campaign to plant a million new backyard and vacant lot gardens.[9]

Wilson opened a second propaganda agency when he put

Herbert Hoover in charge of the Food Administration, organized to stop the rising food consumption. "Go back to the simple life. Be content with simple food, simple pleasures, simple clothes," Hoover urged. Americans were encouraged to patriotically observe wheatless Wednesdays, meatless Tuesdays, and porkless Saturdays so that the nation might ship vital commodities to our European allies. The Food Administration urged reduction of meat and wheat consumption by turning to garden vegetables. The protein of meat should be replaced by beans, peas, and peanuts. For carbohydrates, potatoes should replace wheat. And, for the first time, government agencies recommended eating green vegetables. Before World War I, Agriculture Department nutition experts had laughed at the belief that "greens" were beneficial, thinking it just another silly old superstition that ought to be discarded because greens contained little protein, fat, or carbohydrates. But now nutrition experts had discovered vitamins, which were somehow important for health and growth. So every American now ought to eat lots of green, leafy vegetables — spinach, cabbage, Brussels sprouts, asparagus, and lettuce. And every pound of vegetables grown in a home or community garden relieved railroad congestion, providing more space for munitions, coal, and staples for Europe.[10]

The impact of war garden propaganda cannot be judged with any certainty because the day of the sample poll had not yet arrived. Pack estimated that the number of gardens increased by 300 percent, but his percentages were surely little better than poor guesswork. To declare that 3.5 million gardens in 1917 represented a 300 percent gardening gain, he had to assume that only one family in ten gardened before the war.[11] After the great propaganda year of 1918 — which included more striking color posters, such as "Sow the Seeds of Victory," showing a young woman draped in a sleeveless American flag broadcasting seed on freshly plowed land — Pack declared the number of gardens had risen to more than five million; but that would have been only 25 percent of American families, a percentage too small by more than half. We must assume that neither Pack nor the government was seriously interested in counting the number of gardens in America and used figures only as another means of propaganda.

World War I propaganda. *Reprinted from Charles Lathrop Pack,* War Gardens Victorious *(Philadelphia: National War Garden Commission, 1919).*

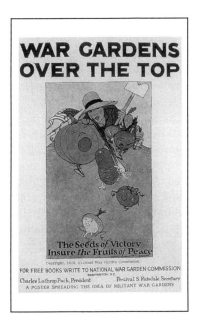

WAR GARDENS OVER THE TOP

The Seeds of Victory
Insure the Fruits of Peace

Copyright, 1919, National War Garden Commission.

FOR FREE BOOKS WRITE TO NATIONAL WAR GARDEN COMMISSION
WASHINGTON, D.C.

Charles Lathrop Pack, President   Percival S. Ridsdale, Secretary
A POSTER SPREADING THE IDEA OF MILITANT WAR GARDENS

What are YOU doing?

THE KAISER IS CANNED—CAN FOOD

CAN Vegetables fruit AND the Kaiser too

Write for Free Book to
NATIONAL WAR GARDEN COMMISSION
WASHINGTON, D.C.

Charles Lathrop Pack, President   P.S.Ridsdale, Secretary

A POSTER WHICH WAS USED FIRST IN 1918 AND WHICH, AMENDED
—FOLLOWING GERMANY'S DEFEAT—WAS ALSO FORCEFUL IN 1919

War Gardens Victorious

Copyright, 1919, National War Garden Commission.

Every War Garden a Peace Plant—
— Charles Lathrop Pack, President.

NATIONAL WAR GARDEN COMMISSION
WASHINGTON, D.C.
A POSTER FOR 1919, SYMBOLIC OF VICTORY

WE HAVE A
War Garden

National War Garden Commission
WASHINGTON, D.C.

THE WAR GARDENERS' BOAST

Certainly Pack received no statistical assistance from the Department of Agriculture, which regarded him as an enemy. His motives, the department suspected, were personal or political rather than patriotic. His gardening booklets, they charged, had been lifted from department bulletins without acknowledgment of the Department of Agriculture. He had chose a name — National Emergency Food Garden Commission — that deliberately deceived the unsuspecting public into accepting it as an official government agency. Department officials grumbled about Pack's media coverage, refused to share their information, and opposed every Pack request. When Pack asked President Wilson to proclaim a special Garden Week, Agriculture Secretary D. F. Houston opposed the request as "likely to stimulate much unwise and unfruitful planting. There has been a great deal of hysterical activity in this field and considerable waste of seeds and fertilizers." Secretary Houston even asked that the president refuse Pack's request for a simple presidential endorsement of war gardens. Any government recognition of the Pack commission might confuse the public and diminish the Department of Agriculture.[12]

Although the Department of Agriculture identified with farmers and not gardeners, they still considered horticulture their turf and resented other government agencies taking any leadership in the war garden work. Hoover's Food Commission had improperly intruded into gardening work, and even more offensive, the Bureau of Education launched a war school gardening program. Education Commissioner P. P. Claxton had been gathering school garden statistics for several years, and now he dreamed of enrolling most of the six million school children between the ages of nine and sixteen in a United States School Garden Army to produce a quarter of a billion dollars of vegetables along with untold amounts of character, health, education, and patriotism. Limited funding for Claxton's dream came only in the second year of the war, but he was able to enroll a million and a half privates in his army. Wearing the army insignia USSGA, armed with garden tools and a thirty-two-page gardening manual, the children marched out to the land singing:

Johnnie get your hoe, get your hoe, get your hoe;
Mary dig your row, dig your row, dig your row;
Down to business, boys and girls,
Learn to know the farmer's joys.
Uncle Sam's in need, pull the weed, plant the seed.
While the sunbeams lurk, do not shirk, get to work.
All the lads must spade the ground,
All the girls must hustle round.

CHORUS
Over there, over there;
Send the word, send the word over there,
That the lads are hoeing, the lads are hoeing,
The girls are sowing everywhere,
Each a garden to prepare,
Do your bit so that we all can share
With the boys, with the boys, the brave boys,
Who will not come back 'til it's over, over there.[13]

Schools with existing gardening programs, such as in Cleveland, Ohio, expanded to include all children. For those who had no home ground to cultivate, the gardening teachers plowed a hundred acres of vacant lots and fertilized with ten carloads of manure from the stockyards. Only Cleveland and 487 other cities had school-directed garden programs before the campaign, but in 1918 the number jumped to 4,390 cities as a million and a half student gardens were planted.

When the war ended, Commissioner Claxton wanted to continue school and home vegetable gardening. But funds for the School Garden Army were promptly eliminated. Even during wartime the Agriculture Department had opposed the program as useless. "Many children are being 'enrolled' and the enrollment is both the beginning and the end of their activity since they are without qualified instructions," the assistant secretary of agriculture had said. "They receive a tin button and that, of course, appeals to their childish fancy, but so far as gardening is concerned they are really doing nothing without proper instruction."[14]

Although the Agriculture Department insisted that only its

professionals were qualified gardening instructors, they had no real interest in urban gardens. The department represented a rural constituency whose gardens made economic sense, but the community and backyard gardens of city people were beyond any concern of the Agriculture Department. Some of the department's free seed went to city school gardens but none of its support went to a Bureau of Education program more interested in developing character, health, thrift, and nostalgia than in producing food.

With a food surplus quickly accumulating after the close of the war, community gardens tended to wither away except for a very few conspicuous examples, such as the Vacant Lots of Philadelphia. Even there the surge of construction gobbled up gardening sites and greatly reduced the number of garden plots. In private backyards many gardens gave way to grass and ornamentals. When the sociologists visited Muncie, Indiana, in the mid-1920s they found the number of backyard gardens had declined to 40–50 percent of local families. A generation before, virtually all, 75–80 percent, had planted large gardens, but now, it was said, the automobile had brought a major decline in home gardening.[15]

The automobile displaced both the horse and stable manure that had been responsible for lush garden growth. When every business family owned a horse and carriage, the animal manure required a garden as a waste disposal system. Manure provided the complete soil additive for superb gardening, and the supply of horse manure from public streets and stables had been abundant enough for even the poor to have fertile gardens. Horse droppings were then considered a major problem on city streets. Sanitary experts calculated that the normal urban horse produced twenty-two pounds of manure each day. New York City's one hundred twenty thousand horses dropped 1,320 tons every day, almost half a million tons a year, or enough to give every family of four in the metropolitan area half a ton of manure. Apartment dwellers, to be sure, would not have wanted their share, leaving more than enough for those with gardens. Health officials were not pleased by the supply of free manure but worried that the mess, stench, and flies on the streets contributed to cholera, typhoid fever, diarrhea, and tetanus. Every city had

Schoolgirl with a wheel hoe, cover of 1918 school gardening textbook. *Reprinted, by permission of Harper Collins Publishers, from Kary Cadmus Davis,* School and Home Gardening, *cover. Illustration by Mrs. Kary Cadmus Davis.* © 1918 by J. B. Lippincott Company.

worried about manure removal. But by 1923 the horse had been replaced. Americans who had purchased two million horse-drawn carriages in 1909, the year Henry Ford began manufacturing his inexpensive Model T, were now buying only ten thousand and were purchasing four million automobiles. By 1923 garden magazines were responding to the crisis of the "modern manureless age" with articles such as "How to Get Along Without Stable Manure," but the remedies—sowing buckwheat or rye for green manures and building compost piles—all required more extra effort than the old horse-garden system.[16]

Some urbanites devoted more thought to their gardens. As the number of urban gardens declined in the 1920s, the literature on gardening strangely flourished. Newspapers added gardening as a regular Sunday feature of their weekend editions. Horticultural articles more than doubled in the periodical literature of the decade. This literature surely never sold to the small-town and country poor who grew food to preserve their standard of living. Only the more affluent purchased magazines, read reports, and grew for therapy as well as food. While many of the affluent had become leisure oriented and ceased to grow their own food, those retaining the old work ethic appear to have increased their consumption of gardening literature and may even have redoubled their efforts to maintain the fertility of their gardens.

The decline in the numbers of gardeners halted when the hard times of the Great Depression turned both the middle class and unemployed back to the land. Country clubs, night clubs, and European travel now seemed beyond the family budget, but Americans in suburbia could still grasp the garden fork and fall back on one of the oldest pastimes since hunting and gathering. Both flower and vegetable gardening regained popularity during the depression, along with church attendance and book reading as many Americans rediscovered the simple pleasures.[17]

Vacant lot gardens, or subsistence gardening as it was called in the 1930s, reemerged as a solution for unemployment. In Detroit, city employees donated monthly contributions from their salaries to raise the ten thousand dollars necessary for financing a free garden program like the Pingree potato patches that had helped the city through the 1890s depression. Now the city plowed school property and vacant lots for five thousand garden plots, along with free seed, for the unemployed. Welfare garden plots blossomed across America from California to Maine as a method of supplying food and work for the unemployed. Sophisticated urbanites of New York City were a little slow in organizing depression gardens for their unemployed, but the state relief administrator, Harry Hopkins, boasted of a New York relief garden program that returned five dollars worth of vegetables for every state dollar invested in its supervised relief gardens. By 1934 the seventy thousand subsistence gardens were said to have yielded $2.8 million worth of food for those on relief. And in 1935 even New York City joined the welfare garden program, preparing plots in every borough except Manhattan to both feed the spirits and nourish the health of its poor.[18]

"Back to the land" became a popular folk movement of disillusioned urbanites during the depression. The radical middle-aged economics professor, Scott Nearing, retreated from urban activism with a vegetarian violinist, Helen Knothe, twenty years his junior, to a homestead in Vermont that was to serve as his storm cellar during the expected collapse of capitalism. The flight from urban breadlines to the rural security of food and shelter extended far beyond literary intellectuals to include more than a million people in the first three years of the 1930s. So popular were subsistence homesteads that the federal government even planned and financed more than a hundred subsistence communities.[19]

The specter of war joined the fear of hunger by the close of the 1930s, sustaining the popularity of kitchen gardening. After the outbreak of war in Europe during 1939, gardening offered even more of a psychological comfort. As the garden editor of the *New York Times* wrote, "We will need the mental and psychological tonic which work with plants and close touch with the soil never fail to bring." Gardening could maintain individual sanity amidst a world insanity and might even be useful in a food scarcity. Although no shortage existed in America in 1941, "such a scarcity developed suddenly during the last war, and 'war gardens' were a boon to hundreds of thousands of their owners, as well as a substantial contribution to America's war effort." [20]

The alarmed Agriculture Department had learned its lesson in the First World War—appeasement of volunteer garden organizers never paid. Strike first and kill off all enemies of the department who might seize for the war garden leadership. With the enormous growth of the national government during the depression, control of gardeners now seemed within the Department of Agriculture's grasp. After Pearl Harbor—December 7, 1941—Secretary Claude Wickard called a special National Defense Gardening Conference in Washington for December 20–21 to both seize control of the victory garden leadership and kill any war garden enthusiasm. Wickard intended to label garden enthusiasm unpatriotic.

"I hope there will be no move to plow up the parks and the lawns to grow vegetables as in the First World War," Secretary Wickard asserted to representatives of the media, the garden association clubs, and the seed, horticultural, and trade associations. City backyards and uninstructed growers seldom raised successful gardens. Excessive zeal in war gardening would only result in waste of seed, fertilizer, and insecticides. Waste in chemicals was unpatriotic; the government needed nitrogen for explosives, and besides, homegrown vegetables were unnecessary when the nation held the greatest food surplus in human history. So Wickard organized a Victory Garden Program to propagandize against ripping up flower beds, front yards, golf courses, and park land. America needed no new gardeners. If amateurs insisted on vegetable growing, they ought to first attend lecture and demonstration courses conducted by trained horticulturists.[21]

Restraint urged by the Agriculture Department did not prevent seed sales from going up by 300 percent in 1942. Despite the greatest food surplus in history, prices did skyrocket, turning more Americans to gardening. War anxiety drove others into the vegetable garden for relief from nervousness. In North Carolina a forty-five-year-old judge, Sam J. Ervin, bought a pair of bib overalls and went out every morning to work in his victory garden. Ervin, who three decades later won fame as chairman of the Senate Watergate hearings, had tried to enlist in the army but had been rejected as an antique, so he made his war contribution and found release from "nervous tension" in the garden.

In New York City digging in the dirt also relieved anxiety. "You make a war garden to be doing a little something extra for your country," one new gardener told the *New York Times*, "and first thing you know you are getting rewards out of it that you didn't look for. It has cured my war jitters, for one thing."[22]

Perhaps medical doctors rather than farmers should have planned the war garden program because the U.S. Public Health Service knew gardening relieved tension and provided relaxation. Public Health's Dr. Samuel W. Hamilton explained the connection between mental hygiene and gardening: Life's many frustrations, disappointments, and failures are damaging to one's self-esteem, but success in providing one of the essential needs, food, gives satisfaction and confidence. Exercise of the muscles and mind in the garden gives a sense of power and feeling that the conflicts of life can be mastered and emergencies met. The expectation of the garden harvest gratifies the human spirit and induces sound sleep.[23]

The heavy agricultural hand of Secretary Wickard even prevented Eleanor Roosevelt from having her victory garden. When the wife of the president of the United States asked Wickard to find her a suitable gardening site on the White House lawn, Wickard's two experts were so severe that they rejected all possibilities. The site near the tennis courts had such tight red clay that only years of adding barnyard manure could turn the soil into a garden. Moving some of the flowers from the Rose Garden would violate the secretary's recommendation against tearing up ornamentals to grow vegetables. So the Department of Agriculture informed the White House that there was no proper victory garden site.[24]

Across America in 1942 gardeners purchased Burpee's Victory Garden packets—the Kitchen Garden selection of fifteen packets for one dollar, the Suburban Garden selection of twenty-five packets for two dollars, and the Country Garden selection of thirty seed packets for three dollars. The Rockefeller Center uprooted flowers and ornamentals for demonstration vegetable gardens. Victory gardens appeared in parking lots, playgrounds, college campuses, vacant lots, and backyards. But less hysteria existed than in 1917, and the media, parroting the Agriculture Department's restraint policy, complimented Americans for being wiser than their parents had been. The general negativism of the department did not go unchallenged. The Illinois Victory Garden Commission bluntly accused Wickard of "sabotage" while even the secretary's own Victory Garden Committee grew impatient. Andrew S. Wing pressured Wickard into approving his Victory Garden Harvest Shows, and Governor Prentice Cooper of Tennessee urged the secretary to recognize the increasingly critical world food problem by endorsing a real victory garden program. Secretary Wickard resisted until early 1943 and then gave in to victory gardeners and admitted the real need for amateur growers.[25]

Now the Agriculture Department spread the word that food shortages were coming; commercial growers were being instructed to produce only high protein foods, eliminating lettuce, celery, cucumbers, peppers, cauliflower, eggplant, and watermelon. Secretary Wickard urged every town, city, and suburban family with a sunny fertile plot to plant a victory garden. And his new chairman of the Committee on Victory Gardens, H. W. Hochbaum, called for spading up larger gardens. "It is time for the amateur to get away from the pocket-handkerchief garden idea," Hochbaum said, "and to realize that if he is to grow enough for both summer and winter requirements of even a small family he has got to cultivate more than a handkerchief size plot of ground."[26]

When canned foods joined the list of rationed items in March, 1943, the seriousness of a vegetable crisis created four million new gardeners. The percentage of gardening families rose from 48 to 54 percent, creating a buyers' panic in the seed market. Twenty million victory gardens were planted in 1943, including one on the White House lawn. Although Eleanor Roosevelt herself did not plant the beans, carrots, tomatoes, and cabbages, her husband's adviser, Harry Hopkins, gardened with his family and posed for photographs beside the executive mansion. So 1943 became the year for plowing up golf courses, park land, and front yards.[27]

In the white-collar town of West Hartford, Connecticut, victory garden enthusiasm reached far beyond the national average to include 72.2 percent of all local families. These suburbanites had begun well below the national gardening average when their city recreation department hired a market gardener to head their war garden campaign. Along with the War Ration Book No. 2, residents received a garden questionnaire and then an information sheet with phone numbers of plowmen and manure and garden suppliers. For those without land, community garden plots were offered on vacant lots. A garden lecture series in the Town Hall and a new radio program, "Uncle Jim's Victory Garden Program," dramatized the patriotic craft. For the close of the gardening season, a Harvest Show in the local high school boasted West Hartford's success at victory gardening.[28]

Chicago revived the school garden army idea that year with Sears Roebuck distributing buttons declaring membership in the School Children's Victory Garden Army for every fifth through eighth grader. Marshall Field contributed packets of seed — lettuce, radish, kohlrabi, bush beans, Swiss chard, carrots, beets, petunia, and zinnia. For inner-city children without land, the city parks provided gardening plots.[29]

Victory gardeners in 1943 waged a holy war on the garden pests, following the advice, "Dust that plant and spray that row, keep those insects on the go." The tobacco-based Black Leaf 40 provided the heavy poison. For soon-to-be-harvested crops, rotenone and pyrethrum were weapons of destruction to the insect hordes but less poisonous to humans. For the larger pests — birds, rabbits, squirrels, chipmunks, woodchucks, and deer — gardeners were urged not to be soft on the enemy. If mothballs or nicotine spray failed to repel the intruders, garden authorities insisted that the enemies must be reduced by other means. Homemade traps were described for birds, squirrels, and rabbits, and the gas treatment — calcium cyanide — was urged for burrowing rats, woodchucks, and chipmunks.[30]

To garden successfully with the reduced nitrogen content in Victory fertilizer, gardeners were encouraged to build a compost heap as part of their patriotic duty. Saving all leaves and vegetable waste, dumping it in a pile layered with manure or superphosphate, and watering and turning the pile occasionally with a garden fork produced humus with nitrogen and all the elements necessary for plant growth as well as a soil conditioning magic. Compost could even eliminate the work of hoeing and cultivating when used as a mulch to smother weeds and save moisture.[31]

Gardening enthusiasm peaked in 1943, and then participation slipped as canned foods were dropped from rationing lists in 1944. Even increased government propaganda, including Secretary Wickard's trip north to open the New England campaign by plowing a furrow in the Boston Commons, did not hold the twenty million gardeners, and the number dropped by a million and a half. Neither could later postwar efforts by President Harry Truman and Secretary of State George C. Marshall persuade all former gardeners that food remained important for maintaining peace in the world. The lapsed gardeners would not believe they had an international obligation to contribute to the food supply by backyard or community garden production. By 1948, directors of urban community garden programs were complaining, "People just aren't willing to bend their backs these days." A few community gardens such as five acres in Boston's Fenway Park and Washington D.C.'s National Park Service victory gardens continued, but most community gardens were abandoned from lack of interest.[32]

Vegetable gardening had shifted from serious business to Sunday humor in the media. Rather than a patriotic contribution, gardening was now described as a kind of spring madness one succumbed to following the intoxicating gardening talk of office acquaintances and the smell of fresh-spaded earth from the yard of the neighborhood's eager beaver. Dreams of bountiful harvest, however, were certain to be lost in the "Battle of Suburbia" against the animal, insect, and microbe world that took the harvest, leaving only eleven radishes, four tomatoes, and a single bent cucumber. The intelligent approach to gardening, according to a *New York Times* story, was the neighbor Driscoll system — "an overstuffed garden chair, a shaker of martinis, and a hired man."[33]

Obviously Driscoll lacked the character to be a prosperity gardener. He represented only the 30 percent of dropouts from victory gardening. The hard-core believers were no more apt to give up gardening for martinis than they were to be found in bar lounges instead of the plant lectures while attending garden conventions. The numbers of new gardeners in the spreading suburban developments actually grew so rapidly that vegetable seed sales did not decline as they had in the 1920s. Population growth, love of gardening, and perhaps the inflationary price spiral kept gardeners at seventeen million in the early 1950s, setting new records for peacetime seed sales as well as garden equipment such as rotary tillers and walking tractors. Gardening remained the number one leisure hobby in postwar America. Thirty-nine percent of all families said they planted a vegetable garden. On the farm, 82 percent of the families grew garden vegetables, while 31 percent of nonfarm families gardened.[34]

Government propaganda actually had little control over gardening enthusiasm. Most gardeners grew vegetables in both good and bad times. A national crisis could increase the number of gardeners by 30 percent, but government policy seemed less influential than private perceptions of the advantages of vegetable gardening. If food prices rose, more Americans gardened. The Agriculture Department might restrain gardeners from overselling war gardening, but government propaganda itself actually had little control over the number of Americans who wished to participate in kitchen gardening. Victory gardening came from private rather than government desire.

10 : BACK TO MUCK AND MAGIC

The twentieth century has witnessed a powerful reaction against chemical horticulture, toppling the Department of Agriculture and its professors from the leadership of kitchen gardening. Scientific horticulture had dominated the gardening books and journals for the first half of the twentieth century, but then suspicions shifted against the experts until they were more apt to be distrusted than respected by home gardeners.

The reaction against scientific horticulture should not be dismissed as just another example of the American distaste for experts. Anti-intellectualism surely grows in part from the arrogance of experts who inflate their claims and fail to communicate the limits of their understanding. While the scientific study of garden soil had taken brilliant strides as it grew beyond chemistry to include bacteriology and physics, gardeners were told little of the new understanding, only that soil was "very complicated." And where garden books had once devoted long chapters to manures and none to insects, now the opposite was true. Gardeners were led, perhaps by advertisers more than professors, to believe that they needed to know only insecticides and chemical fertilizers.[1]

Applying chemical fertilizer—nitrogen, phosphorus, and potassium—to good garden soil produces great harvests, but only disappointment results from pouring chemicals on the clay of most new gardens. Clay is a stack of tiny aluminum silicate flakes so minute that only an electron micrscope can separate them for the viewer. Puddled together while wet, clay is fit only for bricks, pottery, or farm ponds. Only when the tiny flakes are separated, preferably with organic material, can the soil become favorable to garden cultivation, the growth of roots, and the passage of water. Organic material—the remains of plants and animals, manure, compost, leaves, and peat moss—not only promotes the desirable loose crumb structure but also provides the food for soil life, worms and millions of microorganisms that digest organic material into dark brown humus, and the simple elements—calcium, potassium, and nitrates—that growing plants can absorb. Humus creates both desirable soil structure and nitrogen-creating bacteria. While the mineral clay lasts forever, humus-building material must be constantly replaced. Thus, overemphasis on soil chemistry, to the neglect of soil biology, led naturally to a reaction against chemical gardening.

Careless urban gardeners had rather easily been led astray by professional derision of "smelly manure" and touting of the presumed superiority of chemical fertilizer. Of course, experts had usually added a note on the wisdom of maintaining a supply of organic matter in soil, but secondary points gain little attention. After some years of adding nitrogen, phosphorus, and potassium, but no humus, chemical fertilizer could no longer produce bountiful crops, disappointing gardeners and making many suspicious of the chemical industry and its scientific advocates. Science, we must remember, still had much to be modest about in the 1930s. Medical doctors, for example, could recognize and identify a disease but were unable to alter the course of the illness. Medicine remained a "profoundly ignorant occupation" with prescriptions that doctors knew could kill no infections.[2] Home remedies in medicine or agriculture then suffered no statistical disadvantage.

Nature had also delivered a shocking blow to agricultural science and technology in the form of ruinous soil erosion. In the spring of 1935 a huge dust storm blew tons of topsoil from the plowed lands of the American West across the nation, even veiling the sun in the Northeast, before blowing out into the

Atlantic. The Dust Bowl aroused fear for the land and the environment, producing a sharp debate between the claims of nature and those of technology. The official Great Plains Committee reported against technology, declaring, "It is our ways, not Nature's, which can be changed."[3]

The return to natural gardening in America came under the leadership of a feisty New Yorker, Jerome I. Rodale, who grew up on the Lower East Side, the son of a grocer, without either a garden or a college education. Poor in eyesight, health, and athletic ability, Rodale compensated by determination and intellectual curiosity. He studied accounting in night school, becoming a federal tax auditor before organizing Rodale Manufacturing Company. Financial success from electrical wiring devices allowed Rodale to indulge his hobby of journalism, publishing *Health Guide* and *Fact Digest,* which reprinted health articles. While scanning the British health literature in 1941 he saw a reference to Sir Albert Howard's *An Agricultural Testament* (1940), sent for the book, and became the leading apostle in America of organically grown food.[4]

Sir Albert Howard rejected agricultural science after having worked as a government professional for almost half a century. Born on an English farm in 1873, Howard studied botany at the Royal College of Science and then worked as a scientific investigator in India. In a less developed nation that lacked the capital for purchasing artificial fertilizers and that burned its cow dung for fuel, Howard turned to other organic materials for fertilizer. He knew the Chinese compost method through Franklin H. King's *Farmers of Forty Centuries* (1911) and the science of decay from the America humus studies of S. A. Waksman. With the assistance of a chemist, Howard mastered the biochemical and biological processes of the compost heap, publishing *Waste Products of Agriculture* (1931), and then became a missionary advocate of his Indore, India, system of mixing vegetable refuse with a little manure to triple the farmer's supply of humus.[5]

The radical aspect of Howard's message asserted that organically fertilized food protected animals from diseases. Organically fed oxen could rub noses with the carriers of hoof and mouth disease, he said, and remain completely healthy. Howard ~neculated that freedom from disease resulted from the living

organism's natural capacity, if in good health, to repel attack. Rather than worrying about fungus and parasites, we should worry about organically grown food. Artificially fertilized food, he declared, lacked the natural health-giving power of organically grown crops.

Howard's call for a return of the old methods found little or no sympathy in the British establishment. His reputation turned from that of a respected scientific investigator to that of a crank agitator who retired from government work to devote the remainder of his life to denouncing chemical fertilizers as devil's dust and the major threat to the health of people and their planet.[6]

Howard explained his faith in *An Agricultural Testament*, which described nature as in revolt against the acceleration of agricultural production. Although the tractor and chemical fertilizer increased the productivity of the farmer, these unnatural methods led to increased human disease and soil erosion. Nature removed worn-out soil by erosion and nutritionally deprived people by disease. Trust nature, Howard said. Nature's methods of soil management could be observed in the forest or on the prairie, where soil did not erode. Rain moved slowly through vegetation, humus, and subsoil with only a small runoff of practically clear water. Nature wasted nothing, neither water, soil, nor organic material. Fungi and bacteria recycled organic waste into humus for a new cycle of plant and animal growth. Nature preserved the land and conferred disease resistance upon the plants and animals, Howard asserted. Consider primitive peoples, such as the Hunzas or the Tristan islanders, whose diet of fresh and unprocessed foods gave them a marked absence of disease. Or consider Howard's own orchard. He acquired diseased, worn-out trees bearing apples of poor quality, but three years of rebuilding the orchard humus drove away the parasites, transformed the trees, and produced first-class fruit. When all people ate such naturally grown fruit and vegetables, Howard predicted, half the illnesses of humankind would disappear.[7]

Even before publication of *An Agricultural Testament* Howard had gained converts in England. A medical doctor in Cheshire County had persuaded his colleagues to endorse a medical testament that "illness results from a life-time of wrong

nutrition." Physician Lionel James Picton conducted a mass meeting on March 23, 1939, asking the entire county to agree that bad teeth, rickets, anemia, and constipation were products of diet which might be eliminated by natural foods. And Picton later edited a *News Letter on Compost* to further organic farming and gardening.[8]

In New Zealand the Mount Albert Grammar School had experimented with Howard's natural diet, feeding its boarding school students organically grown food. Colds and childhood diseases were greatly reduced, according to the results published in the *Lancet*. This case study caught the eye of Jerome Rodale, introducing him to Sir Albert's theory of health. The boarding school experiment might have been understood as proving that a better diet of vegetables reduced illness, but Rodale accepted the compost miracle-maker theory, becoming a convert, reading *An Agricultural Testament,* and purchasing a sixty-acre farm near Emmaus, Pennsylvania, to grow his own organic food.[9]

For most believers, restoring the natural fertility of a miserable piece of land would have been a sufficient challenge, but Rodale had the high energy of a missionary. To handle his farm and compost pile he hired a farmhand while he corresponded with Sir Albert and laid plans to launch the organic revolution in American farming. Rodale intended to publish a new magazine opposing chemical fertilizer, and he sent twelve thousand farmers complimentary copies of his first issue of *Organic Farming and Gardening* (May 1942), the twelve-page journal proclaiming "Back to Nature in Agriculture."

Organic Farming explained not only Sir Albert's compost method but also the more philosophical biodynamic system created in the 1920s as part of the spiritual science of Austrian philosopher Rudolf Steiner. Biodynamic also rejected modern commercial farming for the old methods, including concern for cosmic forces and moon rhythms. The biodynamic compost pile required secret preparations that could be obtained only from a bona fide biodynamic farmer who had been given the elaborate recipe of medicinal herbs—such as chamomile, valerian, nettle, dandelion, and horsetail—which were fermented at specific depths in the earth until they were humus themselves and their bacterial content speeded up decomposition of the compost pile.

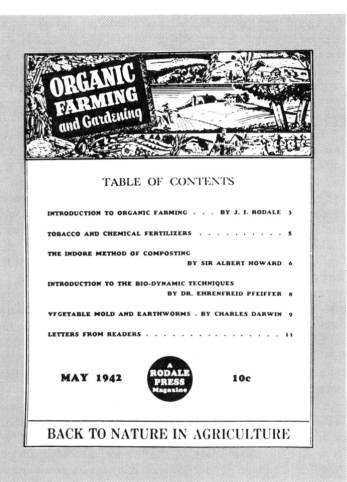

ORGANIC FARMING and Gardening

TABLE OF CONTENTS

MAY 1942   A RODALE PRESS Magazine   10c

BACK TO NATURE IN AGRICULTURE

First edition of Rodale magazine. *Reprinted by permission of Rodale Press, Inc.*

Biodynamic agriculture also taught companion planting of plant varieties to encourage growth while repelling insects. Rodale never claimed to believe in the various biodynamic theories but accepted them as fellow travelers in the war against artificial fertilizers, printed their literature, and recommended Ehrenfried Pfeiffer's *Bio-Dynamic Farming and Gardening* (1940) for those who preferred the more cultist method.[10]

Organic Farming accepted Sir Albert's bacteriological approach to soil, explaining that crops depended on soil bacteria and earthworms to convert organic matter into plant food. Rodale even reprinted Charles Darwin's work on vegetable molds and earthworms while editorializing that artificial chemicals reduced the numbers of these little decomposers, allowed the texture of the soil to harden, and contributed to water and wind erosion. But most important, the food grown with artificials deprived people of the good health that came from natural fertilizers—manure, compost, ashes, and rock phosphate.

Farmers are notoriously reluctant to accept new methods or even subscribe to new periodicals. A mere fourteen subscriptions resulted from the twelve thousand free copies of the first issue. By the end of the year, Rodale lost hope for a farm readership and shifted to kitchen gardeners, moving them up to first place in the journal title. With the January 1943 issue, Rodale's magazine became *Organic Gardening and Farming*.[11]

Organic Gardening offered much practical assistance to kitchen gardeners involved in victory gardens at a time when the government had taken most of the nitrates for explosives. "Hints for the Victory Gardener" provided specific nurture instructions for the major garden vegetables as well as the Jerusalem artichoke and the sunflower, along with instructions for mulching, composting, and controlling bugs. Rodale himself claimed that the organic method kept the problem of destructive insects to a minimum. "In our own organic garden there is so little of it that we do absolutely nothing about it."[12] But for those who feared to trust the birds and the beneficial insects, *Organic Gardening* gave safe old remedies such as hand picking bugs, covering plants with cheesecloth, or dusting with wood ashes.

Artificial fertilizers, not pesticides, were the chief chemical

A 1945 magazine cover. *Reprinted by permission of Rodale Press, Inc.*

villains for *Organic Gardening*. But reader complaints about mindless spraying of lead arsenate, and then DDT, led the magazine to adopt the slogan "Gardening without Chemicals." Even then, in 1948, the artificials remained Rodale's "devil's dust"; the following year he began a series called "Is Cancer Related to Artificial Fertilizers," which ran for more than a year. It made even organic gardeners a little impatient, prompting Rodale to launch an additional journal, *Prevention,* for his longer health essays promoting freedom of disease through organic foods, natural food supplements, and exercise.

Rodale had pumped circulation of *Organic Gardening* steadily higher after the relaxation of wartime paper restrictions. He spread the message of returning to the land without chemical fertilizers, weed-killers, and sprays in his book *Pay Dirt* (1945). If America were to save its land, health, and civilization, citizens must join the organic revolution in farming and gardening. Believers did embrace the faith, forming organic garden clubs in California, Texas, Michigan, and New York. By 1947 paid subscriptions hit sixty thousand and then one hundred thousand two years later. "The first battle is over," Rodale cheered. "There is not a county or even a city in the United States in which there are not some practicing organiculturists. We number millionaire magnates, congressmen, senators, judges, physicians by the many hundreds, educators, and even plain people, the ones who are taking this idea on their shoulders and carrying its torch, among the soldiers in the camp of organiculture."[13]

Rodale grew so confident of victory in 1949 that he resumed his campaign with the farmers, launching a separate *Organic Farming.* By now he had deserted the labor-intensive Indore system for the easier method of spreading organic material directly on the land without composting. "Sheet composting" he called the new system, which transferred humus-making to the land itself and did not exceed the labor capacity of a large-scale farmer.

Rodale even took on the U.S. Department of Agriculture, asking that it cease dismissing organiculturists as a "bunch of misguided crack-pots" and open a series of scientific tests to determine whether organic methods produced greater yields and better health. The department and the university agriculture professors were surely in the pay of chemical companies, Rodale believed. Professors were not pleased and replied in *Horticulture, Country Gentleman, Reader's Digest,* and *Consumer Reports.* "Organic Farming—Bunk!" roared the dean of Kansas State, R. I. Throckmorton, dismissing every claim of the organic method and asserting that chemicals even promoted the growth of bacteria and earthworms. The world would starve without these miracles of agricultural research, Throckmorton said, adding, "Chemical fertilizers stand between us and hunger."[14]

The Agriculture Department's dean of soil science, Charles E. Kellogg, offered a kinder response to organic advocates, viewing them as a natural, if somewhat extreme, reaction to the fallacy of Liebig's chemical storage bin theory. Without organic matter, Kellogg agreed, gardening would be impractical or impossible on most soils. Organic matter had great value in maintaining a friable soil structure, in furnishing a continuous supply of plant nutrients, and as a source of food for microorganisms. But humus had "no mysterious power." Sir Albert's New Zealand boarding school experiment probably owed more to the shift from polished rice to fresh vegetables than to the organic method. Better balanced diets promoted good health, but no nutritional advantages came from organically grown food. Food fertilized by nitrogen, phosphorus, and potassium from a chemical factory did not differ nutritionally from food that obtained those same elements from natural decayed organic matter. Well-nourished crops were all better able to resist disease, with artificially fed plants being just as disease resistant.[15]

The organic versus chemical debate divided gardeners across America in the 1950s as speakers were sternly asked, "Are you an organic gardener or a chemical gardener?" The established gardening journals, such as *Horticulture,* remained hostile, dismissing organic gardening as a cult and a threat to the American way of life.[16] Growth of *Organic Gardening* remained slow in the face of ridicule from the established press. The journal continued to lose money for sixteen years before subscriptions reached one hundred seventy-five thousand in 1958, large companies decided to buy advertising, and Rodale's missionary efforts began to return a profit.[17] During those years *Organic Gardening* had been the major kitchen gardening magazine in America; the other horticultural journals were more devoted to ornamentals than food. *Organic Gardening* devoted most of its space to useful information on growing food plants. Open to both new and old gardening tricks, the journal had become the great advocate of mulch, the shredder, and the rotary tiller.

Mulching plants with waste vegetable refuse to save moisture and keep down weeds had been an ancient technique recommended in the 1940s by *Organic Gardening* as well as *Horticulture*. Then in the 1950s it became an entire gardening philosophy pushed by Ruth Stout, a white-haired Connecticut lady who, when no plowman was available to work her victory garden, impatiently planted in the unplowed ground. The garden grew so well in the deep mulch that she completely gave up not only the plow but also the hoe, spade, and cultivator. She kept only the garden trowel for planting and threw all her organic material — hay, leaves, coffee grounds, eggshells — directly on the garden. In 1954 she urged other organic gardeners to "Throw Away Your Spade and Hoe." The following year she published her classic *How to Have a Green Thumb without an Aching Back* (1955), arguing that mulch gardening could easily be handled by any seventy-year-old lady.[18]

For gardeners who preferred the big machinery, *Organic Gardening* promoted mechanical shredders that broke down vegetable waste, reducing the composting time microbes required for turning waste into humus. In two weeks, a gardener could have finished compost. For working the new humus into the garden, rotary tillers were touted. This new garden tool of the 1950s had been invented in 1910 by a Swiss agricultural engineer watching a dog dig in a flower bed. The idea of mounting claw tines on a rotary wheel and replacing the plow, disk, and harrow with an earth grinder produced electric tillers for Switzerland. Not until the 1930s were gasoline models imported to America; but at $695 they cost more than a new Chevrolet pickup. In the 1940s, smaller models priced at less than $200 came on the market, and after some reluctance for fear the tiller would kill all the earthworms, *Organic Gardening* embraced the

rotary tillers as labor-saving devices for working organic material into the soil. *Organic Gardening* did caution that tilling
could be overdone; soil tilth would be ruined by tilling wet soil
or by tilling too many times a season.[19]

The excellent gardening information alone would never had
made *Organic Gardening* popular if the intellectual climate in
America had not changed in the 1960s. Technology had created
a pollution crisis as use of chemicals escalated after World War
II, with even good old soap losing out to a chemical detergent.
Testing of new atomic weapons in the atmosphere so alarmed
scientists in 1958 that Barry Commoner and others formed the
Committee on Nuclear Information to warn of dangers from
radioactive fallout. Agricultural chemicals also threatened the
environment. Synthetic insecticide use had escalated in agriculture, and as beneficial insects were killed off, pests developed
resistance to sprays and increased spraying brought no better
results. Outcries against DDT had been published in the 1940s,
not only in *Organic Gardening* but also in the *New Republic* and
the establishment garden press such as *Horticulture*. Still the
mass media and the public remained largely unmoved until Rachel Carson's *Silent Spring* (1962).[20]

A quiet naturalist from the federal Fish and Wildlife Service, Rachel Carson created a national alarm over the fate of the
environment. Her specter of disaster documented the effect of
two hundred chemicals created since agriculture moved beyond
arsenic to chlorinated hydrocarbons and organic phosphates for
killing insects, weeds, and rodents. Not only the pests but the
birds, fish, food, water, and land had been contaminated. We
were now more threatened by sickness and death from chemicals
than from insects. Not only commercial farmers but gardeners
had become a danger to human life. "Gardening is now firmly
linked with the super poisons," Carson wrote. "Every hardware
store, garden-supply shop, and supermarket has rows of insecticides for every conceivable horticultural situation. Those who
fail to make wide use of this array of lethal sprays and dusts are
by implication remiss, for almost every newspaper's garden page
and the majority of the gardening magazines take their use for
granted."[21]

To the delight of Jerome Rodale, *Silent Spring* terrified

Americans into concern about chemical pollution of the food chain and all life on the planet. New subscribers flooded into *Organic Gardening,* perhaps one hundred thousand in 1963, for a total of three hundred thousand. *Organic Gardening,* after all, had been carrying the message against chemicals for twenty years, calling for peaceful coexistence or the use of biological controls for insect pests. Biological controls had become even more practical with the development of *Bacillus thuringiensis* in 1958 for eliminating cabbage worms on all the green vegetables.[22]

Concern over pollution and the growing support for an environmental cleanup gave *Organic Gardening* a new respectability with the old as well as the young. When the youth culture turned against the establishment for getting the United States into the Vietnam War as well as polluting the environment, *Organic Gardening* became one of the anti-establishment heroes. The *Whole Earth Catalogue* applauded *Organic Gardening* as the "most subversive" publication in America. "Organic gardeners are in the forefront of a serious effort to save the world," the *Catalogue* proclaimed, "by changing man's orientation to it, to move away from the collective, centrist, super-industrial state, towards a simpler, realer one-to-one relationship with the earth itself."[23] Along with the *Cultivator's Handbook of Marijuana,* the *Catalogue* recommended every young radical should have a copy of *Walden* and *Organic Gardening.*

Perhaps Rodale had a little trouble speaking the language of the young radicals, but he hired the organic nature lover, Euell Gibbons, to write a regular column. And his own son, Robert Rodale, could speak the youth language. Organic gardeners were the Thoreaus of the 1970s, son Robert wrote: "They make a Walden Pond out of their home, their grounds, and their activities. It is the purpose of our compost and our avoidance of poisons to preserve the web of life in our garden."[24] Organic gardeners no longer suffered from an inferiority complex. Now they had allies. They joined hands with the ecologists to protect the environment.

As the environment and the fate of the earth became a dominant concern in the early 1970s, Jerome Rodale finally received fame. He had long gained wealth from the manufac-

J. I. Rodale in his greenhouse. *Reprinted by permission of Rodale Press, Inc.*

turing company and Rodale Press. But his health ideas and his dramas — he wrote thirty-three plays — had been insulted and dismissed. Now that *Organic Gardening* subscriptions were up to seven hundred thousand and the journal had become a hero of the youth culture, Rodale finally received recognition by the *New York Times* with a magazine article, "Guru of the Organic Food Cult," explaining how he had made Emmaus, Pennsylvania, the mecca for organic gardeners, health food eaters, and the youth culture. Sure, the American Medical Association still considered Rodale Press books "quackery," and the chemical companies had not come to love him, but Rodale could now count reputable scientists such as Dr. Barry Commoner as supporters of his *Organic Gardening*.[25]

Management of the multi-million dollar Rodale Press had already shifted to the college-educated son, Robert Rodale, who spoke the language of those who wanted a better, cleaner, more peaceful world by working with nature and applying appropriate technology. *Organic Gardening* even moved close to mainstream opinion in the 1970s as the one old opponent, *Horticulture*, devoted attention to the environment, urging a reduction of pesticides, and another, the Department of Agriculture, worked with Rodale on experiments for more energy-efficient agriculture.[26]

11 : GARDEN AND COMMUNITY

I n the 1970s kitchen gardening ceased to be a private activity outside the concern of the government. A new surge of community horticultural enthusiasm won acceptance for the principle that all Americans should have the right to grow some of their own food. In previous community gardening campaigns — victory, school, or vacant lot — only national crisis or special disadvantage justified gardening assistance, but now the right to a garden plot was declared even more essential than access to a municipal golf course or tennis court. Government became a regular provider of garden plots for all interested citizens.

Gardens and politics have rarely mixed in America. Historically those concerns were so separate that gardening literature avoided all mention of political questions. Since both radicals and reactionaries have planted gardens, magazine editors dared not cross the garden fence to comment on controversial questions beyond horticulture and health. Even ethnic differences in the garden were left alone; vegetables from around the world grew together in the garden, and with a very few exceptions, such as Brussels sprouts or Chinese cabbage, their origins were ignored. So the ethnicity of American gardeners as well as their politics has been ignored by the agricultural press. Speculations outside the garden were bad form in horticultural literature.

Even in the 1970s gardeners managed to call for public action on community gardens without raising controversial political issues. Old right wing conservatives, devoted to individual self-help, could join with young radicals, hostile to control by the corporate state, in helping urban people find land for kitchen gardens. Both groups could unite because local, not federal, government assisted these neighborhood programs. If little bureaucracy or public expense were required in finding vacant land and administering applications for garden plots, then neither the political right nor the left objected to a gardening program that promised so many beneficial results.

For young radicals in the age of ecology, gardening ceased to be merely a private activity and became part of the fate of the universe. When gardeners grew food organically, their action extended beyond their private world, contributing to the health of the planet by reducing the amount of food grown with poisonous chemicals and capitalistic agriculture. The new philosophy of ecology taught, "We are morally obligated to our planet, if not to ourselves, to grow at least part of our food."[1] Ecology and gardening came together, advocating not only a cleaner environment but space for urban Americans to oppose corporate agriculture by growing their own vegetables.

The initial youth response to the problems of the 1960s — the Vietnam War, urban riots, and pollution — had created a rage against the corporate state's exploitation of humanity and nature that promoted turning away from the system rather than continuing to work within the community. Dropping out from civilization and capitalism to the back country were themes of the *Whole Earth Catalogue* and *Mother Earth News*. Just as a return to the land had always been a response to social crisis, so the 1970s began with a youth retreat from the city back to the good earth, rural communes, remote farms, and Walden ponds.

Mother Earth explained "How to Get out of the City and Back to the Land" in 1970 for hip young adults interested in alternate lifestyles, ecology, working with nature, and doing more with less. Edited by an Indiana-born farm boy turned New York advertiser, the magazine had been inspired by the *Whole Earth Catalogue*. Urbanites needed help to get away from the cities, where the atom bomb would fall and economic depression hit, to the simple life of the country. Do like Ted Richmond and move to a worn-out ten-acre farm near Jasper, Arkansas, to remake your life and live better than ever on one hundred dollars a year. With a library of Euell Gibbons's *Stalking the Wild Asparagus* (1962), Barry Commoner's *Science and Survival* (1966), and Ruth Stout's and Jerome Rodale's books, any dropout could escape from the urban rat race of overconsumption and overpollution. "A subscription to *Organic Gardening* will give you that proverbial green thumb within a year," *Mother Earth* promised.[2]

Organic Gardening welcomed the new converts. In response to the double shock of inflation and oil shortages, Robert Rodale promoted "back to the land," arguing that with the passing of cheap energy we must return to the smaller, simpler technology that now proved itself more energy efficient. The fossil fuels required for chemical sprays and fertilizers were more expensive than compost. Organic gardening used only "the free energy of the sun, and valuable minerals in the soil that otherwise would not be transformed into things of value." Endorsing the "small is beautiful" idea, Rodale agreed that cities were never the place to live: "The ones who will suffer the most from population pressures and shortages of food, energy and other resources are those who have always suffered, the very poor, the unfortunates locked into a life of dull routine and desperation in the inner cities."[3]

Even the suburbs no longer offered a real escape, according to Rodale, because they, like the cities, suffered from crowding, crime, and taxes. Urban people had finally began the retreat back to the country that *Organic Gardening* had promoted for thirty years. "Suddenly many of these city folk woke up and realized that they were in a kind of prison," Rodale wrote. "Sure, they still like the bright lights, the plays, the good restaurants, and their friends. And they liked the big money they were making. But often they were afraid to walk the streets at night, and sometimes in the daylight, too. In fact, from a multitude of directions, they saw the cities begin to decline and even degenerate—trapping their occupants in a most unpleasant web of human and physical decay. The prisoners began to seek means of escape."[4] *Organic Gardening* promised to assist by offering not only natural foods but advice on alternative energy production—wood stoves, windmills, solar panels—for the new shelter.

While the retreat back to the land received more press attention in the early 1970s, a community gardening movement emerged in the cities as economic troubles doubled the old inflation rate to more than 4 percent in 1968 and then zoomed the rate to 11 percent after the Arab oil embargo in 1973. The concern over escalating food costs and the dangers of agricultural chemicals produced "guerrilla gardens" along the streets of Berkeley, California. "People are going to have to learn how to grow their own food," a Berkeley student told the press. "Think of the prices and what chemicals are pumped into everything we get at the supermarkets. We have to get ourselves together and learn to do things on our own."[5]

The end of the Vietnam War, accompanied by the twin economic ills of inflation and depression, ended the political activism of the New Left, turning some young reformers to community gardening programs. The voice of highminded activists could be heard in California when community garden organizers came together. "What we're doing by being involved in urban agriculture," Jomo said, "is . . . helping to heal the planet. And we're helping to hold things together. We're helping to hold people together. . . . It goes far beyond the fact that we're raising radishes and raising carrots. It's helping us to realize our unity." The youth goal of community now united with a cultural criticism of the system and its nutrition. "A lot of people are starving and just dying in our culture," Los Angeles community gardener Mark Casady said. "Lots of these people are eating too much sugar, drinking too much booze, and smoking too many cigarettes. And they are not getting enough good food. . . . A lot of them are poor people. They need help, the kind of strength people can get from a garden. I want to go right to these neighborhoods because that's where the human ecology problem is and that's where the gardens belong."[6]

California produced not only advocates of community gardening but a new school of urban intensive gardening. In Berkeley, urban food gurus William and Helga Olkowski taught self-sufficiency with chickens, rabbits, bees, and a rooftop garden grown in old five-gallon containers. The new University of California at Santa Cruz had hired its own gardening guru, Alan Chadwick, a former actor and British naval officer who brought his biodynamic French intensive methods. Essentially raised beds that were double-dug, organically fertilized, closely planted, and hand watered, the Chadwick gardening system achieved fame from its spiritually oriented packaging. Chadwick apparently understood the California youth culture and sold his trenching as "opening the soil to starlight."[7] Gardens were sacred, he said, and gardening was a religion as well as an art. The dash of mysticism mixed with humus and air grew beautiful gardens and created a personal following for Chadwick. New books — John Jevons's *How to Grow More Vegetables Than You Ever Thought Possible on Less Land Than You Can Imagine* (1974) and Duane Newcomb's *The Postage Stamp Garden Book* (1975) — promoted Chadwick's methods of intensive urban gardens on small spaces but without his spiritual packaging.

As the energy crisis joined the inflation spiral, forcing people to stay home because of the gas shortage, gardening appealed to both cultural critics and old traditionalists; the number of gardens increased by 10 percent. The new appeal of gardening even gained access to the popular culture of television and folk music. David Malet composed his "Garden Song." And Boston public television hired professional horticulturist James Crockett in 1974 to begin Crockett's "Victory Garden" program demonstrating that the miracle of harvest would follow seed time if gardeners did their part. Soil preparation with profligate use of organic material was Crockett's key to successful gardening. While not an organic gardener, he had been influenced by the environmentalists and urged caution with chemicals. "If I can possibly do without chemical pesticides, I don't use them," Crockett said in the popular show, which demonstrated that vegetable gardening had wide audience appeal.[8]

As kitchen gardening grew more popular, Americans of all political persuasions moved to assist landless urbanites in much the way that older industrial nations had made garden plots available. English allotments dating back to eighteenth-century plots for the village poor had been formalized in the 1908 law requiring cities to provide inexpensive allotments if none could be furnished from private land. These allotments had, of course, soared during the world wars to 1.5 million and then dropped back to 635,000 plots by the early 1970s.[9] Urban Americans had nothing comparable to European allotment gardens except for a few survivors from the victory gardens, such as Fenway Park in Boston and the National Parks gardens in the District of Columbia.

A new crop of community gardens grew rapidly across America in the early 1970s, sprouting from many local seeds. In Hartford, Connecticut, the charitable Knox Parks Foundation decided to start a community gardening project in 1971, plowing and fertilizing vacant lands so that inner-city inhabitants could grow vegetable gardens with the assistance of a horticulturist. That same year in Appleton, Wisconsin, the pastor of Sacred Heart Church reponded to his congregation's dismay over rising food prices by persuading a dairy farmer with a vacant pasture to plow 10-by-100-foot swaths in the grass and rent these ten-dollar plots to 259 poor families. The 1972 Appleton gardens were so popular that demand increased to twenty-seven hundred plots as the middle class joined the community garden.[10]

In Burlington, Vermont, an older gardener, Bryson H. Thompson, helped two school teachers plow a summer garden in 1972 for thirty-nine families. The next year his community garden grew to nine hundred plots, and Gardens for All, a non-profit organization for encouraging community gardening across America, was created. Hiring an annual Gallup poll to estimate the millions of Americans who would garden if they had the land, Gardens for All then gave its information to the news media, which advertised the popular demand for community gardens. In addition to Gallup polls, Gardens for All offered gardening seminars, workshops, and a manual of instructions for establishing community gardening.[11]

In 1973 Chicago launched its Neighborhood Farms Program as a productive use for some of the sixteen hundred unsightly vacant lots the city government owned. The city cleared twenty-one sites of debris, rototilled the soil, and provided seed, fertilizer, tools, and water for 140 families. The program grew to ninety-nine sites the following year, with 228 families and at least one kindergarten class growing vegetables on city land. At the Hyde Park Farm, next to Sojourner Truth Child Care Center, fifty-six preschoolers grew lima beans and carrots. Each year the program expanded, with private companies paying much of the cost. International Harvester plowed the plots and Zayre donated seeds for the program, in which twelve hundred families — black, Mexican, and European American — participated and were praised for improving their neighborhoods. "I love to work in my garden," said one sixty-five-year-old about the plot next to her home. "There used to be lots of garbage, rats and bedsprings in the places — now there is beauty, beauty, beauty. I love to just walk over there and smell the land. It reminds me of Poland; so nice, so nice."[12]

In addition to the vacant lot farms, Chicago had a separate garden program for 2,015 of its public housing tenants. Housing authorities had promoted garden contests among their various projects for more than a decade because they understood the value of plants in improving morale and reducing vandalism. The housing gardens were carefully maintained, with problem children enlisted as garden guards and as participants in the competition for the fall prize awards. When horticulturists, along with psychologists and architects, won a grant to study this human aspect of gardening, they rediscovered what gardeners had always known — gardening enhances self-esteem because growers identify with their plants and take credit for their growth. They feel better about themselves and where they live. Thus gardening heals in the ghettos as well as in the mental hospitals, prisons, and suburbs. Vegetables are more than food, fiber, and visual pleasure; they also promote mental and physical health.[13]

When Los Angeles Mayor Tom Bradley launched a community gardening program in 1974 he turned to a young Ph.D. candidate in agronomy, Mark Casady, who not only believed in organic gardening but also preached that chemiculture was destined to be replaced by bioculture within ten to twenty years. Casady ran his fifty acres for three thousand gardeners, including Hollywood entertainers, on compost, natural insect remedies, and a disdain for the U.S. Department of Agriculture.[14]

In 1976 the federal government had appropriated $1.5 million to promote gardening among the poor in six large cities.

The money all went for publicity and administrating and advising by Agriculture Department employees. These agents, with their degrees in agriculture and faith in chemicals, were viewed with more than a little suspicion by community leaders who believed the money would have been better spent for land, seed, and fencing, which the federal appropriations specifically prohibited.

Another government program, Community Development, had permitted money to be used by neighborhood groups to purchase city-owned vacant lots. In Boston, Mayor Kevin White's program turned over to neighborhood groups vacant lots that were bulldozed clean, covered with new topsoil, and fenced. One example was in Ed Cooper's Highland Park area of Roxbury. Cooper had become a volunteer neighborhood organizer after retiring at the age of seventy. To give the senior citizens in his neighborhood something more to do than look out the window, he organized the Highland Park 400 Club. One of the first club projects began a community garden around the corner on a burned-out lot with the charred remains of two houses. Cooper and four others, like himself black migrants from the rural South who enjoyed vegetable growing, planted gardens. The next year they persuaded the city of Boston to bulldoze the burned-out houses, fence the lot, and truck in topsoil for an expanded neighborhood garden of twenty-three plots measuring fifteen-by-thirty feet.[15]

Cooper's community garden movement has been described by urban historian Sam Bass Warner, Jr., as a civil rights effort to take over vacant public lands. Some two thousand acres of inner-city Boston land stood vacant because of arson, urban renewal, and cleared but abandoned highway corridors. Yet these vacant acres were unavailable for neighborhood use until a black nationalist in the state legislature, Melvin H. King, sponsored his Massachusetts Gardening Act of 1974, permitting free use of vacant public land. Helping the community to make use of the newly available land became a priority for community activists, who organized to obtain topsoil, water, and fencing from local government along with horse manure from the Suffolk Downs racetrack.[16]

As the number of garden groups multiplied, Ed Cooper

joined others from Roxbury, South End, and Jamaica Plain in an umbrella organization, Boston Urban Gardeners (BUG), to secure community development funds as well as a larger voice in Boston politics. To further the practical interests of community gardening, BUG's ninety thousand dollar grant funded a paid staff for some very practical assistance with rototilling and soil toxicity research as well as workshops in organic gardening. The young horticulturists not only taught organic methods but also believed that community gardens, which gave people land and control over their own lives, were a radical challenge to the "economically and ecologically destructive policies of agribusiness and local politics, which put profit before human needs — greenery, open space, and fresh food."[17]

One distinctive contribution of BUG offered a scientific investigation of the heavy metals problem for urban gardeners. The primary cause of high levels of lead in urban soil came not from automobile exhaust but from old lead-based exterior paint, the Boston study reported in 1978. Lead entered the soil by both acid rain leaching and the scraping and repainting of older homes. Once there, the lead toxicity in the soil might persist for seven hundred years. An urban gardener should not grow leafy greens in contaminated soil, but fruiting vegetables — tomatoes, squash, and beans — were relatively unaffected by soil lead levels. Keeping the soil pH neutral and the humus level high also inhibited plant lead intake. And keeping a garden at least fifty feet back from a busy street reduced the airborne lead exhausts from automobiles.[18]

Under BUG's sponsorship twenty-five acres of vacant land turned into a hundred community gardens for several thousand black, Spanish, white, and Chinese residents who worked together, helping to heal the long-neglected scar through Boston neighborhoods and to unite the communities in other self-help activities — recreational playgrounds and health, social, and educational programs. Neighborhoods improved their communities, making them friendlier, healthier, and more pleasant places to live. When land developers and politicians sought to take gardens away from the people, BUG organized protests to sensitize those in power to the needs of inner-city residents for gardens and open space in their neighborhoods.[19]

Inner-city gardens contributed to the environmental cleanup by educating people about the problems of chemical pollution and giving them an opportunity to do something to end the abuse of their surroundings. Gardens converted polluted, rubble-covered lots into productive green space where plants restored oxygen to tired city air, and they recycled leaves and organic waste, turning problems into assets. In the process of working together on a common task, gardeners gained a sense of community, replacing feelings of isolation and loneliness with confidence and pride, which often grew beyond the garden into general neighborhood cleanups and tree plantings.[20]

The number of community gardeners across America had increased dramatically from a handful in 1971 to three million a decade later. Those who gardened in community plots were a small minority, 8 percent of the 38 million American gardeners in 1982, but their growth across urban America from the suburbs to the inner city demonstrated a special appeal of vegetable gardening that surely went beyond concern for food prices. The 1970s were not only the decade of inflation but also the decade of the environment. Growing plants had always contributed food, exercise, and health but now promised to make the environment a better place to live; and this promise made community gardening more popular than it had ever been in peacetime.

Community gardeners persisted in their craft even though the inflation cycle turned down in the 1980s. Community numbers declined less than did the number of backyard gardeners, who quickly lost those attracted by economic considerations. As inflation declined and backyard produce seemed less rewarding, four million gardeners dropped out by 1984. Thirty-four million families, however, continued to share the promises and joys of growing food; and community gardeners were especially persistent when city governments sought to dispossess them. Consider the Clinton Community Garden, for example, in the old Hell's Kitchen area of New York City, where a rubble-strewn 150-by-75-foot vacant lot had been an eyesore for twenty-eight years before it bloomed as a community garden in 1978. Residents of West 48th Street turned a wasteland into a community park and garden with small 6-by-8-foot plots. Soon after the first garden flowered, land values began to soar, doubling every year. The lot, which had once been appraised at little more than one hundred thousand dollars reached a value of nine hundred thousand dollars by 1984. When the city attempted to take the land back, a "Save the Garden" campaign persuaded the mayor to give Clinton Garden to the community, keeping New York City's number of community garden sites at 319 and the number of community gardeners at thirty-four thousand.[21]

Gardening surely offered an art and craft for urban people in the age of ecology. Both journals of vegetable growing in the 1980s — *Organic Gardening* and *National Gardening* — stressed that the craft improves our environment. Traditional food production had acquired a new philosophy and creativeness that kept it relevant even to the young. If kitchen gardeners believed they were doing good, creating beauty, making themselves and their universe a little better, then surely the struggle to grow gardens in hostile environments would remain in style.

12 : EPILOGUE: GARDENING AND NOSTALGIA

Gardeners see themselves as serious and practical. Intent on saving money and eating more wholesome food, they pose as simple earthy producers who grow their own vegetables. But could food growing really be thrifty if nongardeners dismiss it as hard work without significant reward? A typical dismissal, that of Josephine von Miklos in *Gardener's World* (1968), declares: "Most amateurs agree that it costs them more to grow their own produce than it would to buy it even at the most superior markets; that the culture and care can be back-breaking; that rabbits and woodchucks and crows often reap the harvest before the owner has had a chance to find out if the lettuce is coming up bitter." Could urban gardening be a kind of madness that rests as much on nostalgia as on thrift and frugality? Perhaps the revival of gardening in the 1970s could be explained as a product of the same sentiment that made the good old days chic and led Hollywood to sentimentalize the past in such films as *The Sting* and *The Way We Were*.[1]

Gardeners stoutly deny the charge of nostalgia. Who would want to be accused of suffering a diseased state of mind, a form of melancholia caused by prolonged absence from home? First diagnosed among seventeenth-century Swiss mercenaries fighting in foreign countries, nostalgia continued to have a connotation of disease until the mid-twentieth century when the word gained popularity as a sentimental yearning for the past, a fond memory of early years. A nostalgic view of one's bygone years censors out the pain or hardship and recalls the good old days as having been happier, healthier, and more beautiful. While no longer implying a diseased state of mind, nostalgia still suggests a certain reactionary refusal to fully accept the modern world.

Psychologists say men are more nostalgic than women. Presumably their studies reflect the views of an earlier generation of women who remained in the home rather than pursuing careers in the outside world. Men, more subject to status changes, job anxieties, and more responsible for governing the world, were therefore more inclined to recall personal memories as one of their indispensable psychological resources. Recollections of a happy childhood could fortify against those insecurities of the present. Firm roots in the memory of a secure and virtuous childhood could maintain self-esteem and composure while one lived in the outside world of chaos and personal insecurity. These blessings of nostalgia, to be sure, came only to those past the arrogance of youth. Loving memories flow only to those beyond the age of thirty-five or forty. Looking to the past characterizes only those with the wisdom, and perhaps the frustrations, of maturity.[2]

Nostalgia is usually depicted as fond memories of fads, songs, and styles that were current during our late teens, but the private recollections of a childhood garden have also been precious memories. What but nostalgia led country-born horticulturist L. H. Bailey to write "A Reverie of Gardens," urging urbanites to spade their own spring garden: "Yourself thrust the blade deep into the tender earth. Bear your weight on the handle and feel the earth loosen and break. Turn over the load. You smell the soft, moist odor, an odor that takes you back to your younger and freer days and sends you dreaming over the fields."[3] Bailey's daydreams were pure nostalgia for that rural past he and his fellows had lost.

A generation earlier, Charles Dudley Warner expressed much the same nostalgia in *My Summer in a Garden* (1871), declaring delight in gardening to be a characteristic of people who had reached their mature wisdom. "Fondness for the ground comes back to a man after he has run the round of pleasure and business, . . . sown wild-oats, drifted about the world, and taken the winds of all its moods," the farm boy turned newspaper editor observed. Having experienced the world, and presumably been disillusioned by it, Warner found greatest satisfaction while digging in his own three acres. "To own a bit of ground, to scratch it with a hoe, to plant seeds, and watch their renewal of life—this is the commonest delight of the race," Warner said; "the most satisfactory thing a man can do." Agrarian literary types since the days of the Romans have portrayed agriculture as one of the pleasures of old age, and Warner supported the ancient wisdom by explaining that gardening gave him a therapeutic feeling of productive usefulness. "The man who has planted a garden feels that he has done something for the good of the world. He belongs to the producers. It is a pleasure to eat of the fruits of one's toil, if it be nothing more than a head of lettuce or an ear of corn," Warner said.[4] The contrast of wholesome, productive country life and artificial, parasitic urban life runs through nostalgic agrarian literature from Virgil to the moderns. Only the size of the retirement homestead has changed. Population pressure in the nineteenth century reduced romantic husbandry to garden size while retaining its supposed virtue of plain living and high thinking.

Sentimental gardeners have always been those town and city dwellers. Traditional farmers, with large fields to plant, hold small plots in contempt, as observers have commonly noted, but those farm boys who deserted the wide acreage for the small urban lot frequently discovered affection for a miniature garden and the memories it invoked of a lost childhood. City gardeners have taught their children, and grandchildren, to love growing plants, perpetuating in urban America a part of the rural folk culture. The garden writer Stanley Schuler, for example, declared, "One of my oldest and pleasantest memories is of the vegetable garden behind my grandfather's summer cottage."[5] The grandfather gave Stanley a small plot for his own seeds, and the two worked together happily in their gardens. Later, as a mature adult, Stanley realized that food gardening still thrilled him far more than flowers and ornamentals.

Women gardeners, when writing of childhood memories, often are less likely to single out the vegetable garden. Consider

Clare Leighton, who wrote for the Garden Club of America in 1948, declaring: "There is nothing more satisfying than the rituals of the year. They don't let you down. The rituals of the first harvest of one's apples and one's strawberries! There is nothing that makes me more homesick than my old ritual of picking the first primrose of the year." While flowers and fruit remained vivid, vegetables may not have danced at all in Leighton's memories. The Leighton recollections express a point not unlike those of a later midwestern male who said: "Now, when it's gardening time, the first thing that comes to my mind is radishes, onions, lettuce and tomatoes. . . . For Marian, its petunias, marigolds, impatiens." But many women do recall the vegetables and say, "I did just what my mother used to do," just as men declare, "I mostly just garden the way my dad gardened."[6]

If nostalgia is indeed an important reason for growing plants, then gardening should have a special appeal for older people. Certainly the retirement garden has been a favorite recurring topic for garden magazines. Surveys of leisure have found that few teenagers, no more than 20 percent, have regarded garden work as anything like a leisure activity, while 42 percent of people over sixty have found pleasure in the garden. In Britain we can be certain that vegetable growing appeals far more strongly to the old. Of more than half a million holders of allotment gardens in Britain in the past generation, 82 percent were men over forty years of age. American gardening polls show a younger group predominating; not the senior citizens but the thirty to forty-nine year olds are the largest American group of gardeners. Surely the craft appeals to many in all age groups but has a special appeal to the mature.[7]

Nostalgia could explain the reluctance of vegetable growers to read books on their hobby. No kitchen garden book has ever been a best-seller. Among home reference books, Benjamin Spock's *Baby and Child Care* easily takes first place, and the next best-sellers are all the cookbooks, which have sold millions of copies. A mass-market *Better Homes and Gardens* can sell eleven million copies of its cookbook before selling two million copies of its *Garden Book* devoted to ornamentals as well as vegetables.[8] Nostalgic vegetable gardeners simply have not cared to purchase information on gardening; they learned the craft in childhood. It is the new gardener, the one who comes to the craft without parental instruction, who feels the need for a printed manual. New gardeners need science and information, while the old ones need only memories.

Traditional gardeners have also been reluctant to subscribe to kitchen garden magazines; during most of American history none were available. Magazine choices were limited to farming journals, which carried some gardening information, and horticultural magazines, which concentrated on orchards and ornamentals. Those who planted ornamentals were certainly more in need of informational literature because childhood never provided a mastery of the style changes in the horticultural world of flowers, shrubs, and trees with all their Latin names and arrangements by architectural design. Not until Jerome Rodale's organic crusade would kitchen gardeners be offered a magazine of their own, and so few responded that *Organic Gardening* did not become profitable until the 1960s. Only when American society seemed to come apart at the seams, suffering shock after shock, did substantial numbers of Americans turn to gardening literature. Could the new demand for horticultural writing have had anything to do with nostalgia?

As Americans suffered a barrage of disasters that overturned fundamental assumptions about their government and themselves, many did retreat from public to private preoccupations. This move to private survival strategies has been characterized as the national "malaise" and the psychological disorder of "narcissism."[9] Narcissus, the mythical Greek character who symbolized self-absorption, alienation, and self-destruction, supplies the label for those whose selfishness destroys commitment to others. Dropouts of the 1970s who turned to personal gurus, sex therapy, or perhaps even jogging may have suffered from such an impoverished psyche. But the gardener claimed to grow for family, friends, and the planet, as well as self. Could gardening be just the nostalgic self-indulgence of a narcissist?

When economic and political systems fail to work, sustaining psychological comfort may be found in private resources. As Americans approached their Bicentennial year of 1976 many turned not to the national past but to their own personal recollections for support. *American Horticulturist* observed a general retreat from national and world preoccupations to private gardens.[10] Plants promised no miracles for society, but they paid individuals off in the old absolutes of food, therapy, and nostalgic memories. Working with food plants renewed folk roots and restored faith in one's virtue, strength, and sense of community. Backyard gardeners could share the same sense of fellowship enjoyed by community gardeners. Neighbors might have nothing else in common, but if they gardened, backyard fences were bridged with a new sense of sharing, information, tools, and vegetables. Gardening helped to recreate the sense of community recalled from childhood.

Perhaps it was no coincidence that America's Bicentennial decade saw both a revival of gardening and the emergence of a folk crusade to save garden heirloom varieties of seeds from extinction. The old vegetable varieties that had passed from one generation to the next were then announced to be in such danger that home gardeners had to rally to save them. Since World War II seed catalogues had been replacing the traditional open-pollinated vegetable varieties with new hybrids. Each hybrid seed resulted from the seed industry hand-pollinating two different varieties. The new seed produced vigorously but could not reproduce itself; hybrids grew either sterile or genetically unpredictable seed. Hybrid seed could not be saved by the home gardener. Most gardeners, of course, had long since ceased to care about saving seeds, and their uninterest created an alarming threat to gardening. When seed catalogues replaced an old variety with a new hybrid, the old plant faced sudden extinction as its seeds were discarded from our treasury of vegetables.

Complete extinction of hundreds of seed varieties would have occurred had not a few traditional garden seed savers continued the old methods. An Oklahoma Cherokee, John Wyche, had retired from dentistry to grow and distribute the seeds of his ancestors. Wyche maintained a private collection of purple and white squaw corn along with more than two hundred other garden seeds, freely distributing them without charge to thousands of gardeners. "I have kept the seeds of my fathers," he said. "I gave seed to my people so that they would have food to eat, and I give seed to old people to bring a little happiness."[11]

The heirloom seed crusade began as these older seed savers were joined by younger gardeners inclined to denounce commercial seed companies as villains who conspired to deprive America of its seed heritage. When old family seed companies such as Burpee, Harris, Northrup King, or Ferry Morse were bought by conglomerates such as General Foods, ITT, Celanese, and Purex, suspicious gardeners feared they were to be sacrificed to corporate profit. Greater corporate dividends could be gained by narrowing seed lists and concentrating on hybrids created for the commercial growers, who were the largest seed purchasers. Agribusiness cared less for vegetable taste than for a plant that matured uniformly for a single harvest day and possessed the tough durability to survive mechanical picking, shipping, and the grocery bin. Because tough commercial hybrids were depriving gardeners of their seed heritage, heirloom crusaders called for seed exchanges to locate, share, and multiply all endangered varieties[12]

The best-known heirloom crusader, Kent Whealy, organized a Seed Savers Exchange in Iowa. This midwestern journalist, who had inherited three German heirloom varieties, feared food plants were disappearing from seed catalogues not because they lacked uniqueness or delicious taste but because corporate seed companies earned larger profits by offering only a few leading varieties. Whealy offered to trade heirloom seeds in the mid-1970s, announcing in garden magazine bulletin boards and then circulating a list of seed varieties that his first twenty-nine correspondents would share. Growing numbers of gardeners joined the cooperative group, responding to Whealy's call to save the old seeds because, he said, "the standard varieties that are available today are the best home garden varieties that we will ever see. The vast majority of the vegetable breeding being done today is for commercial application and such varieties are seldom suited to the needs of the home gardener. The old varieties are the vegetable gardener's heritage."[13] By the 1980s Whealy's *Seed Savers Winter Yearbook* had grown to two hundred pages of seeds for exchange.

One gardener joined the Seed Savers Exchange with more than a thousand varieties of beans. John Withee had grown up in Maine with gardens and baked beans but, as an adult, could no longer purchase the old Yellow Eye beans of his childhood. Withee then began to collect, grow, and save the rare old varieties. The beautiful diversity of colors and sizes surely made beans the most collectable seed, and by the 1970s Withee's collection included almost twelve hundred varieties. The beans were easy to grow and usually did not cross-pollinate, yet the effort of maintaining such an extensive collection grew too much for him, and he wanted to share his massive collection with other gardeners who would assist in growing and saving the beans for the next generation.[14]

Growing interest in heirlooms stimulated a crop of small new seed companies willing to offer extensive lists of regional varieties, selling only a few hundred packets a year. Gardeners desiring a choice from fifty tomatoes, thirty corns, ninety beans, or thirty squashes could turn to the new seedspeople who ignored hybrids and sold only the old open-pollinated varieties. More than fifty seed companies competed for the heirloom business by the 1980s, ranging from the Vermont Bean Seed Company, with the most extensive selection of lentils, to older seed firms such as Gurney, which continued to stock some of the folk varieties.

Historical museums of the 1970s joined in the nostalgia of heirloom gardens, planting the old seeds to produce more authentic kitchen gardens of the past. Plimoth Plantation, Monticello, Genesee Country Museum, Old Salem, as well as thirty other living history farms and museums advertised heirloom gardens. The energetic Genesee Country Museum in Rochester, New York, not only planted an old-fashioned garden but held annual agricultural fairs for home gardeners to compete for prizes with their heirloom produce. Interested growers were offered, for twelve dollars, a seed package of thirty-six antique varieties along with a bulletin, *The Heirloom Vegetable Garden,* written by the Genesee team.[15]

The two horticulturists advising the Genesee Country Museum, Roger Kline and Robert F. Becker, took the detached scientist's view that heirlooms were not really superior to the modern varieties, which were bred to be tasty as well as more disease resistant. These agricultural scientists worried only about the genetic loss if seed varieties became extinct. Seed diversity offered insurance against serious crop destruction from new plant diseases. Genetic uniformity of hybrids left these plants more vulnerable to blights such as the smut, which had taken 15 percent of the corn crop in 1970, or the earlier great disaster to the Irish potato crop of the 1840s. A rich and diverse genetic pool drawn from many varieties offered seed breeders a wider range of traits on which to draw when future disasters require a specific resistance built into a plant threatened by disease. The Department of Agriculture had recognized the merit of saving seed varieties, building a National Seed Storage Laboratory at Colorado State University to preserve garden as well as field seed.[16]

While Robert Becker of the Department of Agriculture served as a seed expert for living history museums and collected the old heirlooms as a personal hobby, he filled his own vegetable garden with modern varieties from the commercial seed houses. New vegetables were better, Becker and Roger Kline thought. Except for a very few old plants, such as Hubbard and Boston Marrow squash or Long Keeper beets, most modern hybrids were superior in vigor and flavor, the vegetable scientists asserted. Professional horticulturists rejected all suggestions that seed companies were corporate villains because they had dropped heirlooms.[17]

Professionals took a bemused attitude toward old gardeners' complaints of declining vegetable flavor. Consider *Horticulture*'s pretense of taking seriously an old professor's protest that supermarket vegetables don't taste like they did back in Pin Hook, Texas. To test whether tomato taste had been ruined by the conglomerate invasion of the seed industry, a professional horticulturist bought seed for thirteen tomato varieties. Seed from half a dozen foreign countries were chosen, along with that of major American companies and one American heirloom. When the ripe tomatoes were tasted that summer, Burpee's "Big Girl" beat all the foreign competition. Even the old history professor agreed American tomatoes were best. Of course, they were not quite what his family had grown from heirloom seed back in the old days, but the horticulturist had an explanation. The special flavor supplied by a child's excitement at the first harvest can never be reproduced; old memories only seem sweeter than real flavors.[18]

Heirloom gardeners never concede. The taste panel, they say, is an industry ploy: "There are tasting panels that would prefer canned orange juice to freshly squeezed, or Campbell's soup to that of a good home cook." Besides, they say, why admit defeat by a contest comparing only seeds of the world's commercial companies while ignoring the old folk varieties. Nor would they concede defeat by fruits that were not grown by old-fashioned methods: "Old fashioned strains especially need to have old fashioned methods in order to demonstrate their superiority in flavor to those that are bred to grow in chemicals. The nonsense that 'old memories only seem sweeter than real flavors' is an industry ploy to convince us of it."[19] Natural gardeners who have traveled in France, Italy, and Morocco point to recent tasting sensations in addition to their childhood memories. The question of taste remains an open one, and gardeners refuse to let scientists disqualify their recollections from the taste debate.

Gardeners savor the past, indulging in a craft that stirs the mystic chords of memory; and yet, yearning for the past does not fully characterize the gardener. Sentimental self-indulgence is too glib and superficial a description of the motivation for this craft in which two-thirds of American gardeners in the late 1980s were less than fifty years of age. Nostalgia would be no motivation at all for most of those younger gardeners and a poor explanation for that quarter of gardening families who dropped out during prosperous times. The thirty-eight million vegetable growing families of the early 1980s declined to twenty-nine million by 1988, according to the National Gardening Survey. Sentiment surely had no controlling influence with the nine million dropouts from food gardening.

The word *nostalgia* is insufficient to convey the power of a craft that has experienced five folk revivals in the past century. Nostalgia implies a more constant emotion of the mature, but the gardening renewals have come and gone, often backward looking and sentimental, preferring the country to the town, but surely demonstrating the appeal of a conservative food tradition inadequately conveyed by the explanation of a psychological yearning for the past.

The persisting power of kitchen gardening in difficult times must stem from its folk survival as a practical skill inherited from our peasant ancestors. Frugality, thrift, and kitchen gardening are survival habits learned in former ages of scarcity. All folk wisdom of the household economy tradition required the kitchen garden. The religions of the poor, from Western Methodism to the Eastern Japanese Tokugawa tradition, have taught "Work much, earn much, and spend little." The frugal habit of tending "useful gardens" has been a virtue taught by traditionalists through the centuries. When the American Society for Thrift organized two frugality projects in 1914, it taught school children to grow vegetable gardens and to save their money in school thrift banks. Gardening, as a utilitarian tradition, has persisted from the days of native Americans to the present. Home gardening has even been declared an "economic indicator" by the *Wall Street Journal:* the number of backyard gradens declines in economically prosperous years but rises again when financial difficulty encourages the return of frugality.[20]

When modern gardeners are asked by pollsters why they garden, frugality and thrift usually prove the most popular explanations.[21] People say they grow vegetables to reduce the cost of their food. Almost 70 percent claim they grow to save money, while only half the gardeners point instead to health, recreation, or better-tasting food as a major explanation for practicing their craft. Rather than dismiss these explanations, we might agree that the presence of a little nostalgia need not imply that gardeners distort the past to the point of deceiving themselves. A majority probably do plant within the utilitarian inheritance of their frugal ancestry and would applaud those who say: "I garden to put food on our table. Just like Mama." "My love of gardening started back when my father was a farmer and gardening was a way of survival to feed family and neighbors." "I'm from a small town and everybody had a garden to make ends meet."[22] Those fond childhood memories of hours spent with parents and grandparents in the garden most likely suggest that the careful hand of the ancestors had then nurtured a habit of frugal virtue, teaching a valued heritage.

Any kitchen gardener can tell you that homegrown vegetables are cheaper than supermarket produce if the grower has a site with abundant sunshine and fertile soil. Those urban gardners with adverse growing conditions have smaller harvests and more expensive produce. Cheap vegetables are no reality for gardeners plagued by shade, tree roots, and surburban wildlife. But even if such gardening is poor in production, it may still be within the thrift tradition. Kitchen gardens cost less than ornamental gardens: gardeners usually spend more for ornamental plants than for their garden seed. Some modest return on vegetable seed is possible even in the most adverse conditions. But clearly, many urban gardeners care less about actually saving money than about experiencing that special excitement that comes from continuing in the utilitarian tradition and growing some of the family food.

The appeal of kitchen gardening obviously includes not only the virtue of thrift and comfort from the past, but also hope for the future. Hope—the life-renewing spirit—begins anew with every garden, restoring optimism and bringing new joy. While millions of gardeners plant by memory, so do countless millions experiment for the future. The future may be dark and uncertain, but gardening promises therapy, bountiful good, good health, and a better environment. An optimistic group, gardeners pursue their craft with the hope and faith of the young. They are fascinated by new techniques—clear plastic grow tunnels for planting in winter, floating row covers to shield spring plants from frost and insects, drip irrigation systems to continue growth during the drought of autumn. It is a rare gardener who never falls for new experiments. Most gardeners plant not only heirlooms and old reliables but also new seed catalogue novelties just as they experiment with new growing techniques: they value the past but also plan for the future while enjoying this wonderful craft from rural America that survives amidst the affluence of urban civilization.

NOTES

CHAPTER 1 : NATIVE AMERICAN GARDENERS

1. Mark Nathan Cohen, *The Food Crisis in Prehistory: Overpopulation and the Origins of Agriculture* (New Haven: Yale University Press, 1977); Ernestine Friedl, *Men and Women: An Anthropologist's View* (New York: Holt, Rinehart & Winston, 1975), 12–18.

2. Recent students of the Near East tend to reject both the food crisis explanation for the origins of agriculture and the inventive role of women in gardening. See Donald O. Henry, *From Foraging to Agriculture: The Levant at the End of the Ice Age* (Philadelphia: University of Pennsylvania Press, 1989), 3, 229–236, and Hans J. Nissen, *The Early History of the Ancient Near East* (Chicago: University of Chicago Press, 1988), 21. Peter Dreyer provided this Near East perspective, along with the name of the earliest known gardener, mythological Sumerian Shukalletuda—distinctly male; see Samuel Noah Kramer, *The Sumerians* (Chicago: University of Chicago Press, 1963), 162. The first written evidence appeared some five thousand years after the invention of gardening and as close in time to us as the original gardener, whomever that person may have been. For the gourd family, see Michael Nee, "The Domestication of Cucurbita," *Economic Botany* 44 (July–September, 1990): 56–68.

3. Paul C. Mangelsdorf, *Corn: Its Origin, Evolution and Improvement* (Cambridge: Harvard University Press, 1974), 165, 167, 179; Mangelsdorf told a great story, but molecular biologists have discarded his theory that maize never descended from the wild grass teosinte; see John Doebly, "Molecular Evidence and the Evolution of Maize," *Economic Botany* 44 (July–September, 1990), 12–14; for the evolution of garden crops see R. Douglas Hurt, *Indian Agriculture in America* (Manhattan: University Press of Kansas, 1987), 1–27.

4. William L. Langer, "American Foods and Europe's Population Growth, 1750–1850," *Journal of Social History* 8 (Winter, 1975), 56–61; Thomas McKeown, *The Modern Rise of Population* (London: Edward Arnold, 1976), 131–142.

5. Harold E. Driver, *Indians of North America* (Chicago: University of Chicago Press, 1961), 54, 78.

6. Ibid., 50–53; Charles Hudson, *The Southeastern Indians* (Knoxville: University of Tennessee Press, 1976), 290–297.

7. Lynn Ceci, "Fish Fertilizer: A Native North American Practice?" *Science* 188 (April 4, 1975), 26–30; Howard S. Russell, *Indian New England Before the Mayflower* (Hanover, N.H.: University Press of New England, 1980), 166–167; Nicholas P. Hardeman, *Shucks, Shocks, and Hominy Blocks: Corn as a Way of Life in Pioneer America* (Baton Rouge: Louisiana State University Press, 1981), 17–18; Paul Weatherwax, *Indian Corn in Old America* (New York: Macmillan Company, 1954), 124–125.

8. David Douglas, *Journal Kept by David Douglas During his Travels in North America 1823–1827* (New York: Antiquarian Press, 1959), 141.

9. Lynn Ceci, "Watchers of the Pleiades: Ethnoastronomy Among Native Cultivators in Northeastern North America," *Ethnohistory* 25 (Fall, 1978), 301–317; Charles C. Willoughby, *Antiquities of New England Indians* (Cambridge: Harvard University Press, 1935), 296–297.

10. William N. Fenton, ed., *Parker on the Iroquois* (Syracuse: Syracuse University Press, 1968), 29, 126.

11. Ruth M. Underhill, *Red Man's Religion* (Chicago: University of Chicago Press, 1965), 173–182; for an anthropologist's study of native garden magic among traditional South Pacific people, see Bronislaw Malinowski, *Coral Gardens and their Magic* (London: George Allen & Unwin Ltd., 1935).

12. Fenton, *Parker on the Iroquois,* 28–29; U. P. Hedrick, *A History of Horticulture in America to 1860* (New York: Oxford University Press, 1950), 15.

13. John T. Omohundro, "The Folk Art of the Raised Bed," *Garden,* May 1987, 10–14.

14. James Everett Seaver, ed., *Deh-he-wa-mis; or, A Narrative of the Life of Mary Jemison* (Batavia, 1842), 50.

15. Fenton, *Parker on the Iroquois,* 92; Daniel K. Onion, "Corn in the Culture of the Mohawk Iroquois," *Economic Botany* 18 (January, 1964), 60–66; for the ancestor of garden beans, see Howard Scott Gentry, "Origin of the Common Bean, *Phaseolus vulgaris,*" *Economic Botany* 23 (January, 1969), 55–69, and Ollie Berglund-Bruchen and Heinz Brucher, "The South American Wild Bean: An Ancestor of the Common Bean," *Economic Botany* 30 (July, 1976), 257–271; Paul Gepts, "Biochemical Evidence Bearing on the Domestication of Phaseolus Beans," *Economic Botany* 44 (July, 1990), 28–38.

16. Mangelsdorf, *Corn: Its Origin,* 1–2.

17. M. S. Kaldy et al., "Nutritive Value of Indian Breadroot, Squaw Root, and Jerusalem Artichoke," *Economic Botany* 34 (October, 1980), 352–357; Charles B. Heiser, Jr., "The Sunflower Among the North American Indians," *Proceedings of the American Philosophical Society* 95 (1951), 432–448.

18. Fenton, *Parker on the Iroquois,* 93; Richard I. Ford, "Ethnobotany in North America," *Canadian Journal of Botany* 59 (November, 1981), 2178–2188.

19. Hedrick, *A History of Horticulture,* 9–16; U. P. Hedrick, ed. *Sturtevant's Edible Plants of the World* (New York: Dover Publications, 1972), 612–615, 418–424, 212–217; Fenton, *Parker on the Iroquois,* 89–90.

20. William Bartram, *Travels* (Philadelphia: James Johnson, 1791), 192; Russell, *Indian New England,* 167–171.

21. Russell, *Indian New England,* 76–81.

22. Onion, "Corn in the Culture of the Mohawk Iroquois," 63; John Heck-

ewelder, *History, Manners, and Customs of the Indian Nations who once Inhab-ited Pennsylvania* (Philadelphia: Historical Society of Pennsylvania, 1876), 194–195.

23. Fenton, *Parker on the Iroquois,* 31–35; Mangelsdorf, *Corn: Its Ori-gin,* 208; Charles C. Willoughby, "Houses and Gardens of New England In-dians," *American Anthropologist* 8 (January, 1906), 131–132.

CHAPTER 2 : ENGLISH BEDS

1. Keith Thomas, *Religion and the Decline of Magic* (London: Weidenfeld and Nicholson, 1971), 1–8, 283–285, 293–294; Derek Parker, *Familiar to All: William Lily and Astrology in the Seventeenth Century* (London: Jonathan Cape, 1975), 47–68; for a discussion of astrology and gardening, see Thomas Hill, *A Most Brief and Pleasant Treatise Teaching how to Dress a Garden* (Lon-don: T. Marshe, 1563).

2. Thomas, *Religion and the Decline of Magic,* 25–48, 51–76, 113.

3. Peter Laslett, *The World We Have Lost* (London: Methuen and Com-pany, 1971), 66–69; Joan Thirsk, *The Agrarian History of England and Wales,* vol. 4 (Cambridge: University Press, 1967), 401, 413, 450–452; G. E. and K. R. Fussell, *The English Countrywoman: A Farmhouse Social History* (New York: Benjamin Blom, 1971), 30–31.

4. Gervase Markham, *The English Hus-Wife* (London: R. Jackson, 1615), 36; Alicia Amherst, *A History of Gardening in England* (London: Bernard Quaritch, 1896), 100.

5. Thomas Tusser, *Five Hundred Points of Good Husbandry: A Book of Huswifery 1557–1580,* ed. William Mavor (London: Lackington, Allen & Co., 1812), 129.

6. Ibid., 52–53, 177.

7. Thomas Hill, *The Proffitable Arte of Gardening, Now the third tyme set fourth* (London: Thomas Marshe, 1568), 13, 27; G. E. Fussell, "Crop Nutri-tion in Tudor and Early Stuart England," *Agricultural History Review* 3 (1955), 95–106.

8. Tusser, *Five Hundred Points,* 108.

9. Hill, *The Proffitable Arte of Gardening,* preface.

10. Ibid., 51, 158–160.

11. Conrad Heresbach, *Four Books of Husbandry,* trans. Barnabe Googe (London: Richard Watkins, 1577), 67–68.

12. Teresa McLean, *Medieval English Gardens* (New York: Viking Press, 1980), 197–208; Tusser, *Five Hundred Points,* 118–119; for recipes, see Markham, *The English Hus-wife,* 36–48.

13. Hill, *The Proffitable Arte of Gardening,* 95–116.

14. Tusser, *Five Hundred Points,* 124.

15. Ibid., 121.

16. Richard Gardiner, *Profitable Instructions for the Manuring, Sowing and Planting of Kitchen Gardens* (London, 1603); for the British roast beef diet, see Keith Thomas, *Man and the Natural World: A History of the Modern Sensi-*

bility (New York: Pantheon Books, 1983), 26.

17. Jean de La Quintinye, *The Compleat Gard'ner,* trans. John Evelyn (London: Matthew Gillyflower, 1693), 11–15, 22, 138.

18. Actually, the British royal gardener, George London, seems to have done the translation, but the book was attributed to Evelyn for better sales; see W. G. Hiscock, *John Evelyn and His Family Circle* (London: Routledge & Kegan Paul, 1955), 168.

19. John Evelyn, *Acetaria: A Discourse of Sallets* (London: B. Tooke, 1699), 136, 185.

20. John Evelyn, *Kalendanium Hortense: or the gardener's almanac,* 8th ed. (London: R. Chiswell, 1691), preface.

21. Evelyn, *Acetaria,* 78–79.

22. Annette Kolodny, *The Land Before Her: Fantasy and Experience of the American Frontiers 1630–1860* (Chapel Hill: University of North Carolina Press, 1984), 17, 37, 48, 146, 177.

23. For the restored kitchen gardens of Plymouth, Massachusetts, see M. H. Mason, "Plimoth Plantation," *Gardens For All* 6 (February, 1983), 8–9. Americans continued reading English gardening books for two hundred years and then for another century read countrymen who had borrowed heavily from English garden writers.

CHAPTER 3 : THE GARDEN OF THE GOODWIFE

1. Laurel Thatcher Ulrich, *Good Wives: Image and Reality in the Lives of Women in Northern New England 1650–1750* (New York: Alfred A. Knopf, 1982), 11–13.

2. Ibid., 70, 280.

3. Anne Grant, *Memoirs of an American Lady,* vol. 1 (London: Longman, 1808), 39–41; English garden size is taken from Philip Miller, *The Gardeners Dictionary* (London, 1754), 725.

4. Benjamin Rush, *Essays,* (Philadelphia, 1798), 218, 231–232.

5. Sarah F. McMahon, "A Comfortable Subsistence: The Changing Composition of Diet in Rural New England, 1620–1840," *William and Mary Quarterly* 42 (January, 1985), 26–65; for the introduction of the potato, see Redcliffe N. Salaman, *The History and Social Influence of the Potato* (Cambridge: Cambrige University Press, 1949), 188–189; Howard S. Russell, *A Long, Deep Furrow: Three Centuries of Farming in New England* (Hanover, N.H.: University of New England, 1982), 71–72.

6. Peter Kalm, *Travels into North America,* trans. John Reinhold Foster (Barre, Mass.: The Imprint Society, 1972), 97–98; William Strickland, *Journal of a Tour in the United States of America 1794–1795* (New York: New York Historical Society, 1971), 57.

7. St. John de Crevecoeur, *Sketches of Eighteenth Century America* (New York: Benjamin Blom, 1972), 145.

8. "Clamp" seems to be an Anglicized version of the Dutch word for hill. Salaman, *The History and Social Influence of the Potato,* 235–236, provides the

traditional Irish potato storage method. Bernard McMahon, *The American Gardener's Calendar* (Philadelphia: Phil Graves, 1806), 546–547, gives clear instructions for root hills. Cellars seem to have been universal as far south as New Jersey: see Hubert G. Schmidt, *Agriculture in New Jersey* (New Brunswick: Rutgers University Press, 1973), 44, 74.

9. Karen Hess, ed., *Martha Washington's Booke of Cookery* (New York: Colombia University Press, 1981), 161; English sand hill preservation is treated as common knowledge in John Worlidge, *Systema Agriculturae* (London: F. W. Gent, 1687), 164–165; McMahon, *The American Gardener's Calendar,* 546–547.

10. Kalm, *Travels into North America,* 45, 77, 488; Frances Phipps, *Colonial Kitchens, Their Furnishings, and Their Gardens* (New York: Hawthorn Books, 1972), 111–115, 118, 120, 127.

11. Kalm, *Travels into North America,* 343; J. P. Brissot De Warville, *New Travels in the United States of America 1788* (Cambridge: Harvard University Press, 1964), 267.

12. Ann Leighton, *American Gardens in the Eighteenth Century* (Amherst: University of Massachusetts Press, 1986), 363–364; Miller, *The Gardeners Dictionary,* provides helpful essays on walks and walls.

13. William M. Kelso, "Landscape Archaelogy: A Key to Virginia's Cultivated Past," and Elizabeth McLean, "Town and Country Gardens in Eighteenth-Century Philadelphia," in Robert P. Maccubbin and Peter Martin, eds., *British and American Gardens in the Eighteenth Century* (Williamsburg: Colonial Williamsburg Foundation, 1984), 162, 140; for a Connecticut farm garden, see Rudy and Joy Favretti, *For Every House a Garden: A Guide for Reproducing Period Gardens* (Chester: The Pequot Press, 1977), 15–23.

14. McMahon, *The American Gardener's Calendar,* 100–109.

15. In none of Benjamin Latrobe's house sketches is a garden visible: see Edward C. Carter II, ed., *The Virginia Journals of Benjamin Henry Latrobe* (New Haven: Yale University Press, 1977); Peter Kalm observed that gardens were either behind the house or back between neighboring houses in *Travels into North America,* 116, 119; British advice is found in John Parkinson, *Paradise* (London, 1629), 461, and Miller, *The Gardeners Dictionary,* 724.

16. John Rogers Williams, ed., *Philip Vickers Fithian Journal and Letters 1767–1774* (Freeport: Books for Libraries Press, 1969), 121–131, 77, 105, 126, 61–62.

17. Williams, *Fithian Journal,* 151; Elizabeth Fox-Genovese, *Within the Plantation Household* (Chapel Hill: University of North Carolina Press, 1989), 116–118; Betty Wood, *Slavery in Colonial Georgia 1730–1775* (Athens: University of Georgia Press, 1984), 147.

18. Philip M. Hamer et al., *The Papers of Henry Laurens,* vol. 3 (Columbia: University of South Carolina Press, 1968–1981), 458–459; vol. 5, 227, 352, 702. David Ramsay, *Ramsay's History of South Carolina,* vol. 2 (Newbury, S.C.: Duffie, 1858), 128–129.

19. Ramsay, *Ramsay's History of South Carolina,* 128; *South Carolina Historical and Genealogical Magazine* 20 (July, 1919), 205; Mary B. Prior, "Letters of Martha Logan to John Bartram, 1760–1763," *South Carolina Historical*

Magazine 59 (January, 1958), 38–46; Logan's calendar is printed in *Palladium of Knowledge; or, The Carolina and Georgia Almanac 1798* (Early American Imprints, Evans No. 33255).

20. Herbert Leventhal, *In the Shadow of the Enlightenment: Occultism and Renaissance Science in Eighteenth-Century America* (New York: New York University Press, 1976), 14–15, 40–41, 262–264.

21. Suzanne Lebsock, *The Free Women of Petersburg: Status and Culture in a Southern Town 1784–1860* (New York: W. W. Norton, 1984), 149–151.

CHAPTER 4 : THE ENLIGHTENMENT GARDEN OF THOMAS
JEFFERSON

1. For the American Enlightenment see Daniel J. Boorstin, *The Lost World of Thomas Jefferson* (New York: Henry Holt and Company, 1948), and Herbert Leventhal, *In the Shadow of the Enlightenment: Occultism and Renaissance Science in Eighteenth-Century America* (New York: New York University Press, 1976).

2. Dumas Malone, *Jefferson and His Time,* vol. 1 (Boston: Little Brown and Company, 1948), 101–103; Merrill D. Peterson, *Thomas Jefferson and the New Nation* (New York: Oxford University Press, 1970), 46–49.

3. Boorstin, *The Lost World of Thomas Jefferson,* 10.

4. Edwin Morris Betts, ed., *Thomas Jefferson's Garden Book* (Philadelphia: American Philosophical Society, 1944), 357, 364–365, 47; James A. Bear, Jr., *Jefferson at Monticello* (Charlottesville: University Press of Virginia, 1967), 46–47; Margaret Bayard Smith, *The First Forty Years of Washington Society* (New York: Charles Scribner's Sons, 1906), 68; reconstruction of the garden is explained and photographed in Peter Hatch, "Thomas Jefferson as Gardener," *Flower and Garden* 27 (July, 1983), 7–9, and Robert West Howard, "America's Greatest Gardener—Our Third President," *Gardens For All* 6 (August, 1983), 10–11; for the historical archaeology that confirmed and restored Jefferson's garden, see William M. Kelso, "Landscape Archaeology: A Key to Virginia's Cultivated Past," in Robert P. Maccubbin and Peter Martin, eds., *British and American Gardens in the Eighteenth Century* (Williamsburg: Colonial Williamsburg Foundation, 1984).

5. Betts, *Thomas Jefferson's Garden Book,* 377.

6. Ibid., 388–393; for Jefferson's 1812 garden layout, see plate 33, p. 474.

7. U. P. Hedrick, *A History of Horticulture in America to 1860* (New York: Oxford University Press, 1950), 460; the same mistaken view is continued in Sam Bowers Hilliard, *Hog Meat and Hoecake: Food Supply in the Old South 1840–1860* (Carbondale: Southern Illinois University Press, 1972), 173.

8. The recipe is from Mary Randolph, *The Virginia Housewife* (Philadelphia: E. H. Butler, 1871), 17–18; Jefferson to Dr. Vine Utley, March 21, 1819, in John M. Dorsey, ed., *The Jefferson-Dunglison Letters* (Charlottesville: University of Virginia Press, 1960), 98–99.

9. Marie Kimball, ed., *Thomas Jefferson's Cook Book* (Richmond: Garrett & Massie, 1949); I was saved from relying on Marie Kimball by Karen Hess,

who has photocopies of the original handwritten manuscript; Thomas Jefferson, *Notes on the State of Virginia,* ed. William Peden (Chapel Hill: University of North Carolina Press, 1955), 152.

10. Betts, *Thomas Jefferson's Garden Book,* 279.

11. Ibid., 507.

12. Ibid., 208; Dorsey, *The Jefferson-Dunglison Letters,* 105; Daniel Boorstin, *The Americans: The Colonial Experience* (New York: Alfred M. Knopf, 1958), 218.

13. Betts, *Thomas Jefferson's Garden Book,* 47–56, 456, 440, 481, 261, 5, 483, 439.

14. Ibid., 534.

15. Ibid., 461.

16. Ibid., 198; Jefferson recommended botany rather than chemistry, 380.

17. Ibid., 189, 579, 627.

18. Benjamin Smith Barton, *Fragments . . . The Natural History of A Country* (Philadelphia, 1799), 21–23.

19. Betts, *Thomas Jefferson's Garden Book,* 577, 619–620.

20. Ibid., 616.

CHAPTER 5 : GARDENING FOR HEALTH

1. Keith Thomas, *Man and the Natural World: A History of the Modern Sensibility* (New York: Pantheon Books, 1983), 26; Sarah McMahon examined wills for Middlesex County, Massachusetts, and charted the meat allowance willed by 292 documents between 1654 and 1830: see Sarah F. McMahon, "A Comfortable Subsistence: A History of Diet in New England, 1630–1850," (Ph.D. dissertation, Brandeis University, 1981), 44.

2. Estate inventories in rural Massachusetts listed salt meat 97 percent of the time, while only 63 percent of inventories listed any vegetables: see Sarah F. McMahon, "A Comfortable Subsistence: The Changing Composition of Diet in Rural New England, 1620–1840," *William and Mary Quarterly* 42 (January, 1985), 58; Timothy Dwight, *Travels in New England and New York* (London: William Baynes & Sons, 1823), 341–343.

3. Sereno Edwards Dwight, "Memoir of the Life of the Author," in Timothy Dwight, *Theology,* vol. 1 (New Haven: T. Wright & Son, 1833), 1–61; "Moral Tendency of Horticulture," *Cultivator,* March 1838, 11; Charles E. Cunningham, *Timothy Dwight 1752–1817* (New York: Macmillan Company, 1942), 43–50, 132–134.

4. Timothy Dwight, *Greenfield Hill* (New York: Childs & Swaine, 1794), 124–125.

5. Dwight, *Travels in New England and New York,* 462.

6. "Gardens," *New England Farmer,* November 9, 1827, 126.

7. Shadrack Ricketson, *Means of Preserving Health and Preventing disease* (New York: Collins, Perkins & Co., 1806), 103, 105, 156; *Journal of Health,* September 23, 1829, 22–23; September 9, 1829, 6–7; March 10, 1830, 208.

8. J. S. Chambers, *The Conquest of Cholera* (New York: Macmillan, 1938), 63–64; Charles E. Rosenberg, *The Cholera Years* (Chicago: University of Chicago Press, 1962), 1–4.

9. Rosenberg, *The Cholera Years,* 66–67, 74–75, 81.

10. James C. Whorton, *Crusaders for Fitness: The History of American Health Reformers* (Princeton: Princeton University Press, 1982), 38–45.

11. Stephen Nissenbaum, *Sex, Diet and Debility in Jacksonian America: Sylvester Graham and Health Reform* (Westport, Conn.: Greenwood Press, 1980), 4–8.

12. Whorton, *Crusaders for Fitness,* 49–61.

13. William A. Alcott, *The Young House-Keeper; or Thoughts on Food and Cookery* (Boston: George W. Light, 1838), 47, 83–84, 213, 220.

14. Ibid., 134–135, 165, 167, 183.

15. Luther V. Bell, "Diet," *Boston Medical and Surgical Journal* 13 (December 2, 1835), 265–268.

16. Catherine Beecher, *A Treatise on Domestic Economy* (Boston: T. H. Webb & Co., 1842), 44, 94, 10; women who gardened in Petersburg, Virginia, took more pleasure there than in any other home task, according to Suzanne Lebsock, *The Free Women of Petersburg* (New York: W. W. Norton, 1984), 150–151.

17. *Southern Agriculturist,* December 1831, 627–631.

18. Sam Bowers Hilliard is good on the evolution of Southern gardens but would have us believe that the tomato was only an ornamental: see his *Hog Meat and Hoecake: Food Supply in the Old South 1840–1860* (Carbondale: Southern Illinois University Press, 1972), 173; the classical statement of the Southern diet is Richard Osborn Cummings, *The American and His Food* (Chicago: University of Chicago Press, 1940), 14–15, 86, 87; for those garden vegetables recommended for the Southern plantation, see the series in the *Southern Agriculturist* beginning in August, 1830, and running through March, 1831.

19. For tomato popularity in the North, see Robert Buist, *The Family Kitchen Gardener* (New York: C. M. Saxon & Co., 1855), 125–128; for early tomato popularity in the South, *Southern Agriculturist,* February 1829, 79–82; for a catalogue of early tomato citations, see U. P. Hedrick, ed., *Sturtevant's Edible Plants of the World* (New York: Dover Publications, 1972), 343–348.

20. Frances Trollope, *Domestic Manners of the Americans* (Barre, Mass.: The Imprint Society, 1969), 49–50.

21. *Genesee Farmer and Gardener's Journal,* July 30, 1831, 233; August 27, 1831, 266; September 2, 1834, 143; January 24, 1835, 29; September 19, 1835, 304; December 17, 1836, 402; *Farmer and Gardener,* February 10, 1835, 326.

22. *Farmer and Gardener,* April 19, 1836, 406.

23. *Genesee Farmer and Gardener's Journal,* September 23, 1837, 301; *Southern Agriculturist,* April 1837, 191–192.

24. *Southern Agriculturist,* August 1832, 407–409; *New England Farmer,* September 5, 1832, 59; *Farmer and Gardener,* September 6, 1836, 148–149; the first rhubarb in the colonies was apparently sent to John Bartram from England by Peter Collinson in 1739.

25. The recipe is from *Farmer and Gardener,* September 6, 1836, 149.

26. *New England Farmer,* May 18, 1831, 348; *Southern Cultivator,* June 1857, 188–189; Harry J. Carman, ed., *Jesse Buel: Agricultural Reformer* (New York: Columbia University Press, 1947), 198.

27. Jeffrey and Leabeth Abt, "The Gardening Sentiments of an Early Texas Pioneer," *Magnolia: Bulletin of the Southern Garden History Society* 6 (Summer, 1989), 4–9.

28. Carman, *Jesse Buel,* 197.

29. Merton M. Sealts, Jr., ed., *The Journals and Miscellaneous Notebooks of Ralph Waldo Emerson,* vol. 10 (Cambrige: Harvard University Press, 1973), 93.

30. A. W. Plumstead and Harrison Hayford, ed., *The Journals and Miscellaneous Notebooks of Ralph Waldo Emerson,* vol. 7 (Cambridge: Harvard University Press, 1969), 525.

31. Henry David Thoreau, *Walden* (Boston: Tichnor and Fields, 1854), 175.

32. Nathaniel Hawthorne, *The American Notebooks,* ed. Claude M. Simpson (Columbus: Ohio State University Press, 1972), 328–329.

33. Henry Ward Beecher, *Plain and Pleasant Talk About Fruits, Flowers and Farming* (New York: Derby & Jackson, 1859), iii–v; Jane Shaffer Elsmere, *Henry Ward Beecher: The Indian Years, 1837–1847* (Indianapolis: Indiana Historical Society, 1973), 129–137, 195–201.

34. U.P. Hedrick, *A History of Horticulture in America to 1860* (New York: Oxford University Press, 1950), 505–507.

35. *Cultivator,* July 1840, 115.

36. Andrew Jackson Downing, *Rural Essays,* ed. George William Curtis (New York: H. W. Hagemann, 1894), 13–17.

37. Ibid., 110–115; Edward K. Spann, *The New Metropolis: New York City 1840–1857* (New York: Columbia University Press, 1981), 193–198.

CHAPTER 6 : SEED CATALOGUES AND STRAIGHT ROWS

1. U. P. Hedrick, *A History of Horticulture in America to 1860* (New York: Oxford University Press, 1950), 40–41; a seed trade existed in thirteenth-century British fairs and markets. By the sixteenth century, London shopkeepers sold seeds grown by local market gardeners as well as imported from the continent; see Malcolm Thick, "Garden Seeds in England before the Late Eighteenth Century," *Agricultural History Review* 38 (1990), 58–71.

2. Robert F. Becker, "American Vegetable Seed Industry — A History," *HortScience* 19 (October, 1984), 610; Edward and Faith Andrews, *Work and Worship: The Economic Order of the Shakers* (Greenwich, Conn.: New York Graphic Society, 1974), 53–60.

3. *Indiana Farmer and Gardener,* April 5, 1854, 92–93.

4. *Horticulturist,* January 1863, 12–13; April 1869, 128.

5. Anna Warner, *Miss Tiller's Vegetable Garden and the Money She Made By It* (New York: A. D. F. Randolph & Co., 1873), 11–31.

6. Edward Halsey Foster, *Susan and Anna Warner* (Boston: Twayne Publishers, 1978), 74, 19–21; Buckner Hollingsworth, *Her Garden Was Her Delight* (New York: Macmillan, 1962), 91–101.

7. Anna B. Warner, *Gardening by Myself* (West Point, N.Y.: Constitution Island Association, 1972), 17–22, 168–181.

8. William W. Tracy, "Vegetable Seed Growing as a Business," *Yearbook of the United States Department of Agriculture 1909* (Washington, D.C.: Government Printing Office, 1910), 273–284.

9. J. M. Thorburn and Co., "The Seed Trade in America," *Standard Cyclopedia of Horticulture,* vol. 3 (New York: Macmillan, 1928).

10. Seed catalogue ads may be located in January–April copies of any farm, garden, or popular journal; Frank Presbrey, *The History and Development of Advertising* (Garden City: Doubleday, Doran & Company, 1929), 338, 416; for the Burpee story, see Ken Kraft, *Garden to Order* (Garden City: Doubleday and Company, 1962), 5–19.

11. In the 1980s Burpee reproduced copies of its *Farm Annual 1888.*

12. Bob Birkby and Janice Nahra Friedel, "Henry, Himself," *The Palimpsest* 64 (September, 1983), 151–169.

13. The eleven hundred varieties are all discussed by seedsman Fearing Burr, *The Field and Garden Vegetables of America* (Boston: J. E. Tilton, 1865); the history of the dwarf lima is told in L. H. Bailey, *Plant Breeding* (New York: Macmillan Company, 1895), 138–139.

14. Charles Dudley Warner, *My Summer in a Garden* (Boston: Fields, Osgood & Co., 1871), 172–173.

15. Ridicule can be found in *American Garden* 7 (May, 1886), 135; support for seed saving can be found in *American Farmer,* August 1, 1892.

16. For early advocates of the plow in the garden, see *New England Farmer,* September 19, 1828, 70; *Southern Agriculturist* December 1854, 459; *Horticulturist,* April 1849, 471–472; Henry Ward Beecher, *Plain and Pleasant Talk about Fruit, Flowers and Farming* (New York: Derby & Jackson, 1859), 199–201; mostly old-style gardens were still found by George Thompson in 1868, *Gardeners Monthly,* January 1868, 12.

17. For patent medicines, see James Harvey Young, *The Toadstool Millionaires: A Social History of Patent Medicines in America before Federal Regulation* (Princeton: Princeton University Press, 1961), 32–33, 40, 104, 110; Rudyard Kipling, *Rewards and Fairies* (Garden City: Doubleday, 1915), 261.

18. The end of the English bed is proclaimed in *American Garden,* January, 1890, 28; W. J. Beal of the Michigan Agriculture College noted the fall of garden fencing in *American Garden* 11 (August, 1890), 445–448; for old fencing preferences, see William Cobbett, *The American Gardiner* (Claremont, N.H.: Manufacturing Co., 1819), 20–32, and William N. White, *Gardening for the South* (New York: O. Judd & Co., 1868), 16.

19. For early hand cultivators, see *New England Farmer,* July 10, 1839, 11; *Cultivator,* January 1843, 23–24; July 1843, 114; *Arkansas Gazette,* March 7, 1885; for illustrations of garden plows, see Fred L. Israel, ed., *Sears Roebuck Catalogue 1897* (New York: Chelsea House Publishers, 1968), 160–161.

20. Warner, *My Summer in a Garden,* 91–92.

21. Quoted in L. H. Bailey, *Garden Making* (New York: Gosset & Dunlap, 1898), 25–28.

22. "Gardening without Backache," *Garden Magazine* 1 (February, 1905), 28; T. Griener, "The Home Vegetable Garden," *Country Life in America* 3 (March, 1903), 196–198.

23. Professor Rudy Favretti is my authority for the Italian American garden practice. For the general movement of Italians to urban fringes where they raised goats and vegetables, see Nathan Glazer and Daniel Patrick Moynihan, *Beyond the Melting Pot* (Cambrige: MIT Press, 1970), 187; Luciano J. Iorizzo and Salvatore Mondello, *The Italian Americans* (New York: Twayne Publishers, 1971), 127–127.

CHAPTER 7 : BALANCE OF NATURE IN THE GARDEN

1. Keith Thomas, *Man and the Natural World: A History of the Modern Sensibility* (New York: Pantheon Books, 1983), 17–20.

2. Benjamin Smith Barton, *Fragments . . . The Natural History of a Country* (Philadelphia, 1799), 21–23.

3. *New England Farmer,* June 28, 1823, 379; May 27, 1825, 350; April 20, 1827, 310; *Cultivator,* May 1835, 40–41; June 1835, 178–179; *Southern Agriculturist,* October, November 1844, 384–386, 421–425.

4. Nathaniel Hawthorne, *American Notebooks,* ed. Claude M. Simpson (Columbus: Ohio State University Press, 1972), 388.

5. *New England Farmer,* June 29, 1827, 386; April 4, 1828, 289; June 17, 1840, 416; *Southern Cultivator,* June 21, 1843, 96.

6. Henry Ward Beecher, *Star Papers or Experiences of Art and Nature* (New York: J. C. Derby, 1855), 196.

7. *Horticulturist,* August 1864, 253; July 1862, 307–308.

8. Ibid., January 1869, 24.

9. Walter B. Barrows, *The English Sparrow in North America* (Washington, D.C.: Government Printing Office, 1889), 17–98, 318.

10. Peter Henderson, *Gardening for Pleasure* (New York: Orange Judd, 1875), 115–120.

11. *American Garden,* February 1885, 34; February, 1892, 91–93, 282–283.

12. Robert C. Bannister, *Social Darwinism: Science and Myth in Anglo-American Social Thought* (Philadelphia: Temple University Press, 1979), 9–11; Donald Worster, *Nature's Economy: The Roots of Ecology* (San Francisco: Sierra Club Books, 1977), 144.

13. Charles Dudley Warner, *My Summer in a Garden* (Boston: Fields, Osgood & Co., 1871), 47–50, 58–59, 79–80.

14. *Garden Magazine* 1 (December, 1905), 229–230; Philip Dorf, *Liberty Hyde Bailey: An Informal Biography* (Ithaca: Cornell University Press, 1956); Andrew Denny Rogers, *Liberty Hyde Bailey: A Story of American Plant Sciences* (Princeton: Princeton University Press, 1949).

15. *American Garden* 14 (February, 1893), 102–103; Dorf, *Liberty Hyde Bailey,* 88–89.

16. *American Garden* 11 (January, 1890), 35.

17. James Whorton, *Before Silent Spring: Pesticides and Public Health in Pre-DDT America* (Princeton: Princeton University Press, 1974), 4–67.

18. Margaret W. Rossiter, *The Emergence of Agricultural Science: Justus Liebig and the Americans, 1840–1880* (New Haven: Yale University Press, 1975), 1–17; *Horticulturist,* August 1846, 99; Robert Buist, *The Family Kitchen Gardener* (New York: C. M. Saxon & Co., 1855), 9; Peter Henderson, *Gardening for Profit: A Guide to the Successful Cultivation of the Market and Family Garden* (New York: Orange Judd Company, 1866), 35.

19. *Scribner's Monthly* 3 (December, 1871), 241–242.

20. *New England Farmer,* December 20, 1843, 198; *Western Farmer and Gardener,* July 1, 1846, 202; Sucheng Chan, *This Bitter-Sweet Soil: The Chinese in California Agriculture 1860–1910* (Berkeley: University of California Press, 1986), 79, 82–84, 90–94.

21. Chan, *This Bitter-Sweet Soil,* 104–105; Samuel Bowles, *Our New West* (Hartford: Hartford Publishing Co., 1869), 402; A. W. Loomis, "The Chinese as Agriculturists," *Overland Monthly* 5 (June, 1870), 526–532.

22. Chan, *This Bitter-Sweet Soil,* 99–100.

23. For studies of Chinese exclusion, see Gunther Barth, *Bitter Strength: A History of the Chinese in the United States, 1850–1870* (Cambridge: Harvard University Press, 1964), and Alexander Saxton, *The Indispensable Enemy: Labor and the Anti-Chinese Movement in California* (Berkeley: University of California Press, 1971). As Chinese moved east, their market gardens followed. To supply New York City's Chinatown, Asians acquired land on Long Island about 1887 and began planting some twenty varieties of native vegetables — *American Garden* 11 (October, 1890), 607–609.

24. *American Garden,* May 1886, 154; January, August 1889, 69, 288; March 1890, 228–230; Eastern market gardeners reduced their use of stable manure by half, forcing the price down from three dollars in 1881 to less than a dollar a wagon load by 1889. During summer months demand became so slight that stables gave away their manure. Some New York City stables even paid to have their waste hauled away — *New England Farmer,* January 19, 1889, 2.

25. L. H. Bailey, *Manual of Gardening* (New York: Macmillan Company, 1910), 110–114.

26. L. H. Bailey, "A Reverie of Gardens," *Outlook* 68 (June 1, 1901), 171.

27. L. H. Bailey, "An Evolutionist's View of Religion," *The Independent* 51 (February 2, 1890), 335–339.

28. L. H. Robbins, "Behind the Scenes in Smiling Gardens," *New York Times Magazines,* May 1, 1932, 14.

CHAPTER 8 : COUNTRY LIFE IN THE SUBURBS

1. For English nostalgia, see Keith Thomas, *Man and the Natural World: A History of the Modern Sensibility* (New York: Pantheon Books, 1983), and

Jan Marsh, *Back to the Land: The Pastoral Impulse in England from 1880 to 1914* (London: Quartet Books, 1982); for American nostalgia, see Peter J. Schmitt, *Back to Nature: The Arcardian Myth in Urban America* (New York: Oxford University Press, 1969); Morton and Lucia White, *The Intellectual versus the City: From Thomas Jefferson to Frank Lloyd Wright* (Cambridge: Harvard University Press, 1962); and Leo Marx, *The Machine in the Garden: Technology and the Pastoral Ideal in America* (New York: Oxford University Press, 1964).

2. Grace Peckham, "Infancy in the City," *Popular Science Monthly* 28 (March, 1886), 683–688; Judith Walzer Leavitt, *The Healthiest City: Milwaukee and the Politics of Health Reform* (Princeton: Princeton University Press, 1982), 37; John L. Coffin, "The Suburban Baby and His City Cousin," *Suburban Country Life* 4 (January, 1907), 13.

3. *American Garden* 7 (October, 1886), 293; February 1888, 58; March 1889, 69.

4. Felix L. Oswald, "The Remedies of Nature," *Popular Science Monthly* 24 (February, 1884), 454–460; Herr Dr. Bilsinger, "Modern Nervousness and its Cure," *Popular Science Monthly* 42 (November, 1892), 90–93; Peter Henderson, *Gardening for Pleasure* (New York: Orange Judd, 1875), 175–177.

5. Sam Bass Warner, Jr., *Streetcar Suburbs: The Process of Growth in Boston 1870–1900* (Boston: Harvard University Press, 1962); Edward K. Spann, *The New Metropolis: New York City, 1840–1857* (New York: Columbia University Press, 1981), 183, 188–189; Everett Chamberlin, *Chicago and its Suburbs* (Chicago: T. A. Hungerford & Co., 1874), 188.

6. Kenneth T. Jackson, *Crabgrass Frontier: The Suburbanization of the United States* (New York: Oxford University Press, 1985), 54; *American Garden* 3 (December, 1882), 186.

7. *American Garden,* October 1883, 190.

8. Frank J. Scott, *The Art of Beautifying Home Grounds* (New York: D. Appleton & Co., 1870), 23.

9. Henry Lincoln Clapp, "School Gardens," *Popular Science Monthly* 52 (February, 1898), 445–456; Augusta Tovel, "A Plea for Increased Study of Nature in the Common School," *Education* 8 (January, 1888), 310–314; Cary Cadmus Davis, *School and Home Gardening* (Philadelphia: J. B. Lippincott, 1918), 1–5; Dora Otis Mitchel, "A History of Nature Study," *Nature Study Review* 19 (September, 1923), 258–274; Schmitt, *Back to Nature,* 77–79, 90–92; Dora Williams, *Gardens and Their Meaning* (Boston: Ginn and Company, 1911), 43.

10. John Burroughs, *Time and Change* (Boston: Houghton Mifflin, 1912), 246; Liberty Hyde Bailcy, "John Burroughs at Home," *American Gardening* 14 (January, 1893), 1–4; Hans Huth, *Nature and the American* (Berkeley: University of California Press, 1957), 88–103.

11. H. Roger Grant, *Self-Help in the 1890s Depression* (Ames: Iowa State University Press, 1983), 23–31.

12. New York Association for Improving the Condition of the Poor, "Cultivation of Vacant City Lots by the Unemployed," *Notes* 1 (December, 1895), 29.

13. Ibid., 19.

14. Frederic W. Speirs, "Vacant Lot Cultivation," *Charities Review* (April, 1898), 1–28.

15. Ibid., 28.

16. See the Philadelphia Vacant Lot Cultivation Association, *Annual Reports for 1912*, p. 7, and 1929, p. 3, for ethnicity; for ethnic taste, see Peter Farb and George Armelagos, *Consuming Passions: The Anthropology of Eating* (Boston: Houghton Mifflin, 1980), 185; Jewish and Italian responses are reported in Thomas Kessner, *The Golden Door: Italian and Jewish Immigrant Mobility in New York City 1880–1915* (New York: Oxford University Press, 1977), 211.

17. Philadelphia Vacant Lots Cultivation Association, *Sixth Annual Report* (1902), 9.

18. Laura Dainty Pelham, "The Chicago City Gardens Association," *Survey* 22 (June 19, 1909), 423–425; Bolton Hall contributed regularly to *Survey*.

19. Roy Lubove, *Community Planning in the 1920s; The Contribution of the Regional Planning Association of America* (Pittsburgh: University of Pittsburgh Press, 1963), 5–15; *Survey* 26 (September 9, 1911), 828–829; 35 (December 4, 1915), 228.

20. "What This Magazine Stands For," *Country Life in America* 1 (November, 1901), 24–25; Andrew Denny Rodgers, *Liberty Hyde Bailey: A Story of American Plant Sciences* (Princeton: Princeton University Press, 1949), 297.

21. *Country Life in America,* August 1907, 426; "Cutting Loose from the City" ran August–January, 1910–11.

22. L. H. Bailey, "The Landward Movement," *Country Life in America* 19 (March 15, 1911), 379–381.

23. Ibid., August 1, 1911, 72–76.

24. "What We Stand For," *Suburban Country Life* 1 (December, 1904), 20.

25. Charles R. Sanford, "The Gentle Art of Killing Bugs," *Suburban Country Life* 1 (April, 1905), 14.

26. "How to Make a Garden—Digging in the Dirt," *Country Life in America* 1 (April, 1902), 218; L. H. Bailey, "A Reverie of Gardens," *Outlook* 68 (June 1, 1901), 171.

27. Allen French, "Gardening versus Golf," *Country Life in America* 8 (May, 1905), 960.

28. Robert C. Bannister, Jr., *Ray Stannard Baker: The Mind and Thought of a Progressive* (New Haven: Yale University Press, 1966), 108–125.

29. Ray Stannard Baker, *American Chronicle: The Autobiography of Ray Stannard Baker* (New York: Charles Scribner's Sons, 1945), 160–162, 214–215, 246–247.

30. Dallas Lore Sharp, "Our Uplift Through Outdoor Life," *World's Work* 8 (July, 1904), 5043–5045; Sharp, *The Face of the Fields* (Boston: Houghton Mifflin, 1911), 236–237, 239–242; Sharp, "Five Days and an Education," *Harper's* 151 (August, 1925), 273–280.

31. Schmitt, *Back to Nature,* 181–182; Wilhelm Miller, "What England Can Teach us about Garden Cities," *Country Life in America* 17 (March, 1910), 531–534; William E. Smythe, *City Homes on Country Lanes* (New York: Macmillan, 1921); Paul K. Conkin, "The Vision of Elwood Mead," *Agricultural History* 34 (April, 1960), 88–97.

32. David E. Shi, *The Simple Life: Plain Living and High Thinking in American Culture* (New York: Oxford University Press, 1985), 231–232; Lewis Mumford, *The Culture of Cities* (New York: Harcourt, Brace & World, 1938), 210–211, 428.

33. The new hostility to suburbia is discussed in Scott Donaldson, *The Suburban Myth* (New York: Columbia University Press, 1969), and John Kramer, *North American Suburbs: Politics, Diversity and Change* (Berkeley: Glendessary Press, 1972), 5–18.

CHAPTER 9 : VICTORY GARDENING

1. *New York Times,* February 22, 1917, 1; Mary Dewhurst, "The Food Demonstrations in New York," *Outlook* 115 (March 7, 1917), 405–406.

2. *New York Times,* March 20, 24, 31, 1917; April 14, 1917; and May 16, 1917.

3. *Daily Oklahoman,* March 1–2, 1917.

4. Ibid., March 8, 9, 11, 1917.

5. Ibid., April 22, 1917.

6. Ibid., September 9, 1917.

7. For the story that Pack published and distributed, see Charles Lathrop Pack, *The War Garden Victorious* (Philadelphia: J. B. Lippincott, 1919).

8. Woodrow Wilson, *The Public Papers of Woodrow Wilson,* vol. 1, ed. Ray Stannard Baker and William E. Dodd (New York: Harper & Brothers, 1927), 22–27.

9. Stephen Vaughn, *Holding Fast the Inner Lines* (Chapel Hill: University of North Carolina Press, 1980), 190.

10. Craig Lloyd, *Aggressive Introvert: A Study of Herbert Hoover and Public Relations Management* (Columbus: Ohio State University Press, 1972), 45; Maxcy Robson Dickson, *The Food Front in World War I* (Washington, D.C.: American Council on Public Affairs, 1944), 24, 142; Richard Osborn Cummings, *The American and His Food* (Chicago: University of Chicago Press, 1940), 130–131, 140; U.S. Food Administration, *Food Guide for War Services at Home* (New York: Charles Scribner's Sons, 1918), 56–59.

11. Pack, *War Garden Victorious,* 23; *New York Times,* July 23, 1917.

12. Clarence Owsley to P. S. Ridsdale, February 13, 1918; Bradford Knapp to Dr. True, March 20, 1918; D. F. Houston to the president, April 10, 1918; Houston – to the president, October 4, 1918; Secretary's Incoming Correspondence – Gardens 1918, Department of Agriculture, National Archives, Washington, D.C.

13. *School Life,* October 1, 1918, 12; Lewis Paul Todd, *Wartime Relations of the Federal Government and the Public Schools 1917–1918* (New York: Columbia Teachers College, 1945), 151–158; Charles Lee Lewis, *Philander Priestly Claxton: Crusader for Public Education* (Knoxville: University of Tennessee Press, 1948).

14. Clarence Owsley to the secretary, October 10, 1918, Secretary's Incoming Correspondence – Gardens 1918, Department of Agriculture, National Archives, Washington, D.C.

15. Robert S. and Helen M. Lynd, *Middletown: A Study in Contemporary American Culture* (New York: Harcourt Brace, 1929), 95, 251–260, 309.

16. Elmer O. Fippin, "How to Get Along Without Stable Manure," *Garden Magazine* 36 (February, 1923), 220–222; Joel A. Tarr, "Urban Pollution—Many Long Years Ago," *American Heritage* 22 (October, 1971), 65–69.

17. Robert S. and Helen M. Lynd, *Middletown in Transition* (New York: Harcourt Brace, 1937), 250; *New York Times Magazine,* March 15, 1931, 8.

18. *New York Times,* March 22, 1931; March 20, 1933; April 9, 1934; July 14, 1935.

19. Stephen J. Whitfield, *Scott Nearing: Apostle of American Radicalism* (New York: Columbia University Press, 1974), 173–177; Paul K. Conkin, *Tomorrow A New World: The New Deal Community Program* (Ithaca: Cornell University Press, 1959), 28–29, 106–113.

20. F. F. Rockwell, "Round About the Garden," *New York Times,* January 5, 1941, sect. 2, 10.

21. *New York Times,* December 20, 1941; "Program for Victory Gardens," *Horticulture* 20 (January 1, 1942), 5; James B. Williams, "Gardening for Victory," *Recreation* 35 (February, 1942), 683–686.

22. L. H. Robbins, "15,000,000 Victory Gardens," *New York Times Magazine,* August 23, 1942, 15–25; Dick Dabney, *A Good Man: The Life of Sam J. Ervin* (Boston: Houghton Mifflin, 1976), 127–128.

23. Samuel W. Hamilton, "Mental Hygiene and Gardening," *Gardener's Chronicle* 46 (February, 1942), 51.

24. H. W. Hochbaum to H. G. Crim, April 17, 1942, Secretary's Office Correspondence—Gardens 1942, Department of Agriculture, National Archives, Washington, D.C.

25. R. Milton Carleton to Claude R. Wickard, February 12, 1942; H. W. Hochbaum to Samuel Bledsoe, April 22, 1942; Prentice Cooper to Wickard, August 10, 1942; Carl Hamilton to H. W. Parrsius, December 18, 1942, Secretary's Office Correspondence—Gardens 1942, Department of Agriculture, National Archives, Washington, D.C.

26. *New York Times,* January 3, 1943.

27. Ibid., May 11, 1943; for photographs of victory gardens in front lawns, see *House and Garden* 84 (November, 1943), 60–62.

28. Harry T. Arens, "West Hartford's War Gardens," *Recreation* 37 (February, 1944), 620–622.

29. "Gardening—Modern Three-Faced Janus," *Recreation* 37 (March, 1944), 647–651.

30. "Guarding the Garden Crops," *Horticulture* 22 (May 15, 1944), 224; "Gaining the Victory," *Gardener's Chronicle* 47 (June, 1943), 155; *New York Times,* August 2, 1942.

31. *Gardener's Chronicle* 46 (October, 1942), 274; "Taking the Back-ache out of Gardening," *Horticulture* 21 (June 15, 1943), 245–246.

32. *New York Times,* May 31, 1944; March 25, 1945; February 22, 1946; February 3, May 31, 1948; "What's Next in Victory Gardening?" *House and Garden* 87 (January, 1945), 36; Richardson Wright, "Food for Peace," *House and Garden* 87 (May, 1945), 53.

33. C. B. Palmer, "Memoir Written by a Non Green Thumb," *New York Times,* June 12, 1949, sect. vi, 20.

34. U.S. Department of Agriculture, Extension Service Statement on Gallup Poll, September 21, 1951; Arthur W. Baum, "Thirty Million Gardeners," *Saturday Evening Post* 226 (August 8, 1953), 64.

CHAPTER 10 : BACK TO MUCK AND MAGIC

1. The derision of manure by academic professionals never extended to such practical garden advisers as *Wise's New Garden Encyclopedia* (1941) or Montague Free's *Gardening* (1937). Manure and compost remained popular with these garden writers and with the *Gardener's Chronicle,* but the L. H. Bailey tradition ridiculed manure, as did such articles as William S. Haynes, "Feeding the Garden on a Budget," *Horticulture* 12 (May 15, 1934), 179–180.

2. Lewis Thomas, *The Youngest Science: Notes of a Medicine Watcher* (New York: Viking Press, 1983), 13, 15, 29.

3. Donald Worster, *Nature's Economy: The Roots of Ecology* (San Francisco: Sierra Club Books, 1977), 231, 237; Russell Lord, *The Care of the Earth* (New York: Thomas Nelson, 1962), 278–279.

4. James C. Whorton, *Crusaders for Fitness: The History of American Health Reformers* (Princeton: Princeton University Press, 1982), 332–338; Wade Greene, "Guru of the Organic Food Cult," *New York Times Magazine,* June 6, 1971, 30; Jerome Rodale "Autobiography," *Organic Gardening* 13 (March, 1966), 105–107.

5. Louise E. Howard, *Sir Albert Howard in India* (London: Faber & Faber, 1953).

6. E. John Russell, *A History of Agricultural Science in Great Britain* (London: George Allen & Unwin Ltd., 1966), 467–468.

7. Albert Howard, *An Agricultural Testament* (London: Oxford University Press, 1940), 1–4, 17–21, 37–38, 167, 177, 224.

8. Miss E. B. Kirkham, "Lionel James Picton," *Organic Gardening* 17 (October, 1950), 25–27.

9. J. I. Rodale, "Autobiography," *Organic Gardening* 13 (March, 1966), 105–106.

10. *Organic Farming and Gardening,* May 1942, 3–5; Ehrenfried Pfeiffer, *Bio-Dynamic Farming and Gardening* (New York: Anthroposophic Press, 1940); H. H. Koepf and C. J. Budd, "Bio-Dynamic Agriculture," in John Davy, ed., *Work Arising from the Life of Rudolf Steiner* (London: Rudolf Steiner Press, 1975), 151–169.

11. J. I. Rodale, "Looking Back," *Organic Gardening* 9 (November, 1962), 59–60.

12. *Organic Gardening,* December 1944, 3–6.

13. J. I. Rodale, "Radical Change in Organic Method," *Organic Gardening,* December 1949, 26–27.

14. R. I. Throckmorton, "Organic Farming—Bunk!" *Readers Digest* 61 (October, 1952), 45–48; Ray Koon, "This Organic Farming Business," *Horticul-*

ture 28 (May, 1950), 183; "Organic Gardening" *Consumer Reports* 17 (July, 1952), 341–342; "Organic vs. Inorganic Gardening," *Consumer Reports* 18 (January, 1953), 47–48; J. I. Rodale, *The Health Finder: An Encyclopedia of Health Information from the Preventive Point-of-View* (Emmaus: Rodale Books, 1954), 198–204.

15. Charles E. Kellogg, "Conflicting Doctrines about Soils," *Scientific Monthly* 66 (June, 1948), 475–481; Kellogg, *Our Garden Soils* (New York: Macmillan Company, 1952), 2–3.

16. Arthur B. Beaumont, "Biochemical Gardening," *Horticulture* 30 (October, 1952), 388; Dean Collins, "I Call It Microcosmic Gardening," *Horticulture* 33 (July, 1955), 342.

17. J. I. Rodale, "20 Years of Organic Gardening," *Organic Gardening* 9 (June, 1962), 17–19, an *Organic Garden* series of 1956–57 radio programs in the Northeast surely contributed to more rapid growth in readership.

18. Ruth Stout, "Throw Away Your Spade and Hoe," *Organic Gardening,* July 1954, 18; Betsy Mitchell, "Ruth Stout: The No Work Gardener," *Gardens for All* 6 (March, 1983), 10–11.

19. Warren Schultz, Jr., "Tillers on Parade," *Organic Gardening* 30 (August, 1983), 50–55; *Organic Gardening,* April 1955, 26–30; May 1967, 53–55.

20. James Whorton, *Before Silent Spring: Pesticides and Public Health in Pre-DDT America* (Princeton: Princeton University Press, 1974), 253; Barry Commoner, *The Closing Circle: Nature, Man and Technology* (New York: Alfred Knopf, 1971), 49–54, 128, 151–153; Worster, *Nature's Economy,* 339–341.

21. Rachel Carson, *Silent Spring* (Boston: Houghton Mifflin, 1962), 176.

22. Robert Rodale, "Rachel Carson's Masterpiece," *Organic Gardening* 9 (September, 1962), 17–19; Rodale, "The New Look in Insect Killers," *Organic Gardening* 6 (July, 1959), 30–31.

23. *Whole Earth Catalogue* (N.P.: Portola Institute, 1973), 50.

24. Robert Rodale, "How Big Is the Organic Idea?" *Organic Gardening* 15 (October, 1968), 19–21.

25. Wade Greene, "Guru of the Organic Food Cult," *New York Times Magazine,* June 6, 1971, 30.

26. See Carleton B. Lee's editorials in *Horticulture,* March and August 1971; Robert Rodale, "What Would J. I. Rodale Say?" *Organic Gardening* 31 (June, 1984), 28–32.

CHAPTER 11 : GARDEN AND COMMUNITY

1. Mary Lee Coe, *Growing with Community Gardening* (Barr, Vt.: Countryman Press, 1978), 7; for the belief that our survival depends on replacing capitalist agriculture, see Richard Merrill, ed., *Radical Agriculture* (New York: New York University Press, 1976).

2. *Mother Earth News* 1 (January, March 1970); John N. Cole, "Mr. Mother," *Horticulture* 55 (February, 1978), 20–30.

3. Robert Rodale, "Gardening for Security," *Organic Gardening* 22 (January, 1975), 44–47.

4. Robert Rodale, "Rural Renaissance on the Way," *Organic Gardening* 22 (September, 1975), 42–43.

5. Los Angeles Times, June 10, 1973, part 3, 17; *Washington Post,* July 5, 1973, 61; Helga and William Olkowski, *The City Peoples Book of Raising Food* (Emmaus: Rodale Press, 1975).

6. Jamie Jobb, *The Complete Book of Community Gardening* (New York: William Morrow, 1979), 22, 38–39.

7. Robert Rodale, "Alan Chadwick," *Organic Gardening* 30 (April, 1983), 24–27; J. Tevere MacFadyen, "The Call to Dig," *Horticulture* 63 (March, 1985), 38–47.

8. James Underwood Crockett, *Crockett's Victory Garden* (Boston: Little, Brown, 1977), 152; the "Garden Song" can be found in Lynn Ocone, *The Youth Gardening Book* (Burlington, Vt.: Gardens for All, 1984), 108.

9. H. Thorpe, "The Homely Allotment, From Rural Dole to Urban Amenity: A Neglected Aspect of Urban Land Use," *Geography* 60 (July, 1975), 169–183.

10. *Wall Street Journal,* July 18, 1975, 24; *New York Times,* June 10, 1977, sect. 23, 11; James Daniel, "Gardens for All," *Readers Digest* 106 (April, 1975), 41–44.

11. *Gardens for All* 6 (May, 1983), 20; Larry Sommers, *The Community Garden Book* (Burlington, Vt.: Gardens for All, 1984), 120–121.

12. *Chicago Tribune,* March 23, 1975, sect. 9, 16; June 22, 1978, sect. 7, 7.

13. Charles A. Lewis, "Plants and People in the Inner City," *Planning* 45 (March, 1979), 10–14.

14. *Los Angeles Times,* July 4, 1976, sect. 7, 1; Coe, *Growing with Community Gardening,* 70–75.

15. Susan Naimark, ed., *A Handbook of Community Gardening* (New York: Charles Scribner's Sons, 1982), 15, 160.

16. Sam Bass Warner, Jr., *To Dwell Is to Garden: A History of Boston's Community Gardens* (Boston: Northeastern University Press, 1987), 30–40.

17. Naimark, *A Handbook of Community Gardening,* 9–10.

18. Eileen McConough, "Heavy Metals and the Urban Garden," in *Community Gardening,* vol. 35 of Brooklyn Botanic Garden Record *Plants and Gardens* (Spring, 1979), 62–64.

19. Warner, *To Dwell Is to Garden,* 34–40.

20. Naimark, *A Handbook of Community Gardening,* 15; Lewis, "Plants and People in the Inner City," 10–14; Sommers, *The Community Garden Book,* xi.

21. Judy Chaves, "Garden Plots in Manhattan," *Gardens for All* 7 (September, 1984), 34–35; for other New York City gardens, see *Wall Street Journal,* April 23, 1985, and the special issue of New York Botanical *Garden* 9 (December, 1985).

CHAPTER 12 : EPILOGUE: GARDENING AND NOSTALGIA

1. Josephine von Miklos, *Gardener's World* (New York: Random House, 1968), 192; for 1970s nostalgia, see Fred Davis, *Yearning for Yesterday: A Sociology of Yesterday* (New York: The Free Press, 1979), 103–107, 118–142; David E. Shi, *The Simple Life: Plain Living and High Thinking in American Culture* (New York: Oxford University Press, 1985), 263–275.

2. Davis, *Yearning for Yesterday,* 55–56, 31–50.

3. L. H. Bailey, "A Reverie of Gardens," *Outlook* 68 (June 1, 1901), 271.

4. Charles Dudley Warner, *My Summer in a Garden* (Boston: Fields, Osgood & Co., 1871), 1–3.

5. Stanley Schuler, *Gardens Are for Eating* (New York: Macmillan, 1971), 1–3.

6. Clare Leighton, "The Philosophy of Gardening," in Alice Sloane Anderson, ed., *Our Garden Heritage* (New York: Dodd, Mead, & Co., 1961), 8–11; Jane Anne Staw and Mary Swander, *Parsnips in the Snow: Talks with Midwestern Gardeners* (Iowa City: University of Iowa Press, 1990), 153, 1–2.

7. Sebastian de Grazia, *Of Time, Work and Leisure* (New York: Twentieth Century Fund, 1962), 460; H. Thorpe, "The Homely Allotment: From Rural Dole to Urban Amenity: A Neglected Aspect of Urban Land Use," *Geography* 60 (July, 1975), 175; "Gallup Survey," *National Gardening* (March, 1988), 6.

8. Alice Payne Hackett, *70 Years of Best Sellers* (New York: R. R. Bowker, 1967), 12, 19.

9. Christopher Lasch, *The Culture of Narcissism* (New York: W. W. Norton, 1978).

10. "Horticulture Has Arrived," *Horticulture* 52 (September, 1974), 16; "American Gardening Revolution: 1976," *Horticulture* 53 (April, 1975), 24; "Plant/People Symbiosis," *American Horticulturist* 55 (June 1976), 2.

11. Carolyn Jabs, *The Heirloom Gardener* (San Francisco: Sierra Club Books, 1984), 34–35.

12. For the folk movement back to seed saving, see John F. Adams, *Guerrilla Gardening* (New York: Coward-McCann, 1983).

13. Jabs, *The Heirloom Gardener,* 47–55.

14. Ibid., 24–6, 176–177.

15. Ibid., 97–121; Ellen Cohen, "A Fair Shake for Heirloom Vegetables," *Organic Gardening* 30 (October, 1983), 40–43.

16. Jabs, *The Heirloom Gardener,* 123–147.

17. Ibid., 103–105, 172–173.

18. Thomas Christopher, "The Great Tomato Quest," *Horticulture* 63 (March, 1985), 19–22. "Big Girl" won another taste contest without heirloom competition, scoring 8.45 points while a nameless store-bought tomato earned only 1.75 for its tough, mealy, tasteless character: see Cathy Wilkinson Barash, "The Great Tomato Taste-Off," *National Gardening* 11 (August, 1988), 30–58.

19. Karen Hess to author, March, 1989.

20. Wesley's quote, "useful gardens," can be found in *The Works of John Wesley,* vol. 6 (London, 1874), 131; for frugality in the Japanese tradition, see

Robert N. Bellah, *Tokugawa Religion: The Values of Pre-Industrial Japan*
(Glencoe: The Free Press, 1959), 116–130; for the American Society on Thrift,
see S. W. Straus, *History of the Thrift Movement in America* (Philadelphia:
J. B. Lippincott, 1920), 68–70; *Wall Street Journal,* May 22, 1980, 1.
   21. *The Futurist* 10 (June, 1976), 161; Larry Sommers, *The Community
Garden Book* (Burlington, Vt.: Gardens for All, 1984), ix; Cecil Blackwell,
"Why Folks Garden," *Gardening for Food and Fun* (Washington, D.C.: U.S.
Department of Agriculture, 1977), 2–3; pollsters heard that better-tasting food
rather than saving money was the reason for gardening in 1986: see, *National
Gardening* 10 (January, 1987), 1.
   22. Staw and Swander, *Parsnips in the Snow,* 44, 189, 195.

NOTE ON SOURCES

   Finding sources for garden history is one of the more difficult research
challenges. Only twentieth-century gardening journals and manuals are found in
most public libraries. To explore for other materials consider the following hints.
   Old English books are available on microfilm in research libraries. The
process of locating the proper reel requires looking in two books. First go to
A. W. Pollard and G. R. Redgrave, *A Short Title-Catalogue of English Books
1475–1640* (London: Bibliographical Society, 1969), and find the number that
has been assigned to your book. Then take your number to *Early English Books
1475–1640 Cross Index* (Ann Arbor: University Microfilms International, 1977),
where the number is paired with the microfilm reel number you need. Books
published after 1641 are easier to locate. Go to *Accessing Early English Books
1641–1700* (Ann Arbor: University Microfilms International, 1981) where book
titles and reel numbers are listed together.
   Many early American garden books can be found in two microform collec-
tions. The *Microbook of American Civilization* (Chicago: Library Resources,
1972) includes the works of William Cobbett, Fearing Burr, and John Randolph.
The *American Culture Series 1493–1875* (Ann Arbor: University Microfilms
International, 1979) adds the work of Robert Squibb. Unfortunately both collec-
tions ignore Bernard McMahon and Martha Logan.
   The garden work of McMahon and Logan can be located on microcards of
the Evans and Shaw-Shoemaker Early American Imprints. For Martha Logan's
Gardener's Calendar, see Evans No. 33255. For Bernard McMahon's *The American Gardener's Calendar,* see Shaw No. 10771. The full citations of the indexes
are Charles Evans, *American Bibliography 1639–1800* (New York: Peter Smith,
1941–1955), and Richard R. Shaw and Richard H. Shoemaker, *American Bibliography 1801–1819* (New York: Scarecrow Press, 1955–1965).
   Garden and horticulture journals for nineteenth-century America are available in the microfilm collection *American Periodicals 1741–1900: An Index*
(Ann Arbor: University Microfilms International, 1979). Despite the collection
dates, horticultural titles are generally omitted after 1865.
   To find Gilded Age (1870–1900) journals, the best solution is to visit the

National Agricultural Library in Beltsville, Maryland, where the Department of Agriculture provides a complete collection of garden literature, or visit the library of a botanical garden or horticultural society. Outstanding garden libraries are provided by the Massachusetts Horticultural Society, Pennsylvania Horticultural Society, New York Botanical Garden, Arnold Arboretum, and Missouri Botanical Garden.

INDEX

201